W9-AUB-260

Alfred Runte

Yosemite

The Embattled Wilderness

University of Nebraska Press:

Lincoln

and

London

The paper in this book meets
the minimum require-
ments of American National
Standard for Information
Sciences – Permanence of Paper
for Printed Library
Materials, ANSI Z39.48-1984.

Library of Congress
Cataloging-in-Publication Data
Runte, Alfred, 1947-
Yosemite: the embattled wilder-
ness / Alfred Runte.
p. cm.   Bibliography: p.
Includes index.
ISBN 0-8032-3894-0 (alk. paper)
1. Natural history – California –
Yosemite National Park.
2. Nature conservation – Cali-
fornia – Yosemite National
Park. 3. Yosemite National Park
(Calif.) – Management.
4. Natural resources – California –
Yosemite National Park.   I. Title.
QH105.C2R86   1990
508.794'47-dc20   89-35128 CIP

Frontispiece:
Hikers pause to marvel at the
power and majesty of Vernal Falls,
June 1938. Photograph by
Ralph H. Anderson, courtesy of
the National Park Service.

For Christine, with love;

For Mary Vocelka, with gratitude;

And for my bother, August,

In special memory of Mom,

Who showed us both the way.

Contents

ILLUSTRATIONS

Frontispiece: Vernal Falls

I. *Incomparable Yosemite* (following page 34):
Half Dome; Thomas A. Ayres's *Yo-Hamite
Falls*; Yosemite Falls; Glacier Point; View from
Glacier Point; Giant sequoias of the Mariposa
Grove; Hikers at Mount Lyell; Frederick Law
Olmsted.

II. *The Art of Promotion* (following page 76):
Albert Bierstadt's *Lake in Yosemite Valley*;
Thomas Hill's *Yosemite Valley*; Cover of *Sunset*
magazine featuring Yosemite; Railroad pro-
motional brochure covers; Horseshoe Route;
Firefall produce label; Yosemite Park and
Curry Company promotions.

III. *Visitation and Development* (following
page 140): John Muir and Theodore
Roosevelt; David and Jennie Curry; Alcoholic
beverages at Desmond's Camp Yosemite;
Yosemite Lodge; Indian Field Days; Frederick
Law Olmsted, Jr.; Automobiles and campers
at Stoneman Meadow; Dredging paving
materials from the Merced River; Bridge across
Wildcat Creek; Painting the rock face above
Wawona Tunnel.

IV. *Wildlife Management and Ecology* (following page 176): Ed Beatty with ice-preserved
bighorn sheep; Grizzly Giant; Visitor's
confrontation with bear; Bear capture; Feeding
deer; Joseph Grinnell; Yosemite Valley "zoo";
Elk herd.

V. *Urban Distractions and Influence* (following
page 216): Hetch Hetchy Valley; Ahwahnee
Hotel; Bracebridge Christmas pageant; Winter
Carnival; Badger Pass ski area; Freeing bear
from milk can; Killing bear by lethal injection;
Causes of visitors' deaths; Yosemite Valley jail;
Yosemite Village Courthouse; Tioga Road;
Yosemite Valley at night.

Map of Yosemite National Park (facing 177).

❧ *Acknowledgments*

Although writing is a very personal undertaking, no historian could begin setting facts and ideas to paper without the assistance of many other individuals. As I recall their names and contributions, I am reminded of an observation made by Mary Vocelka, former director of the Yosemite National Park Research Library. "Why is it," Mary once asked me, "that most writers never mention their husbands or wives until the very last?" A good question, I responded, and a fault that I promised not to repeat. Indeed, no one has meant more to me than my wife, Christine. I would not have started this book, let alone have finished it, without her encouragement and support. Writing may be a cloistered and lonely occupation, but again, thanks to Christine, I was never really alone.

The same, however, must also be said of Mary Vocelka. I do not know anyone, other than my wife, who was more committed, both personally and professionally, to the success of this book. From the beginning of my research in the summer of 1980 through the completion of the final drafts of the manuscript, Mary worked tirelessly to ensure that I saw everything of importance in Yosemite's archives. That meant, on Mary's part, hours and hours of rummaging through stored files; xeroxing countless pages of reports and correspondence; locating photographs, advertisements, and classic ephemera; and, long after I had returned home, discovering and forwarding me even more information on those issues I had brought to her special attention. Just before I completed this book, in the summer of 1988,

Mary resigned from the Yosemite Research Library, noting, in her words, that it was time to move on. I can say only that her absence is a big, big loss to every serious scholar of the national parks. Her knowledge of her collection was deep and insightful, and she shared her discoveries with unbridled enthusiasm and dedication. Believe me, Mary will be missed.

Mary, I would further suggest, symbolizes the dedication and professionalism of archivists everywhere. Special thanks are also due Renee M. Jaussaud, with the Scientific, Economic, and Natural Resources Branch, the National Archives, for guiding me through the complexities and inconsistencies of Record Group 79, the files of the National Park Service. Renee is another of those unsung heroes, cutting days, if not weeks, from a researcher's time at the National Archives simply by knowing its collections inside and out. I am also grateful to the staff of the Bancroft Library of the University of California at Berkeley, and especially to Walter Brem, for much advice and assistance I received while examining the Sierra Club Papers. Finally, on the archival side of the ledger, I thank Dr. David Wake, director of the Museum of Vertebrate Zoology of the University of California at Berkeley, and Dr. Marvalee Wake, chairman of the Department of Zoology, for permission to examine all of the museum's files, including the papers and correspondence of Joseph Grinnell. David and Marvalee, I might add, allowed me access to the museum on weekends and after normal business hours. I deeply appreciate their confidence and trust, and underscore again how fortunate I have been to benefit from the time and assistance of such dedicated people.

Financial support, like archival assistance, has also proven crucial to the realization of this book. Fifteen years ago, Resources for the Future in Washington, D.C., extended me a fellowship to write my doctoral dissertation, which led to my first history of the national parks. In 1985 Resources for the Future awarded me a Small Grant to complete this book as well. The title Small Grant was perhaps a misnomer, at least from my perspective, since the amount was sufficient to allow me a full year for research and writing. In either case, I am honored that this book, like my first, won the support of RFF, indeed that I was so well treated and encouraged as a member of RFF's extended research family. A Herbert E. Kahler Fellowship from the Eastern National Park and Monument Association also speeded the book's completion. Both Resources for the Future and the Eastern National Park and Monument Association can be proud of their contributions to historical research. In my own case, I know this book would not have appeared in time for the Yosemite Centennial had it not been for their willingness to back scholars by providing financial assistance.

I have also benefited, along the way, from the assistance of many other institutions and individuals. The National Park Foundation agreed to administer my grant from RFF without taking any overhead. Indirectly, a film project under the auspices of the Burlington Northern Foundation further contributed financial assistance to locate and reproduce important photographs. Similarly, Leonard McKenzie, chief park interpreter in Yosemite National Park, generously agreed to give me lodging in the Ranger Club dormitory, allowing me to realize substantial savings while concluding my archival investigations in the Yosemite Research Library.

Linda Eade, Mary Vocelka's successor in the library, came to my aid repeatedly as I tried to fill in my data and obtain elusive photographs. Likewise, I have benefited from the assistance of other Park Service personnel, including Stephen Botti, Vicki Lawson, Dean Shenk, Michael Webb, Mallory Smith, Marla LaCass, Sue Beatty, Lisa Dapprich, Don Fox, Eileen Berrey, Fermin Salas, Roger McGehee, Jeff Samco, Bruce Fincham, Jeff Keay, David Forgang, Barbara Beroza, Robert Woolard, and the late Richard Riegelhuth, former chief of resources management. Two former superintendents, Robert Binnewies and John M. Morehead, also facilitated special requests for research information.

I respect the opinions of these and other people; I stress, however, that the interpretations in this book are strictly my own. I did, beginning in 1980, work seasonally in Yosemite Valley through 1983, giving walks, campfire lectures, and seminars as a Park Service naturalist. My knowledge of park history, I admit, was sometimes uncomfortable for management personnel, who expected history to vindicate their actions rather than suggest a possible need for more critical review. Nevertheless, I respect the Park Service for allowing me to bring real scholarship to the public, for giving me the opportunity to educate from within. As I hope this book will show, that opportunity itself is in the highest traditions of Yosemite.

Meanwhile, present friends and former colleagues in university circles, in truth people too numerous to mention all by name, will agree that scholarship cannot flourish without freedom of expression. For sticking by me through the years, I thank especially Frank Freidel, Carlos Schwantes,

Harold Kirker, Roderick Nash, Richard Oglesby, Lisa Mighetto, Arthur Martinson, Michael Frome, Mott Greene, William Goetzmann, Caroline Bynum, Tom Dunlap, Susan Schrepfer, Richard Bartlett, W. Turrentine Jackson, Donald Pisani, Carl Bajema, Michael Allen, Robert Burke, Frank Conlon, Lewis Saum, Grant Sharpe, Wilbur Jacobs, Richard Orsi, and Barry Schuyler. All extended me that most important aid—faith in one's self, even in the face of reversal and adversity. Again, that always lonely enterprise—research and writing—has been made all the more bearable by friends such as these.

And just when you think your book is finished, you find, to your dismay, that you have overlooked an important illustration. So it is back to your sources for a final rush order. Michael Dixon and Brian Grogan in Yosemite; Karen DePonceau Flint at the Rockwell Museum in Corning, New York; Thomas A. DuRant of the National Park Service, Office of Library and Archival Services, Springfield, Virginia; Barbara Stein, the Museum of Vertebrate Zoology, Berkeley, California; Joyce Connolly, the Frederick Law Olmsted National Historic Site, Brookline, Massachusetts; and Joanne Avant, with the Haggin Museum, Stockton, California, all came gladly to my assistance that one last time.

My family, as well, understood my deadlines and immersion in this project and therefore cheerfully endured my habit of staring off into space, mentally lost on some fogbound paragraph or chapter that just wouldn't come together. My mother, although dying of cancer, was no less insistent that I stick with my writing. Naturally I found that impossible, although after her death I did return to the book with a retrospective sense of purpose. It was thirty years ago, in early August 1959, that she took my brother and me to Yosemite Valley, never dreaming that somewhere between the Donald Duck comic books and our daily refrain of "But Mom, when do we get to Disneyland?" the glory of Yosemite was indeed shining through. Unlike her sons, she never went back to Yosemite Valley. We trust, however, that the Yosemite she sees now is even greater and more beautiful than the one we mortals know.

❧ *Introduction*

Among all of the debates affecting America's national parks, the most enduring—and most intense—is where to draw the line between preservation and use. This is an account of that classic confrontation, as told from the perspective of natural resources and environment. The focus is Yosemite, where debating environmental change is now a century and a quarter old. Yosemite, as the oldest park of its kind, has the longest history of modification. Tourists were familiar with Yosemite Valley well over a decade before the Grand Canyon and Yellowstone were even explored. The issues of park development were raised and debated first in Yosemite. Even today, no other national park more dramatically reflects America's alleged failures to reconcile nature protection with the wants and demands of the visiting public.

The subject, to be sure, is by no means new or unfamiliar. The record is nonetheless incomplete, especially concerning natural scientists, their opinions, and their attempts to influence resource management. The National Park Service Organic Act of 1916 itself left every methodology for management deliberately vague, calling simply for protection of scenery and wildlife "in such manner and by such means as will leave them unimpaired for the enjoyment of future generations." But just what was meant by "unimpaired"? In effect, a definition that imprecise extended protection to park resources only by implication. It remained for each generation of Americans to bring its own perspective to the issue, invariably, if only subtly, imposing another viewpoint on existing philosophies of park management and use. Concessionaires in particular, seeking greater profits from increased visitation, consistently advocated visitor comfort and convenience over resource preservation.

That contradiction, among others, forms one basis of this study. I have also examined divergent points of view about what Yosemite *ought* to be and what it in fact became as each generation of Americans reevaluated the park's purpose and future. The ideal of sanctuary—that Yosemite National Park should represent a vignette of primitive America—has rarely been put to greater test than in Yosemite Valley itself. It is here that the goals of preservation contrast sharply with the expectations of a mobile, affluent society. Nor have preservationists, despite their overriding commitment to the ideal of park sanctuary, been entirely free of responsibility for the effects of human change. Merely by their presence, it stands to reason, preservationists themselves have contributed to a modified environment.

Regardless, studies of environmental change have largely been ignored. In the existing literature about Yosemite, most writers have traced the human history of the park, noting, for example, its colorful explorers, aboriginal inhabitants, innkeepers, and early publicists. In this volume, the social history of the national park is subordinate to the emerging debate regarding the proper management of the natural resource. What follows is an environmental history. People, buildings, and traditions are treated only as they pertain to evolving philosophies of park management and use. To reemphasize, I have focused on two issues: the ideal that Yosemite National Park ought to be managed and enjoyed as a natural sanctuary, and that ideal's simultaneous erosion, caused by increased development pressures generally divorced from biological considerations.

I have therefore tried, wherever possible, to avoid familiar ground. I do not, for example, retrace the footsteps of John Muir. Nor is this a chronology of every person or event in the history of Yosemite National Park. If the reader's favorite individual, anecdote, or story is missing, I stress again that this is a study of the natural environment. Similarly, I have avoided giving another long account of the Hetch Hetchy reservoir, except to underscore its significance as a policy and resource issue. Like biographies of John Muir, detailed histories of the Hetch Hetchy controversy are numerous and easily obtained. There would be little point in my repeating an already familiar theme.

My choice of resource subjects has likewise been selective, determined in part by the importance and availability of original source materials. For

2

example, there is much to be found on bears but considerably less for all other wildlife. My own emphasis is on bears not only because more sources are available but also because no other animal has sparked such sustained and revealing debate. Fire ecology, another important issue, receives greater attention for the earlier history of the park. Modern approaches to natural fire are extensively documented elsewhere; then too the future of fire ecology is once more in doubt, especially in the wake of extensive fires bordering Yosemite in 1987 and the outspoken reaction against fire management policies implemented in the Yellowstone fires of 1988. The issue requires more time for definitive conclusions. One thing is certain: Natural fires will be even more closely monitored than they have been in the past and, it would appear, more often contained or suppressed.

Natural resources, like people and events, appear in the narrative as barometers of change. More than an inventory of every resource, this book examines those resources and environmental issues that provoked redirections in management. Meanwhile, the observance of the centennial of Yosemite National Park, established on October 1, 1890, lends special significance to every resource controversy and its intended or thwarted outcome. So too, June 30, 1989, marked the 125th anniversary of the Yosemite Park Act of 1864, which set aside sixty square miles of territory surrounding Yosemite Valley and the Mariposa Grove of giant sequoias. Although the legislation of 1890 established a national park roughly twenty-five times as large, the park act of 1864 was the first instance of scenic preservation in the United States and thus represented the conceptualization of the national park idea.

In that regard, as well as others discussed here, Yosemite's history is both symbolic and distinctive. Proclaimed a public trust as early as 1864, Yosemite bears the longest evidence of the tension, found in every major park, between preservation and use. As the twentieth century now draws to a close, there is renewed concern about the future of the national parks; any reassessment logically must begin with their philosophy and history. A study of Yosemite's natural environment and resources, as viewed against the backdrop of the park's longest and oldest debate, should help guide modern Americans as they grapple to realize the preservation ideals of their own generation. Among them, perhaps the most significant is the determination that *living* wonders of the national parks, and not only dramatic scenery, must survive intact through the twenty-first century and beyond.

3

The Incomparable Valley

CHAPTER ONE

From above, the view of Yosemite Valley can be very deceptive. Roads, buildings, cars, campgrounds, and parking lots are only partially visible or are entirely lost among the trees. Especially from overlooks such as famed Glacier Point, 3,214 feet higher than the valley floor, the world of Yosemite moves slowly and in miniature. At this elevation, the viewer finds it even harder to imagine that the landscape below has long been the subject of intense and sometimes bitter controversy.

Perhaps the problem of protection has indeed been one of lasting but misleading first impressions. John Muir himself, writing of his first look into the valley from the top of Yosemite Falls, did nothing to prepare his followers for the landscape's imperfections. "The level bottom seemed to be dressed like a garden," he wrote, "sunny meadows here and there, and groves of pine and oak; the river of Mercy sweeping in majesty through the midst of them and flashing back the sunbeams." The date of his description was July 15, 1869, and already trails, fences, barns, and houses linked or abutted the meadows and riverbanks below. But although these structures were intrusions on the landscape, Muir said nothing about them years later when he published his journal. Instead he turned immediately to a description of "Tissiack, or Half-Dome, rising at the upper end of the valley to a height of nearly a mile, . . . holding the eye in devout admiration, calling it back again and again from falls or meadows, or even the mountains beyond." Half Dome was all "marvelous cliffs, marvelous in sheer dizzy depth sculpture." Thus even for Muir, a dedicated botanist, the geology of Yosemite Valley was no less overpowering and distracting. "Hereafter," he remarked, he would "try to keep away from such extravagant, nerve-straining places" as his perch on a narrow ledge at the brink of Yosemite Falls. "Yet such a day is well worth venturing for," he concluded. "My first view of the High Sierra, first view looking down into Yosemite, the death song of Yosemite Creek, and its flight over the vast cliff, each one of these is of itself enough for a great life-long landscape fortune."[1]

Much as Yosemite Valley viewed from above appears deceptively spacious, so the observer standing on the valley floor is often overwhelmed by sensations of compactness and immensity. Joseph LeConte, the renowned geologist, alluded to this commonplace perception while leading a party of his students on a Sierra field trip in August 1870. "Started this morning up the valley," the entry in his journal for August 2 began. "As we go, the striking features of Yosemite pass in procession before us. On our left, El Capitan, Three Brothers, Yosemite Falls; on the right, Cathedral Rock, Cathedral Spires, Sentinel Rock." After a brief pause for a group photograph the party resumed its journey. And "again the grand procession commences," LeConte wrote. "On the left, Royal Arches, Washington Column, North Dome; on the right, Sentinel Dome, Glacier Point, Half Dome." After making camp the adventurers went up Tenaya Canyon to Mirror Lake for a swim. "The scenery about this lake is truly magnificent," the geologist remarked. It was here that Yosemite's cliffs appeared to reach "the acme of imposing grandeur." Half Dome seemed to rise "almost from the water, a sheer precipice, near five thousand feet perpendicular." Opposite, North Dome loomed up "to an almost equal height." Overwhelmed, LeConte, like Muir, seemed somewhat out of touch with the valley floor itself. After all, hemmed in by cliffs and mountains as breathtaking as Half Dome, the geologist and his students did not pay as much attention to what lay at their feet.[2]

More recently, the biological tenets of environmentalism have gradually softened and subdued the standard descriptions of Yosemite. In this vein Ansel Adams, another name linked with promoting the grandeur of the valley, recalled of his first visit in 1916 "not only the colossal but the little things; the grasses and ferns, cool atriums of the forest." But even for Adams, writing in the 1980s, the dominant recollection of his first family outing was one of granite cliffs threaded with "many small shining cas-

6

cades"; Sentinel Falls and Yosemite Falls "booming in early summer flood"; and the mists of Bridalveil Fall glistening in the sunlight. "One wonder after another descended upon us," he wrote. Granted, the vegetation of Yosemite Valley impressed Adams, as it had many others. But there was no hiding the fact that its trees and wildflowers were at best pleasant diversions rather than priorities for his visit. Like so many thousands before him, young Ansel Adams was attracted to Yosemite by its visions of wonderment. The vacation promised him by his parents "MUST be in this incredible place" he had read about.[3] As a leading environmentalist, Adams later learned to pay homage to nature in its totality. His fame nonetheless rested on his preoccupation with the *scenery* of Yosemite. By the time he had personally admonished his followers not to overlook the gentler beauties of the Sierra Nevada, his own photographs had lured millions of Americans to Yosemite in hopes of duplicating the monumental images that he too still found so compelling.

As the focal point of that perception, Yosemite Valley inevitably became the symbol of the national park idea both at its finest and at its worst. Among national parks renowned for their breathtaking scenery, no other offered such a variety of natural features in such a limited space. That one characteristic of Yosemite Valley was to prove both its greatest asset and its biggest problem. The immensity of Yosemite's formations could deceive even its most knowledgeable defenders, among them Ansel Adams, John Muir, and Joseph LeConte. By the time Americans as a whole came to understand the argument that Yosemite Valley had reached or exceeded its desirable limits of growth, the forces of development had themselves become entrenched as part of the Yosemite experience. Henceforth the removal of roads, houses, hotels, and campgrounds seemed to threaten both tradition and history. Certainly the suggestion that Yosemite Valley be turned "back to nature" bore distinct notes of futility and improbability.

Established in 1864 as the first park of its kind, Yosemite Valley suffered from the problems of its own longevity. The biological needs of the valley were neither understood nor appreciated in 1864. The establishment of Yosemite National Park in 1890 added another dimension for complacency by lending credence to the argument that biological and wilderness values could be protected outside the valley. Finally, the reduction of the national park by 542 square miles in 1905, coupled with the loss of the Hetch Hetchy Valley in 1913 to the city of San Francisco for its municipal water supply, strengthened preservationists' resolve to oppose further commercial development within Yosemite Valley itself. Growing debate about its lingering vulnerability to despoliation further swelled, encompassing the national park as a whole and indeed spilling over into discussion about the future of the entire park system. The characteristics of no other park put the question more directly: How do the people of the United States want their national parks to be protected and managed? The national parks, in short, were themselves controversial. Meanwhile, as latent pressures for development in Yosemite Valley would continue to demonstrate, perhaps any attempt to reverse the commercialization of the parks was a goal impossible to reconcile with political and social reality.

* * *

If ever a national park was fated by its geology to be the center of endless controversy, Yosemite is that park. Beginning with the uplift of the Sierra Nevada sixty million years ago, Yosemite Valley began its emergence as a progression of natural wonders barely seven miles in length and only one mile wide. In recent geological history, several periods of glaciation followed by constant weathering further scoured and molded Yosemite's spires and granite cliffs. As each glacier retreated, a great lake probably inundated the valley floor and gradually was filled in with river-borne sediments. Finally the Merced River cut its own distinctive channels of change, meandering back and forth across the former lake bed before it rushed headlong through the foothills to the lowlands of the Central Valley.[4] By now the Yosemite of the American imagination—of Albert Bierstadt, Thomas Hill, Ansel Adams, and many other artists—was in place. If only the valley's size had been equal to its beauty, undoubtedly its history as a national park would have been much less controversial.

In this respect, the size of the national park in comparison with the valley has always been misleading. Much like passing up the *Mona Lisa* at the Louvre in Paris, a visit to the park without seeing the valley remains almost unthinkable. Granted, many visit the Mariposa Grove of giant sequoias, thirty-five miles to the south; in summer thousands more cross the Tioga Road for glimpses of the High Sierra, Tenaya Lake, and Tuolumne Meadows; and perhaps as many as one hundred thousand people a year hike or ride horseback through portions of the backcountry. And yet, even among the backpackers, it is the valley from which most begin their experience and to which they inevitably return before going home.

8

Over the years, the response to greater visitation has been greater development. Concessionaires especially, mindful of Yosemite Valley's disproportionate popularity, have zealously opposed serious limitations on public access or structures. As a result, the public has come to expect roads, hotels, stores, and campgrounds in Yosemite Valley as a matter of course. Unquestionably, more than 125 years of emphasis on visitation has compromised the valley's protection. By the same token, similar problems would probably surface if the United States had to develop the park all over again. After all, in the words of its most noted geologist, François Matthes, the heart of Yosemite National Park is still its valley "incomparable."[5]

The Indians called the valley *Ah-wah-nee,* or "place of a gaping mouth." Invariably, the evidence of their occupation is open to broad interpretation, yet Native Americans probably came to Yosemite Valley well over two thousand years ago. At about the time Columbus made the European "discovery" of North America, Yosemite Valley was occupied by a Miwok-speaking people drifting eastward from the San Joaquin Valley under population pressures from stronger neighboring tribes. In the Sierra the Miwoks probably subdued and mingled with existing Yosemite natives. Thus were formed the Ahwahneechees, the people of the valley whose appearance suggested a great "gaping mouth."[6]

Yosemite Valley's native inhabitants had no conception whatsoever of *scenic* preservation; Yosemite Valley was strictly for the use and survival of the tribe. Survival called for the manipulation of the valley's resources, particularly through the use of fire. Annual fires accomplished a variety of important ends, most noticeably the retention of the valley's open meadows and scattered stands of black oak. From black oak the Ahwahneechees obtained acorns, their single most important source of food. Boiling water poured over acorn meal leached out the tannic acid, providing flour for hot cakes, gruel, and mush. Without periodic fires, dense forest would quickly have reinvaded the meadows and competed with black oak for sunlight and nutrients. Similarly, the lack of trees on the valley floor made hunting and gathering much easier and all the while deprived potential enemies of concealment for furtive movements.[7]

Unfortunately, fire was no deterrent against disease and white encroachment. Around 1800 a disease, probably smallpox, decimated the Ahwahneechees, forcing them to abandon their villages, including those in Yosemite Valley. Survivors of the plague trickled off to join neighboring tribes.

9

Years later, remnants of the Ahwahneechees and other Miwok-speaking peoples returned to Yosemite under Tenaya, whose father, an Ahwahnee-chee chief, apparently had told his son stories of the "deep, grassy valley." Perhaps two hundred strong, Tenaya's band still found "Ahwahnee" impossible to hold indefinitely. Barely a year after the discovery of gold along the American River in 1848, thousands of fortune seekers swarmed throughout the Sierra Nevada foothills. The interests of miners and natives inevitably clashed, and death or dislocation for the Yosemite Indians once more became a frightening possibility.[8]

The process of dispossession began in January 1851 with the formation of the so-called Mariposa Battalion. Its commander, James D. Savage, accused the Yosemite Indians of depradations against his trading outposts along the Merced River, the Fresno River, and Mariposa Creek. If a treaty was not signed, he warned Tenaya the following March, all of the Indians would be killed. With Tenaya reluctantly in the vanguard, Savage led the battalion from its camp near Mariposa up an old Indian trail winding toward Yosemite Valley. Along the way they encountered a group of seventy-two natives; the absence of young men among the refugees undermined Tenaya's efforts to convince the battalion that these women and children were all that remained of his band. Savage sent the chief back to the soldiers' encampment, and with the batallion he pushed on in search of the Ahwahneechee fugitives.[9]

In the late afternoon of March 27, 1851, the men came to a clearing in the trees and for the first time looked down into Yosemite Valley. They were undoubtedly the first organized party of adventurers to do so since the fall of 1833, when Joseph R. Walker, leading a group of mountain men across the High Sierra, had peered down into the valley with members of his detachment from somewhere along the north rim. According to Zenas Leonard, Walker's clerk, the party had "found it utterly impossible for a man to descend, to say nothing of [their] horses," and so had pressed on across the mountains.[10] The Mariposa Battalion, entering from the west at Old Inspiration Point, encountered none of the precipitous terrain that had thwarted the ambitions of Walker's group. On the evening of March 27, Savage and his militia set up camp on the valley floor in Bridalveil Meadows.[11]

That the Indians had already escaped became apparent the next day. Although the battalion scouted far and wide through the valley, even ascending the Merced River above Nevada Fall, the soldiers found only an aged woman, left behind because, as she put it, "I am too old to climb the rocks!"[12] Savage questioned her further, but she refused to tell him where the Indians had gone. In reprisal, the battalion burned everything the natives had been forced to abandon, including their dwellings and large caches of acorns. Without food and shelter the Indians would be forced out of the mountains, or so Savage and his men conveniently assumed.[13]

In fact, Tenaya's band had circled back to the battalion's camp near Mariposa; with Tenaya himself the Indians had slipped out of camp past the militia's sleeping guards. A second expedition, raised in May 1851 under the command of John Boling, finally hunted down the Yosemite Indians and brought them in for punishment. The youngest of Tenaya's three sons had already been killed while trying to escape from his captors.[14] Mournful over his son's death and the loss of his people's freedom, Tenaya soon asked for permission to return to Yosemite Valley. The alternative was permanent assignment to the reservation at Fresno, where he and his band suffered from poor food and government restrictions. The Indian agent granted the chief's request, provided that Tenaya keep his promise to cause no more trouble.[15]

Yet peace in Yosemite Valley proved impossible to secure. In the spring of 1852 the Indians attacked a group of prospectors in the valley; two of the miners were killed and six others barely escaped with their lives. Ostensibly one of the prospectors had incited the natives to attack, hoping in this manner to wrest from his companions sole possession of the claim. In the end only one thing mattered—Indians had killed whites. A detachment of the regular army entered Yosemite Valley and executed five captives allegedly responsible for the miners' deaths, sending Tenaya in flight over the High Sierra to take refuge with the Mono Indians near Mono Lake. There, late in the summer of 1853, Tenaya and several of his band were killed, apparently by the Monos over a gambling dispute.[16] The remainder of the Ahwahneechees scattered east and west of the Sierra, never again to regroup as a distinct and unified people.

Thus did the recorded history of Yosemite open on a discordant note of misery and violence. And yet, through a strange twist of irony, the Ahwahneechees were to leave behind an indelible reminder of their fate. For well over a century, historians assumed the word *Yosemite* to be a corruption of *Uzumati,* meaning "grizzly bear" in Miwok and signifying the larger of the tribe's two social subdivisions. This was the original translation of *Uzumati* offered by Lafayette Bunnell, the noted diarist of the Mariposa Battalion. To the Ahwahneechees, however, the word *husso* meant grizzly bear. *Yosemite* is now believed to be a corruption of *Yo-che-ma-te,* literally meaning "some among them are killers." In any reference to the militia companies of March and May 1851, the meaning would be dramatically obvious. What the soldiers may have mistaken as a comparison of themselves to the revered grizzly bear may in fact have been a warning among members of Tenaya's band to fear for their very lives.[17]

And so the name of Yosemite National Park may subtly yet unmistakably betray the park's origins, a fact that is lost on most of today's visitors. So too, the untrained eye sees little evidence of the modifications that the park, especially the valley, has undergone since the soldiers of the Mariposa Battalion first camped there in 1851. Published in 1880, Lafayette Bunnell's popular account of the expedition was undoubtedly influenced by Yosemite's growing notoriety. Still, his alleged emotions the evening of March 27, 1851, ring true, not only among his contemporaries but also among the thousands of present-day observers seeing Yosemite Valley for the very first time. Above all, it is the geology that still leaves the most lasting impression. "The grandeur of the scene," Bunnell recalled, "was but softened by the haze that hung over the valley,—light as gossamer—and by the clouds which partially dimmed the higher cliffs and mountains. This obscurity of vision but increased the awe with which I beheld it, and as I looked, a peculiar exalted sensation seemed to fill my whole being, and I found my eyes in tears with emotion."[18] Only gradually did Americans come to appreciate more fully the Yosemite environment exclusive of its waterfalls, domes, mountains, and cliffs. Similarly, only in retrospect did Americans understand what had been lost as well as gained by the relentless modification of the natural scene. Initially, even Yosemite's most ardent defenders came to the valley innocently, eager only to see and marvel at its wonders. Observation, not preservation, was the oldest pursuit. Too late Americans realized that seeing was not saving and that making observation easier exacted a price. Conflict and compromise, it followed, would always be part of Yosemite's resource history.

❧ First Park

L ike a precious stone that escapes detection in the sands of a beach, Yosemite was protected over the centuries by its isolation. In turn the Spanish, Mexicans, and mountain men had claimed the High Sierra, but even the few explorers who finally entered the mountains left without publicizing all they may have seen. The miners of 1849 not only invaded California; many stayed and promoted it. Put another way, the Ahwahneechees were not only victims of gold but also casualties of publicity. Even as the gold ran out, tourists quickly replaced miners. The future of Yosemite Valley had already been sealed. As the Ahwahneechees themselves had learned by bitter experience, isolation did nothing to deter invasion once the location of Yosemite Valley was either suspected or known.

It remained for a young Englishman, James Mason Hutchings, to see in the description of Yosemite's wonders a means to fame and fortune. A frustrated miner but keen observer of the California scene (following his failure in the goldfields he turned to publishing a popular newsletter for miners), Hutchings sensed his opportunity in 1855. He retained an artist, Thomas A. Ayres, and with two other companions and two Indian guides entered Yosemite Valley in late June of that year. For Hutchings the five-day excursion marked the beginning of a lifetime involvement with Yosemite as publicist, settler, developer, and concessionaire.[1] Yosemite, in retrospect, had come to its first important threshold of development and had quietly passed over it, all without the slightest hint of public debate or at least some expressions of mild concern.

13

Like any committed publicist, Hutchings welcomed the fast-approaching close to Yosemite's days of isolation. By the end of 1855 several other parties of tourists had experienced the valley's grandeur; all told, the number of bona fide visitors had already reached forty-two.[2] The following July Hutchings did his own part to make certain the number steadily increased. On the strength of his many travels and obvious talent as a journalist, he released the first issue of *Hutchings' California Magazine*. "We wish to picture California, and California life," he wrote in the opening of his introductory note, "to portray its beautiful scenery and curiosities; to speak of its mineral and agricultural products; to tell of its wonderful resources and commercial advantages; and to give utterance to the inner life and experience of its people." In other words, he intended to promote California in every manner possible. Nor did he apologize for his commitment to boosterism, tourism, and economic growth. "Whatever we believe to be for the permanent prosperity of California, we shall fearlessly advocate, in any way that suits us." Of course, as publisher he intended to profit only by increasing his circulation. "Therefore," he concluded, "placing ourselves in the hands of a generous public, we make our bow, and introduce to your kindly notice the first number of HUTCHINGS' CALIFORNIA MAGAZINE."[3]

The subject of many feature articles, Yosemite Valley soon passed from obscurity into state, regional, and national prominence.[4] To be sure, the tide of description quickly swelled as eastern journalists and travelers also discovered Hutchings's favorite topic. Among the most effective publicists was Horace Greeley, editor and publisher of the *New York Tribune*. On a whirlwind visit to the valley in August 1859, he endured endless hours in the saddle, all the while anticipating the thrill of his first glimpse of Yosemite Falls. Typically, however, that late in the season the cataract had almost dried up, prompting Greeley to denounce it as nothing but "a humbug." Yosemite Valley, on the other hand, was well worth "a fatiguing visit." Indeed, he agreed, it was "most unique and majestic," unsurpassed by any other wonder like it "on earth." The following year the Reverend Thomas Starr King of Boston also made a visit and, several months afterward, described his horseback ride up the valley for the *Boston Evening Transcript*. "Is there such a ride possible in any other part of the planet?" He asked his readers to imagine formations such as "The Sentinel," standing 4,347 feet. "Reader, do you appreciate that height?" Similarly, before King's party "had been twenty minutes in the Yosemite Valley," they were "standing at the foot of a fall as high and more beautiful than the celebrated Staubach, the highest in Europe." Further try to comprehend, he asked, "such stupendous rock scenery." Certainly nothing "among the Alps, in no pass of the Andes, and in no Cañon of the mighty Oregon range" could rival it. Perhaps only "the awful gorges of the Himalaya," he finally conceded, could equal the tremendous uplift of the Sierra Nevada.[5]

The more such descriptions appeared in the popular press, the more Americans realized what Yosemite, symbolically, might mean to their culture. Among the few natural wonders renowned throughout the East, the most visited, Niagara Falls, had already been lost to private ownership and the attendant commercial ills. Once trees and wildflowers had framed the Niagara River; by 1850 hotels, shops, stables, signboards, tourist traps, and other eyesores all competed for public attention.[6] In dramatic contrast Yosemite was fresh, mysterious, inspiring, and, above all, unrivaled throughout the world. "Niagara itself," agreed Albert D. Richardson, another popular correspondent, "would dwarf beside the rocks in [Yosemite] valley." Europe itself could claim nothing of comparable grandeur, either natural or human made. In that vein Samuel Bowles, editor and publisher of the *Springfield* (Mass.) *Republican,* asked his readers to imagine how "The Three Brothers," "Cathedral Rocks," and "The Cathedral Spires" each replicated "the great impressiveness, the beauty and the fantastic form of the Gothic architecture. From their shape and color alike," he concluded, straining his analogy to the limit, "it is easy to imagine, in looking upon them, that you are under the ruins of an old Gothic cathedral, to which those of Cologne and Milan are but baby-houses."[7]

In Yosemite Valley, America came closer to ending its long and frustrating search for a distinctive national identity. Accordingly, describing the valley in combination with the giant sequoias proved doubly irresistible. Of the three groupings within a day's ride—the Merced, the Tuolumne, and the Mariposa groves—the latter was by far the largest and most popular. "Here," Horace Greeley informed his readers in 1859, "the Big Trees have been quietly nestled for I dare not say how many thousand years." But "that they were of very substantial size when David danced before the ark, when Solomon laid the foundations of the Temple, when Theseus ruled in Athens, when Aeneas fled from the burning wreck of vanquished Troy, when Sesostris led his victorious Egyptians into the heart of Asia," Greeley had "no manner of doubt." Thus did the giant sequoias further compensate the United States for lacking a national history that sparked interest overseas.

The explorer Clarence King later agreed with Greeley's assessment that the United States had a traditional past; American history simply required occasional measurement in "green old age." King's implication, like Greeley's, once again was obvious; the cultural possibilities of these enduring giants seemingly had no end. Meanwhile, for the traveler, "if he love the tree for its own grand nature," King concluded, "he may lie in silence upon the soft forest floor . . . and spend many days in wonder, gazing upon majestic shafts . . . up and through the few huge branches, and among the pale clouds of filmy green traced in open network upon the deep blue of the sky."[8]

Thoroughly fascinated, Americans thronged to exhibit halls, art galleries, and photographers' studios to see such descriptions lent visual expression. After all, in Hutchings's words, Yosemite Valley, like Niagara Falls, had become fixed in the American mind as another "scene of wonder and curiosity." C. L. Weed made the first photographs of the valley for Hutchings in 1859; romanticized versions appeared that October as engravings in the *Hutchings' California Magazine*.[9] Two years later Carleton E. Watkins, another rising photographer, also visited Yosemite and the Mariposa Grove. The artist Albert Bierstadt followed in the summer of 1863. For seven weeks he sketched Yosemite's cliffs, domes, and waterfalls; on canvas the wonders grew even larger than life against their unmistakably exaggerated backgrounds. But exaggerated or not, Bierstadt's grandiose paintings were the talk of critics and the art-viewing public. "Adventure is an element in American artist-life which gives it singular zest and interest," wrote H. T. Tuckerman, a reviewer, in praise of Bierstadt's work. The artist had captured not only the "bold and true significance" of American scenery but also the spirit of "pioneer enterprise and hardy exploration" that seemed to imbue the nation's art as a whole.[10] Yosemite, it followed, was open to some artistic license. More than a natural wonder, it had become fixed in the national consciousness as an icon of American culture. From Hutchings's early travels to Bierstadt's imaginative paintings, the period of transition spanned a total of barely eight years. Between 1855 and 1863, Yosemite's timeless hold on the American imagination had already become a foregone conclusion.

* * *

If Americans had thought seriously about Yosemite's future in 1855, instead of waiting, as was the case, until 1864, the development of the valley might have been strictly curtailed right at the outset. But the United States as a whole still knew little about the area; more significant, scenic preservation was not yet part of the nation's frame of reference. Americans simply could not debate an issue that had yet to evolve. In the process of transforming Yosemite Valley from natural wonder to icon, Americans naturally assumed that its development for tourism was both legitimate and necessary.

Hardly had the first tourists arrived in 1855 when a few entrepreneurs, sensing the possibilities of the valley as a summer resort, contemplated building the first camps and rustic hotels. By 1857 a primitive structure opposite Yosemite Falls was serving guests; two years later a slightly more elaborate structure, the Upper Hotel, had also been completed, a short distance up the valley.[11] Yosemite had passed over another threshold of change, again without discussion or evidence of widespread concern about the consequences.

The first settler to arrive in the valley was James C. Lamon. A transplanted Virginian who had come west in search of gold, Lamon claimed a portion of the upper, or eastern, end of the valley in 1859. There he put up a cabin, planted an orchard, and tended a garden, all with the intention of selling fruit and produce to summer guests. The importance of establishing a residence in Yosemite Valley as a prerequisite for commercial advantage was also not lost on James Mason Hutchings. In 1860 he published *Scenes of Wonder and Curiosity,* a guidebook further extolling Yosemite's distinctive grandeur; in March 1862, after a heavy winter snow, he made a round trip to the valley, seeking to prove that it could be reached and inhabited throughout the year. In part influenced by Hutchings's reports, Lamon wintered the following season in his cabin on the valley floor. Further encouraged by Lamon's success, Hutchings returned in 1863 and purchased the financially troubled Upper Hotel. Like Lamon, he "preempted," or claimed by right of first occupation, portions of Yosemite Valley covering more than one hundred acres of land.[12]

As Hutchings and Lamon undoubtedly were aware, both of their claims were technically illegal. Under the land laws of the United States, the right of preemption, or homestead, applied only to *surveyed* portions of the public domain. For obvious reasons government surveyors gave highest priority to lands desirable for settlement; the Sierra Nevada, as a result, had not yet been surveyed. And even if it had, Hutchings and Lamon would not have been granted clear title to their homesteads until each had satisfied the General Land Office that his claim was legitimate. To do this, the claimant had to demonstrate either *permanent* residence or improvements over a period of five years, or he had to be willing to pay the federal government $1.25 per acre. The key restriction again was the limitation of any claim to the surveyed public lands expressly designated for settlement. Until Yosemite Valley had been legally surveyed and further designated for settlement exclusive of any other public use, neither Hutchings nor Lamon had a binding claim to permanent ownership.[13]

Bluntly put, both men were squatters who simply hoped their claims would be recognized once Yosemite Valley had been surveyed. Like the location of the latest gold strike, the variables of America's land laws—and how each might be circumvented—were common knowledge all across the advancing frontier. As former gold seekers themselves, Hutchings and Lamon certainly knew the advantages of staking any kind of claim to a disputed piece of property. Having publicized Yosemite Valley and proven it habitable year-round, they now stood to profit from the greater number of tourists certain to follow. Meanwhile, like many other frontier settlers, they further gambled on the inconsistencies of federal land laws. Regardless of the fact that Yosemite Valley had not yet been surveyed, Hutchings and Lamon had settled there first and thereby had positioned themselves to insist on a recognition of their claims. Here again, as the frontier experience showed, the determined settler or speculator who backed his claim to a piece of property by also occupying it was almost certain to have some influence over its final dispensation.

Of course, neither Hutchings nor Lamon could have predicted the campaign for the government preservation of Yosemite Valley, an event that finally occurred during the winter and spring of 1864. Precisely how the campaign evolved remains largely a mystery. It is known that on February 20, 1864, Israel Ward Raymond, the California state representative of the Central American Steamship Transit Company of New York, sent a letter to John Conness, the junior senator from California, urging the preservation of Yosemite Valley and the Mariposa Grove of giant sequoias. Apparently, Raymond's letter elaborated on previous exchanges or discussions among himself, Senator Conness, and several others. "I send by express some views of the Yo Semite Valley to give you some idea of its character," Raymond began. These views included a photograph, taken at

Inspiration Point, showing "about seven miles of the Valley, and the principal part of it." Indicating the elevations necessary for making any effective comparisons, Raymond continued: "You can see that its sides are abrupt precipices ranging from 2500 to 5000 feet high. Indeed there is no access to it but by trails over the debris deposited by the crumbling of the walls."[14]

In retrospect, Raymond's next statement was crucial to the eventual establishment of the park. "The summits are mostly bare Granite Rock," he remarked. "In some parts the surface is covered only by pine trees and can never be of much value." Undoubtedly, as a result, it "will be many years before it is worth while for the Government to survey these mountains." Still, he considered "it important to obtain the proprietorship soon, to prevent occupation and especially to preserve the trees in the valley from destruction."[15] With this statement he underscored that Yosemite's potential economic value, exclusive of tourism, was minimal at best. Meanwhile, the valley obviously had the enormous scenic appeal that justified its being protected from the few individuals who might wish to settle there.

Raymond further included a brief description of the property that ought to be protected in the Mariposa Grove; he then came to the key statement of his entire proposition. "The above are granted for public use, resort, and recreation and are inalienable forever but leases may be granted for portions not to exceed ten years." Perhaps the wording *inalienable forever* was his own terminology; more likely, however, it resulted from discussions with one or more of the persons whom he listed as possible commissioners of the grant, especially Frederick Law Olmsted, the distinguished co-designer and first superintendent of Central Park in New York City. Although Olmsted and Raymond have not been linked directly, Raymond certainly was familiar with Central Park and Olmsted's growing reputation. Similarly, he could have met with Olmsted previously, either in New York or California; in 1863 Olmsted had gone to California to manage the Mariposa Estate, located about a day's ride west of Yosemite Valley in the Sierra Nevada foothills. Although he did not see the valley proper until August 1864, he was already well aware of its existence and fame.[16] Meanwhile, Senator Conness himself was crucial to the survival of the inalienable clause; he forwarded Raymond's letter to the commissioner of the General Land Office, requesting that a bill be prepared, and, significantly, he repeated Raymond's words: "Let the grant be inalienable."[17]

On May 17, 1864, the Senate Committee on Public Lands reported favorably on Conness's bill; he asked for its consideration immediately and was granted his request. "I will state to the Senate," he began his speech, "that this bill proposes to make a grant of certain premises located in the Sierra Nevada mountains, in the State of California, that are for all public purposes worthless, but which constitute, perhaps, some of the greatest wonders of the world." This statement, of course, repeated Raymond's assurance that Yosemite's striking beauty masked nothing of obvious commercial value. The most telling part of the speech, however, was Conness's own. Deviating momentarily from Raymond's original argument, he forcefully reminded the Senate that the British had earlier denied the very existence of the giant sequoias. "From the Calaveras grove some sections of a fallen tree were cut during and pending the great World's Fair that was held in London some years since," Conness noted. "The English who saw it declared it to be a Yankee invention, made from beginning to end; that it was an utter untruth that such trees grew in the country; that it could not be." Even though merely transporting the exhibit had cost "several thousand dollars, we were not able to convince them that it was a specimen of American growth." Few statements more graphically depicted the cultural significance that Americans had since bestowed on Yosemite Valley and the giant sequoias. "They would not believe us," Conness repeated for effect. If the English were so stubborn, America's duty was unmistakably clear. "The purpose of this bill is to preserve one of these groves from devastation and injury," he concluded, although obviously he did not intend to slight the significance of Yosemite Valley as well. "The necessity of taking early possession and care of these great wonders can easily be seen and understood."[18]

Introduced in those words, as a measure in defense of American pride and patriotism, Conness's bill was assured of success. Nor did England's sympathy for the Confederacy during the Civil War, then already in its third and bloodiest year, hurt the bill's chances. By reminding the Senate of England's earlier denouncement of the giant sequoias, Conness also subconsciously reminded his colleagues of Britain's lingering sentiments toward the American South.

Given the expense of the Civil War, his assurance that the park would cost the government nothing for maintenance and support proved equally important in securing the bill's passage. "The object and purpose is to make a grant to the State," he carefully noted, "to be taken charge of by gentlemen to be appointed by the Governor, who are to receive no compensation for their services, and who are to undertake the management and improvement of the property by making roads leading thereto and adopting such other means as may be necessary for its preservation and improvement." The application for protection itself came "from various gentlemen of California, gentlemen of fortune, of taste, and of refinement," who asked simply "that this property be committed to the care of the State." The one and only objective of the bill was the "preservation both of the Yosemite valley and the Big Tree Grove," that each "may be used and preserved for the benefit of mankind. It is a matter involving no appropriation whatever," Conness remarked, underscoring this most important qualification. "The property is of no value to the Government," he also restated, further invoking Raymond's compelling observation. "I make this explanation that the Senate may understand what the purpose is."[19] The House of Representatives speedily ratified the measure; accordingly, on June 30, 1864, President Abraham Lincoln signed the Yosemite Park Act into law.[20]

Its significance, of course, was easily lost at the time, especially since the bill had been passed in the midst of civil war. In retrospect, however, the United States Congress had done nothing less than approve a model piece of legislation leading to the eventual establishment of national parks. Meanwhile, Yosemite's own history as solely a natural wonder had drawn to a close. Its legacy of accomplishment and controversy as a park was about to begin.

* * *

Yosemite surmounted the first of its bureaucratic obstacles with relative ease. The passage of the Yosemite Park Act of 1864 provided for transferring the valley and the Mariposa Grove to the state of California. The official acceptance of the grant required the approval of the state legislature, which would not meet again until 1866. As a result, Governor Frederick F. Low issued an interim proclamation of acceptance on September 28, 1864, and, further in keeping with his prerogatives under section one of the enabling act, announced in the proclamation his first appointments to the Yosemite board of park commissioners.[21]

Of considerable note, the name heading the governor's list was that of Frederick Law Olmsted. Aside from his probable influence on the park legislation itself, his appointment as nominal chairman of the commission underscored his growing reputation in park management and design. The seven other appointees included Israel Ward Raymond and Josiah Dwight Whitney, state geologist. The commissioners immediately authorized a survey of Yosemite Valley and the Mariposa Grove to determine, as required by the act of June 30, 1864, "the locus, extent, and limits" of the grant. The survey was completed that fall by James T. Gardner and Clarence King, whose names were synonymous with exploration of the region. Finally, on April 2, 1866, the legislature and the governor of California jointly approved an act of acceptance, and the transfer of Yosemite Valley and the Mariposa Grove to the state became official.[22]

The Park Commission, in turn, voted on May 21 to make Galen Clark, one of its members, the first official guardian of the grant.[23] In a more serious vein, the commissioners further addressed the problem of outstanding land claims in the valley. Fortunately, a solution, so it seemed, had already been written into the Yosemite Park Act. In keeping with Israel Ward Raymond's original recommendations to Senator Conness, the bill authorized private individuals to apply for the privilege of building and operating tourist accommodations in the park. Leases to this effect were to be granted for ten-year intervals. Accordingly, the commissioners offered James Mason Hutchings and James C. Lamon the right to maintain their existing properties in the valley for a period not to exceed the ten years allowable under the terms of the Yosemite Park Act.[24]

As Josiah Dwight Whitney, the commission's secretary, later reported to the state legislature, the terms offered Lamon and Hutchings were extremely generous. In Lamon's case, for example, the commissioners charged "the nominal rent of one dollar per annum." By 1866 he claimed 378 acres in the upper portion of the valley; of these, 20 had been cleared and planted with fruit trees and berries. The berries especially, Whitney noted, "have found a ready market in the valley among the visitors." The point again was that Lamon had not established clear title to his property prior to June 30, 1864, nor could he have done so regardless of the park act unless Yosemite Valley had been surveyed and opened to settlement. Still, in view "of the useful character of the work done by him," Whitney remarked, and because "his buildings are not at all conspicuous in the valley," the commission agreed that he should be offered a lease in keeping with the most liberal interpretation of the Yosemite Park Act.[25]

In Hutchings's case, the commissioners tried to be no less accommodating. Moreover, they remained sympathetic even though Hutchings, unlike

Lamon, had claimed "the best meadow land, and the best or one of the best sites for building in the valley." Further weighing his investments in and contributions to the valley's notoriety, the commissioners were also disposed to offer him a ten-year lease to his land, house, and hotel, again "at a mere nominal rent."[26]

Nonetheless, neither Hutchings nor Lamon accepted the commission's offer, insisting that the terms instead infringed on their property rights. Thus the commission had "no alternative," Whitney reported, but to begin "legal proceedings against both these gentlemen as trespassers." Simply stated, the question before the courts would be "whether the State really is the proprietor of the grant made by Congress, or, in short, whether the United States have authority to dispose of the unsurveyed and unsold public land."[27] King and Gardner's survey authorized by the Yosemite Park Commission had established only the boundaries and topography of the grant; in any event, federal acceptance of such limited surveys in no way obligated the General Land Office to sanction any previous settlement claims.

Meanwhile, Hutchings and Lamon prepared to take their case to the California state legislature. Early in 1868 the legislature found overwhelmingly in their favor, passing an act of restitution even over the veto of Governor H. H. Haight. On the ratification of the measure by the United States Congress, each claimant would receive clear title to 160 acres of land in Yosemite Valley.[28] The qualification that Congress itself must ratify the award proved, in the end, to be of special significance. Otherwise, the ramifications of the dispute were already becoming obvious. If Hutchings and Lamon won their case, any land claim, no matter how tenuous, could conceivably undermine the Yosemite Grant, not to mention irreparably compromise all future attempts to establish scenic parks on the public domain.

On June 3, 1868, Representative George W. Julian of Indiana asked for consideration of H.R. 1118, "an act to confirm to J. M. Hutchings and J. C. Lamon their preemption claims in the Yosemite valley, in the State of California." Following the line of argument they themselves had repeatedly advanced, Julian depicted Hutchings and Lamon as men whose investments were in fact personal sacrifices in the *national* interest. Long before June 30, 1864, according to the text of H.R. 1118, both claimants had made "permanent and substantial improvements" in the valley "to the great convenience and comfort of visitors." In other words, the United States had Hutchings and Lamon alone to thank for the fact that Yosemite Valley "was no longer a remote and solitary wilderness." The provision in the Yosemite Park Act allowing only ten-year leases to private developers was obviously "wholly inadequate" to attract other innkeepers and investors. Hutchings and Lamon had staked their fortunes on Yosemite Valley regardless of such risks. They "had built their cabins, planted their orchards and vineyards, and expended several thousand dollars in establishing for themselves a comfortable home," Julian stated, further pleading their case on the floor of the House. Adding to his imagery of their alleged wilderness ordeal, he concluded that all the while, they had faced "the privations and hardship incident to a life remote from society and civilization."[29]

In a similar vein, Representative James A. Johnson of California took up the argument where Julian left off, noting that if the government offered "inducements to those who are hardy and enterprising enough to advance ahead into the unbroken wilderness and blaze out a way for civilization to follow," but then reneged on those inducements, "that Government is not a Government of law, of justice, or of right between man and man; but is a plundering despotism, robbing its own citizens." The Yosemite Park Act aside, the Constitution and laws of the United States made no provision "for the creation of fancy pleasure grounds by Congress out of citizens' farms." Here again, the portrayal of Hutchings and Lamon as struggling pioneers rather than frontier opportunists proved compelling. When the speaker ended debate and the vote was called, the motion for restitution was easily approved.[30]

If the bill had carried in the Senate as well, the Yosemite Park Act might have been irreparably undermined by any land claim, no matter how specious. Instead, the Senate held firm to the preservation principles first enunciated by Israel Ward Raymond and John Conness. On July 23, 1868, Senator George H. Williams of Oregon reported to his colleagues that the Committee on Private Land Claims, to whom H.R. 1118 had been referred, had instructed him "to make an adverse report, and to move the indefinite postponement of the bill." The report itself emphasized that Yosemite Valley had "never been surveyed"; accordingly, it had "never become subject to pre-emption or private sale." It followed that Hutchings's and Lamon's rights to the lands they occupied were no more "than might arise from an *expectation* that at some subsequent time they could obtain title from the United States" (italics added). In any event, especially given the topography of Yosemite Valley and its environs, the claimants at least "had some reasons to suppose that there would be delays and difficulties in perfecting their titles" and, more specifically, "that the public surveys would not, for a long time, if ever, be extended to it." Meanwhile, "the remarkable features of the place" should have forewarned Lamon and Hutchings that Yosemite Valley might "not be treated by the government like agricultural lands of an ordinary character."[31] This observation was "especially true of Mr. Hutchings," Williams wrote, emphasizing that his claim was even more tenuous than Lamon's. Hutchings had "commenced his residence there long after public attention had been attracted to the valley, and only a month or two before it was granted by Congress to the State." If anything, Williams continued, Hutchings was entitled "to credit and possibly compensation," but not land. To be sure, he had "visited the valley frequently before 1864, and published interesting descriptions of it"; the point again was that no law provided "for the inception of a title in that way." Settlers residing on the unsurveyed public lands of the United States did so "at their peril," Williams concluded. "The government is under no equitable obligation to maintain their claims to the prejudice of the public interests."[32]

In the instance of Yosemite Valley, "one of the wonders of the world," only its preservation in trust, Williams argued, protected those public interests. "It stands unrivalled in its majesty, grandeur, and beauty," he wrote. "It is one of those magnificent developments of natural scenery in which all of the people of the country feel a pride and an interest, and to which their equal right of access and enjoyment ought to be protected." It was toward "this end," he emphasized, that Congress had granted Yosemite to California in the first place. Clearly, the acceptance of the grant bound California to honor its conditions. As Williams noted, "That State *was required* and expected to take the valley and hold it for 'public use, resort, and recreation,' and Congress in effect by the act of 1864 reserved it for such purposes" (italics added). Instead California had voted to allow the possibility "that ultimately it would go into the hands of those who would levy tribute upon the travelling public, and make this beautiful valley odious for the extortions of its greedy and sordid possessors." Admittedly, it had been said that Hutchings and Lamon were "good and deserving citizens; that they will protect the valley." Then what about the other people who had supposedly made similar claims? Could the same be said for them? In either case, "passage of the bill before the Senate would be to give up the idea of the public enjoyment of the valley, and surrender it wholly to the purposes of private speculation."[33]

The key again, Williams concluded in his report, was the intent of the original legislation to protect Yosemite Valley "inalienable for all time." The California legislation awarding Lamon and Hutchings title to lands in the valley was a breach of that faith, a measure approved "in utter disregard of the conditions and purposes of the grant." The duty of the Senate was unmistakably clear. "All parts of the country are interested in keeping this property out of private hands," Williams reiterated. Congress had no obligation whatsoever "to ratify the act of California granting to Hutchings and Lamon parts of the Yosemite valley." The American people instead overwhelmingly demanded "that it should be protected for their own 'use, resort, and recreation.' "[34]

In retrospect, preservation had withstood its first significant challenge. Above all, the Senate's insistence that California honor its obligation to protect Yosemite Valley in trust for the American people as a whole, "inalienable for all time," gave crucial impetus to the national park idea. Except for the cession of Yosemite Valley and the Mariposa Grove of giant sequoias to California for management, every other guiding principle of the national park idea was already in place by 1864. The petition of Lamon and Hutchings forced Congress to reaffirm those principles as early as 1868, four years prior to the establishment of Yellowstone National Park.

Traditionally considered to be the birthplace of the national park idea, Yellowstone was in fact the beneficiary of the Yosemite Park Act and, equally significant, of its reaffirmation by Congress in 1868. By way of precedent, the Yosemite Grant had already been publicized, established, challenged, and upheld. Under the circumstances, the idea of public parks came more readily into focus; long before Yellowstone had been explored and promoted, the model pointing the way to its protection had been conceived and sustained.

In the final analysis, the matter of ownership was the only major distinction between the two parks.[35] That distinction was reduced to a technicality the moment the United States Senate refused in 1868 to ratify California's legislation allowing private claims in Yosemite Valley. To be sure, it was California in the first place that had submitted the legislation to Congress for final review and approval. In effect, that gesture alone validated the act of June 30, 1864, by indicating that California both recognized and accepted the limitations inherent in the transfer of Yosemite Valley from federal to state ownership. The fact remains that Yosemite Park originated as a piece of *federal* legislation, and was awarded to California only as long as the state observed the express conditions contained in the act. Obviously, if California had pressed the point in 1868, either by failing to submit its legislation to Congress for review or by ignoring Congress's final determination in the dispute, further legislation leading to the revocation of the Yosemite Grant would have loomed as a very real possibility.

Such disparities as its name and ownership aside, Yosemite was in fact the first national park, the first park not only established but also upheld by Congress. The irony was that Congress, having disallowed private ownership in the park, nonetheless openly promoted private investment in its facilities. On the one hand, individual initiative was strictly curtailed; on the other, the Yosemite Park Act legally sanctioned and encouraged it. Only leases were to be granted for public camps and hotels; no properties supporting these concessions could be privately owned. The point is that a major foundation of the park experiment had been grounded in contradiction. Individuals could still profit by promoting development; they simply could not acquire the attractions themselves.

Concessionaires, it followed, would hedge their investments with a greater say in park matters. Indeed, by 1868 potential investors were already complaining that ten-year leases were not long enough.[36] Granted, James Lamon and James Hutchings had apparently lost their battle to claim land in Yosemite outright, but in truth the convictions of private property that they had defended still largely prevailed. Private property remained sacred; it was simply granted in different form. Accordingly, Yosemite Valley, even as it became a park, still faced the critical problem of limiting change and development. With barely a pause for reflection, the nation had allowed business a legal means for exploiting the preserve. What Yosemite might have been had every form of commercialism been excluded from the outset was a riddle therefore left to future generations.

❧ *Prophecy and Change*

CHAPTER THREE

Barely had Yosemite Valley been surveyed as a park when it challenged a basic assumption of every park yet to come. As demonstrated by the lingering controversy over its disputed land claims, Yosemite's protection in name did not necessarily guarantee its preservation in actuality. Rather, considering the likelihood of just the opposite possibility, as early as August 9, 1865, Frederick Law Olmsted warned the Yosemite Park Commission to guard against any comforting but nonetheless misleading suppositions about the future of the valley. On the strength of his foresight his report would be hailed as a classic, a statement that literally anticipated the ideals of national park management. "It is the will of the nation as embodied in the act of Congress," he remarked, summing up the basis of his observations, "that this scenery never shall be private property, but that like certain defensive points upon our coast it shall be held solely for public purposes." The public interest in Yosemite Valley obviously resided "wholly in its natural scenery. The first point to be kept in mind then," he said, arriving at the heart of his report, "is the preservation and maintenance as exactly as is possible of the natural scenery." Allowances for structures should be made only "within the narrowest limits consistent with the necessary accommodation of visitors." Similarly, management should seek to exclude "all constructions markedly inharmonious with the scenery or which would unnecessarily obscure, distort, or detract from the dignity of the scenery." After all, Olmsted predicted, although visitation currently totaled only several hundred people

28

annually, it would eventually "become thousands and in a century the whole number of visitors will be counted by the millions." The significance of this figure should be dramatically obvious: "An injury to the scenery so slight that it may be unheeded by any visitor now, will be one of deplorable magnitude when its effect upon each visitor's enjoyment is multiplied by these millions." The duty of the commission, it followed, was to protect "the rights of posterity as well as of contemporary visitors," for "the millions who are hereafter to benefit by the Act have the largest interest in it, and the largest interest should be first and most strenuously guarded."[1]

Of all the might-have-beens in national park history, the suppression of Olmsted's report was among the most significant. Two prominent members of the Yosemite Park Commission, Josiah Dwight Whitney and William Ashburner, apparently saw to it that Olmsted's report never reached the state legislature. Whitney, the director of the California Geological Survey, and Ashburner, also a geologist with the survey, possibly feared competition for limited state funds if Olmsted's request for thirty-seven thousand dollars to implement his plan was approved.[2] Not until 1952, under the auspices of Olmsted's biographer, Laura Wood Roper, was this most important document finally discovered, pieced together, and then published for the first time.

How the management of Yosemite Valley might have differed if Olmsted's recommendations had been heeded from the outset is a matter of speculation. But undoubtedly its vegetation, not merely its spectacular geology, would have received far better protection. "There are falls of water elsewhere finer," he maintained, obviously thinking of the sheer volume and sweep of Niagara,[3] "there are more stupendous rocks, more beetling cliffs, there are deeper and more awful chasms, there may be as beautiful streams, as lovely meadows, there are larger trees." In other words, Yosemite's "charm" did not derive from any single "scene or scenes." Rather the beauty of Yosemite Valley resided in the combination of many natural elements, of which its vegetation was no less significant than its geology. Granted, Yosemite was "cliffs of awful height and rocks of vast magnitude and of varied and exquisite coloring." But Yosemite was also cliffs "banked and fringed and draped and shadowed by the tender foliage of noble and lovely trees and bushes, reflected from the most placid pools, and associated with the most tranquil meadows, the most playful streams, and every variety of soft and peaceful pastoral beauty." It followed that "no description, no measurements, no comparisons are of much value." Every dependence on statistics fixed "the mind on mere matters of wonder or curiosity" and thus prevented "the true and far more extraordinary character of the scenery from being appreciated." Ultimately, the real test of management was whether the Yosemite Park Commission could maintain "the value of the district in its present condition as a museum of natural science." If not, Yosemite Valley faced "the danger, indeed the certainty, that without care many of the species of plants now flourishing upon it will be lost and many interesting objects be defaced or obscured if not destroyed."[4]

A further basis for objecting to Olmsted's report was now readily apparent. If preservation was to succeed, compromise, in his view, had absolutely no place in Yosemite Valley. Either "laws to prevent an unjust use by individuals, of that which is not individual but public property must be made and rigidly enforced," or the Yosemite Park Commission would be forced to yield "the interest of uncounted millions" to "the convenience, bad taste, playfulness, carelessness, or wanton destructiveness of present visitors." Similar restrictions, it went without saying, should also apply in the Mariposa Grove. The forest surrounding the grove itself was nothing out of the ordinary. The giant sequoias, on the other hand, were unquestionably unique. "Among them," he noted, "is one known through numerous paintings and photographs as the Grizzly Giant, which probably is the noblest tree in the world." Yet the "beauty and stateliness" of all the big trees equally delighted "one who moves among them in [a] reverant mood." To be sure, he remarked, knowledgeable travelers universally maintained "that they would rather have passed by Niagara itself than have missed visiting the grove."[5]

Olmsted's report, to reemphasize, ranks as a classic not only because he outlined strict principles of park management and visitor conduct but also because he believed park vegetation deserved special care. Granted, as a landscape architect he was already predisposed to consider the placement and manipulation of flowers, trees, and shrubs. Yet for Olmsted vegetation was far more than just a designer's tool. As part of any biological whole its absence would be sorely noticed. What Olmsted did not fully comprehend was the degree to which the vegetative cover of Yosemite Valley had previously been altered and manipulated by the Ahwahneechee Indians. Nor would he personally have any role in future management decisions; only three days after delivering his report he left Yosemite Valley, never again to return. Back in New York City where he resumed work on Central Park, he resigned from the Yosemite Park Commission on October 23, 1866.[6]

* * *

With Olmsted's resignation from the Yosemite Park Commission, a most influential and knowledgeable voice for preservation in Yosemite Valley had been all but silenced. In his absence, the priority of the commission shifted subtly but unmistakably from preservation of the park for its own sake to management in the interest of attracting more tourism. As Olmsted had maintained, visitation and protection could be reconciled, but only if strict rules of conduct and imaginative park design worked against abusive practices and behavior. Underscoring the sincerity of his commitment to public use, he proposed three thousand dollars for the construction of thirty miles of trails and footpaths; one thousand six hundred dollars for the construction of bridges; two thousand dollars for cabins, latrines, stairways, railings, and other tourist amenities; and twenty-five thousand dollars to aid in the construction of good access roads to the valley and the Mariposa Grove.[7] Obviously, Olmsted was no purist bent on prohibiting all but the robust and healthy from seeing Yosemite Valley and the giant sequoias. By the same token, he firmly believed that visitation without uncompromising standards of behavior would defeat the very purposes of park preservation.

Although the commissioners as a whole probably sympathized with his views, his departure and resignation from the commission left it without a conscience in succumbing to expedience. Almost immediately, Josiah Dwight Whitney and William Ashburner interpreted Olmsted's report as a possible competitor for the additional funding needed by the California Geological Survey. Even Israel Ward Raymond apparently sided with Whitney and Ashburner to suppress the report's submission to the California state legislature. When James Lamon and James Hutchings threatened an outright confiscation of Yosemite Valley in 1868, Whitney did join forces with Olmsted to have the claimants defeated in the United States Senate. By then, of course, Olmsted was both off the commission and safely across the continent, where his assistance could be either courted or politely refused at will.[8]

Meanwhile, the Yosemite Park Commission turned increasingly to publicizing the grant, an activity more in keeping with the social, political, and financial ambitions of Josiah Dwight Whitney and Israel Ward Raymond.

31

For example, in his first report to Governor Frederick F. Low in 1867, Whitney announced the preparation of the "Yosemite Guide Book" and "Yosemite Gift Book." The former was intended as a general guide for tourists; the latter was to be a luxury edition of the same text and would contain twenty-four plates by the noted photographer Carleton E. Watkins. "It is believed that it will be one of the most elegant books ever issued from an American press," Whitney remarked, "and that it will have no little influence in drawing attention to the stupendous scenery of the Yosemite and its vicinity."[9] Promotion, in other words, was the volume's distinct aim. Had Olmsted been present, he undoubtedly would have conceded the park's economic attractions; he simply considered the "pecuniary advantage" of parks "less important" than their role in furthering human "health and vigor." Granted, he freely admitted, monetary considerations "likely" had first disposed Congress to establish the park. Consistently falling back on his basic principles, he nonetheless warned that without "proper administration," neither the monetary advantages nor the greater good of parks as reservoirs "of refreshing rest and reinvigoration" would be served.[10]

For Olmsted, preserving Yosemite's natural scenery was "*the first point* to be kept in mind"; for Whitney, it was merely "*one* of the most important duties of the Commissioners" (italics added).[11] The difference between the accents of both descriptions was subtle but significant nonetheless. Preservation, in Olmsted's view, was of top priority; according to Whitney, it was only one of several prime objectives. In either case, under Whitney's influence the Yosemite Park Commission gradually adopted a more pragmatic point of view, including publicity among its major obligations. For example, the *Yosemite Book* appeared in 1868, every bit as lavish and elegant as Whitney had promised. "The object of this volume is," he wrote, employing language highly reminiscent of *Hutchings' California Magazine,* "to call the attention of the public to the scenery of California and to furnish a reliable guide to some of its most interesting features, namely: the Yosemite Valley, the High Sierra and its immediate vicinity, and the so-called 'Big Trees'."[12] Preservation for its own sake was the last thing the commission wanted.

It was not that Whitney and his colleagues opposed Olmsted in spirit; it was simply that as politicians and publicists they opposed the landscape architect by degree. What indeed was the proper line between preservation and use? For the next century and a quarter, every controversy regarding the fate of Yosemite and its resources would hinge on this most fundamental and often troubling question. At least this much had been decided as early as 1868: private ownership within public parks was not acceptable as a basis for compromise. Throughout the *Yosemite Book* Whitney himself underscored California's obligations to the American people by virtue of its acceptance of the Yosemite Grant. California had "solemnly promised," he remarked, to hold Yosemite Valley and the Mariposa Grove "inalienable for all time." Accordingly, the land claims of James Lamon and James Hutchings posed a serious internal threat to the principle of public ownership. The recognition of their claims in the valley would make it "the property of private individuals" determined to use it "for private benefit and not for the public good." But California "has no right to attempt to withdraw from the responsibility she has voluntarily assumed," Whitney argued. "This is not an ordinary gift of land, . . . but a trust imposed on the State, of the nature of a solemn compact, forever binding after having been once accepted." Yosemite Valley had never belonged to the state alone; rather it had "been made a *National public park* and placed under the charge of the State of California" (italics added). Californians only risked making "the name of their state a by-word and reproach for all time," he therefore concluded, "by trying to throw off and repudiate a noble task which they undertook to perform—that of holding the Yosemite Valley as a place of public use, resort, and recreation, inalienable for all time!"[13]

The firmness and clarity with which Whitney pronounced "National public park" further corroborates the interpretation that Yosemite and not Yellowstone is the actual birthplace of the national park idea. Between 1864 and 1868, proponents of the park consistently referred to California as the management authority only of a national "trust." Meanwhile, the future of the valley was still shrouded in controversy. Upheld in February 1868 by the California state legislature, Hutchings and Lamon had refused to yield to the Yosemite Park Commission. Instead they had asked the surveyor general of California for an immediate survey of their claims. Reluctantly he agreed; even more reluctantly, he laid out their claims to the valley not in customary blocks of land but, at their insistence, in widely scattered parcels and unusual configurations. Lamon claimed his property in three separate and distinct parcels; Hutchings insisted that his own claim be laid out in the shape of a cross, "extending from mountain to mountain," Governor H. H. Haight later reported, "and blocking up the valley." In a letter of explanation to Governor Haight, the surveyor general bitterly complained about the whole procedure and its probable effect on the future of the park. "If the grants are made to the claimants [by Congress]," Haight concluded, summing up both his concerns and those of the surveyor general, "others will make similar claims, and it would, in that event, be hardly expedient to expend public funds upon the valley."[14]

The Yosemite Park Commission saw no alternative but to take the claimants to court, seeking their final ejection from all park properties. Named as defendant in the test case was James Mason Hutchings. Hutchings stood firm pending the outcome in 1871 of another bill introduced in Congress to ratify the settlers' claims. Drawing on his experience as a writer and publicist, he attempted to overturn the decision made against him in 1868 by petitioning the Senate not to approve "wresting" him and his family from their "little homestead in Yosemite." Congress still was not moved, however, and the bill once more failed to pass.[15] Meanwhile, the state district court decided the case brought against him in his favor, but on appeal to the state supreme court the decision was reversed and the Yosemite Park Commission sustained. Hutchings in turn took his suit to the United States Supreme Court, which, in the opinion of *Hutchings v. Low,* finally and irrevocably ruled against his claim in December 1872.

Considering the origins of the national park idea, the decision of the Supreme Court is especially significant. Historians comparing the Yosemite Park Act of 1864 with the Yellowstone Park Act of 1872 have generally focused on the acts themselves rather than on the eight years of legislative intrigue in between. Essentially, the Supreme Court in *Hutchings v. Low* upheld the right of the federal government to designate the unsold, unsurveyed public domain for any purpose other than settlement, including for the establishment of national public parks. The preemption laws provided settlers only with the privilege of being the first to bid for land if it was in fact surveyed and then offered for sale. "It seems to us little less than absurd," the court remarked, "to say that a settler . . . by acquiring a right to be preferred in the purchase of property, provided a sale is made by the owner, thereby acquires a right to compel the owner to sell." Congress, in other words, had full legal authority to grant Yosemite Valley to the state of California. California, on the other hand, did not have unilateral authority to revoke any portions of that agreement. "The act of Congress of June 30, 1864," the court reported, underscoring the point, passed title of Yosemite

1. Half Dome, at 8,842 feet elevation, rises nearly a mile above the floor of Yosemite Valley, elevation 4,000 feet. The grandeur of Yosemite has long overshadowed its biological heritage, such as the black-tailed deer momentarily distracted in the foreground. Photograph by Ralph H. Anderson, courtesy of the National Park Service.

I. *Incomparable Yosemite*

2. The first published view of Yosemite Valley, in October 1855, was this striking lithograph, *Yo-Hamite Falls,* from a sketch by Thomas A. Ayres. Note the spacing between the trees and extensive meadows clear across the valley floor, confirming pioneers' accounts that Native Americans periodically burned Yosemite Valley to remove undergrowth and retard advancing forests. Courtesy of the Yosemite National Park Research Library.

3. Ayres's view contrasts sharply with this modern photograph of Yosemite Falls. At 2,425 feet, it is actually three separate cascades. Here only the upper fall, dropping 1,430 feet, is clearly visible above the trees and intervening rocks.

Photograph by Richard Frear, courtesy of the National Park Service.

4. Glacier Point has long attracted reckless tourists, such as this party in 1887. Courtesy of the Bancroft Library.

5. The view from Glacier Point, looking east, includes Half Dome and the High Sierra. Courtesy of the National Park Service.

6. The giant sequoias of the Mariposa Grove have fascinated Yosemite visitors since the late 1850s. Photograph by Ralph H. Anderson, courtesy of the National Park Service.

7. The backcountry of Yosemite National Park, much of it declared wilderness in 1984, lures thousands of visitors annually, such as these hikers at the base of Mount Lyell (13,114 feet), the highest point in the park. Photograph by Ralph H. Anderson, courtesy of the National Park Service.

8. Frederick Law Olmsted, as the first chairman of the Yosemite Park Commission, warned in 1865 against treasuring Yosemite Valley for its natural wonders only, as opposed to protecting both its scenery and its native vegetation as equal and inseparable wholes. Courtesy of the National Park Service, Frederick Law Olmsted National Historic Site.

Valley and the Mariposa Grove to California "subject to the trust specified therein." As a result, the "act of California, of February 1868," the court noted, mincing no words in its closing argument, was "inoperative" unless "ratified by Congress." But no ratification of the act granting restitution to Hutchings had ever been approved, "and it is not believed," the court remarked, "that Congress will ever sanction *such a perversion* of the trust solemnly accepted by the State" (italics added).[16]

Hutchings v. Low, in effect, established that national parks were indeed constitutional. The length and intensity of the debate, especially the reconsideration of the Yosemite Park Act by Congress in 1868 and 1871 and the appeal of Hutchings's claims all the way to the United States Supreme Court, further indicates Yosemite's significance in the evolution of national parks. The irony of the controversy was the degree to which the claimants benefited from simply having pressed their case. In 1874 the California legislature voted sixty thousand dollars to compensate Hutchings, Lamon, and several other claimants for their improvements in the park. Of this amount Hutchings and Lamon received the two largest individual awards, twenty-four thousand dollars and twelve thousand dollars, respectively. Yosemite Valley had been freed of private ownership; simultaneously, however, Hutchings's and Lamon's persistence had won them monetary reward considerably greater than what most American settlers would see in earnings during an entire lifetime.[17]

* * *

In retrospect, the elimination of private claims from Yosemite Valley only set the stage for another protracted controversy in national park history. In the eight years of debate preceding *Hutchings v. Low,* the United States had resolved that Yosemite was in fact a component of the national trust. Yellowstone, itself a beneficiary of this long debate, further defined and strengthened the precedent that parks, once established, ought to remain generally secure from private encroachment. It remained for the government to determine how individuals could still do business inside the parks. The arrangement finalized by Congress allowed licensed concessionaires to operate hotels, camps, toll roads, and transportation lines, provided the rules and regulations prescribed by government officials were consistently obeyed.

Among nineteenth-century Americans, no arrangement for resolving the conflict between the government ownership of parks and the nation's commitment to private enterprise made more sense. At the same time, no compromise between the protection and the development of parks was imbued with greater potential for damage to their natural resources. In theory, the government made strict rules, which concessionaires were obliged to follow. Yet in practice, the government's attempt to justify preservation by boosting visitation to the parks signaled concessionaires to negotiate for leniency as well as special privileges. Elected officials, after all, had determined that parks might bring prosperity to their surrounding communities. In coming to that realization, politicians revealed the vulnerable point in park leasing arrangements. By reassuring government officials of their own commitment to increased visitation, concessionaires were in a position either to bend certain rules or to argue for their abolishment altogether. Ostensibly, the overriding obligation of park managers was the protection of the resource. But in truth, both the government and concessionaires wanted the same thing—more visitors. For concessionaires, more visitation might lead to greater profits; for politicians, larger numbers of tourists held forth the promise of more satisfied constituents.

As Frederick Law Olmsted had warned the Yosemite Park Commission in 1865, any such shift in priority from preservation to the accommodation of development for its own sake threatened to accelerate environmental change in Yosemite Valley, especially through the displacement of its original vegetation. "To illustrate these dangers," he remarked, "it may be stated that numbers of the native plants of large districts of the Atlantic states have almost wholly disappeared and that most of the common weeds of the farms are of foreign origin, having choked out the native vegetation."[18] As Olmsted undoubtedly realized, a tide of exotic vegetation had already swept over California, beginning with Spanish exploration in the sixteenth century. In the final analysis, little could be done to prevent the same nonindigenous plants from eventually taking hold in Yosemite Valley. No less than in the sixteenth century, the common means of seed transport and deposition persisted, most notably dissemination by the wind, in clothing, and through the feed and fecal matter of horses and other livestock.[19] The importation into Yosemite Valley of exotic-laden grass and grain alone foretold inevitable changes in the composition of its vegetation. Conceivably, some changes could have been predetermined as early as the Mariposa Battalion's first encampment on the valley floor in March 1851. Only the general lack of major disturbances to the native vegetation between 1851 and 1865—disruptions allowing exotics to gain a visible hold in Yosemite Valley—prevented the extent of their presence in the future from being fully appreciated.[20]

As Olmsted maintained, strict enforcement of park rules was the only means of preventing undesirable changes to the natural environment. Inevitably, the Yosemite Park Commission would increasingly find itself torn between its duty to protect Yosemite Valley and its obligation to make the valley more accessible. The key, again, to striking the proper balance was strict observance of park objectives. Gradually, however, the commission came to see this as an uncompromising point of view, and noticeably swung in favor of promoting visitation. The result, as Olmsted had predicted, was accelerating levels of biological disruption and change.

Among the more visible changes, the overgrowth of Yosemite Valley's meadowlands by an increasing number of trees was especially dramatic. "The valley at the time of discovery presented the appearance of a well kept park," noted Lafayette Bunnell in 1889, recalling the expedition of the Mariposa Battalion in 1851. "There was then but little undergrowth in the park-like valley, and a half day's work in lopping off branches . . . enabled us to speed our horses uninterrupted through the groves." Like a growing number of knowledgeable Americans, Bunnell attributed the valley's openness to fires set annually by the natives "to facilitate the search for game." Galen Clark, appointed state guardian of the Yosemite Grant in 1866, corroborated Bunnell's observations in a letter to the Yosemite Park Commission in 1894. "My first visit to Yosemite was in the summer of 1855," he reported, further establishing himself as one of the valley's earliest explorers. "At the time there was no undergrowth of young trees to obstruct clear open views in any part of the valley from one side of the Merced River across to the base of the opposite wall." In fact, he maintained, the extent "of clear open meadow land . . . was at least four times as large as at the present time." Like Bunnell, Clark credited Indians with maintaining the valley's open appearance. For "their own protection and self-interests," he noted, the Indians annually set fires throughout the entire valley. The practice not only denied potential enemies more places for concealment but also provided "clear grounds for hunting and gathering acorns." And even when "the fires did not thoroughly burn over the moist meadows," Clark concluded, "all the young willows and cottonwoods were pulled up by hand."[21]

As Galen Clark and his contemporaries had come to understand, the manipulation of forests and grasslands by Native Americans had been nearly universal. Far from a random practice, the use of fire in particular helped encourage the propagation of desirable plants and animals.[22] The Ahwahneechees especially prized the black oak for its acorns; without fire to eliminate its competitors, its numbers would have been considerably reduced. The black oak thrived in open sunlight, in the absence of shade-tolerant vegetation. The annual fires did no harm to mature stands of the trees; on the other hand, the seedlings of pines, incense cedars, and other competitive species seldom survived the flames.[23]

Following the expulsion of the Ahwahneechees from Yosemite Valley in 1853, burning continued to be practiced periodically by the few Indians who occasionally returned to settle there or to hunt food and gather acorns. As a result, the vegetation in 1865 probably appeared little different than it had in 1851. In a rare moment lacking his unique gift of foresight, Frederick Law Olmsted accused the Indians of setting destructive fires. Similarly, he recommended that any road laid out to the Mariposa Grove should also "be carried completely around it, so as to offer a barrier of bare ground to the approach of fires."[24]

Olmsted's concern for fire suppression was to be expected in an age of wooden structures and inadequate building codes. The beneficial aspects of fire so well known to the Indians also made little sense to cultivators of differing persuasions. With the settlement of Yosemite Valley by James Lamon, James Hutchings, and several other claimants, the meadows were gradually taken over for cattle and horses. Lamon also brought in the first apple, pear, plum, and peach trees, whereas Hutchings planted an orchard in 1866.[25] Predictably, the maintenance of livestock and orchards called for fencing and barns. The point is that the more Yosemite Valley was readied for tourists, the less its claimants, concessionaires, and guardians welcomed fire as a natural and beneficial occurrence.

By the early 1870s, as a result, perceptible changes in the appearance of the valley floor had begun to occur. According to Hutchings, visitation increased dramatically between 1864 and 1870, when 4,936 people came to the new park, as opposed to 653 between 1855 and 1863.[26] To meet the growing demand for visitor services, permanent valley residents stepped up their farming and construction activities. Most notably, additional portions of the meadows were plowed, fenced, planted, or grazed. In Olmsted's view, better access into the valley would have allowed all provisions and visitor necessities to be supplied from outside "at moderate rates." Even as conditions stood, he undoubtedly would have objected strongly to any alteration of the meadows.[27] But Olmsted was gone. Meanwhile, although the seeds of exotic plants would have found their way into Yosemite Valley regardless of any precautions, the disruption to existing vegetation and soils caused by plowing and grazing definitely accelerated the entire process of biological change.

As people familiar with the valley during the 1850s continued to report, after 1870 it changed most dramatically in its forest density. This common observation of travelers and publicists was further corroborated by Yosemite's artists and photographers. For example, Thomas A. Ayres's sketches, prepared during his sojourn into the valley with James M. Hutchings in 1855, depicted a landscape far less cluttered with shrubbery and trees. Similarly, Carleton E. Watkins's photographs, taken between 1861 and 1866, demonstrate conclusively that the valley floor was generally free of dense undergrowth and thick stands of conifers.[28] In later years, biologists attributed the rapid invasion of pines and cedars not only to the elimination of periodic burning but also to the compaction of the meadows, caused by plowing and grazing. By destroying established grasses, grazing and plowing allowed more seedling conifers to gain an advantage. The elimination of fires was apparently of greater significance, however, since many young pines and cedars had obviously taken root in the meadows years before extensive plowing and other modifications were begun.[29]

In its own anxiety to increase visitation without providing state-supported access, the Yosemite Park Commission encouraged an escalation of the problem. Frederick Law Olmsted had proposed in 1865 that the park commission not only should improve roads and trails within the reserve but also should request twenty-five thousand dollars to improve access to the valley and the Mariposa big trees. The threat his recommendation might have posed to continued funding for the California Geological Survey was enough to convince Josiah Dwight Whitney and William Ashburner to suppress his report. In either case, the commissioners insisted that it was not "any part of their duty to improve the approaches to the valley or Big Trees," as Whitney argued in 1867, justifying his opposition to Olmsted's report as simply an honest effort to save public funds. Building roads could "safely be left to the competition of the counties, towns, and individuals

39

interested in securing the travel."[30] Unfortunately, in the absence of more reliable transportation to and from the park, the commission in effect had no alternative but to allow valley residents and visitors to release their livestock in the meadows.

In addition, pending the resolution of the valley's outstanding land claims, the California state legislature had appropriated nothing for the grant since 1866, not even enough to pay Galen Clark, its first resident guardian. By 1870 his annual salary of five hundred dollars was already four years in arrears. Even Josiah Dwight Whitney and William Ashburner considered such levels of fiscal conservatism much too extreme. But in formulating their argument for improving the grant, they, unlike Olmsted, relied on its economic potential. For Olmsted, that consideration was at best only secondary; it was not, in any case, a primary reason for establishing public parks. In contrast, Ashburner reported to the state legislature in 1871 that Yosemite's annual value had already risen to a quarter of a million dollars. As a result, evidently it was now advisable to remove the "embarrassing and vexatious restrictions to travel" within the park, especially the trail and road tolls imposed by private entrepreneurs. Only then did he dismiss "the mere pecuniary considerations" of his report, maintaining that "the State should have a pride in treating this property—its magnificent public park—in a liberal spirit" not restricted "to the mere question of dollars and cents."[31]

Nonetheless, having resorted once to the argument, the Yosemite Park Commission found good reason to rely on it indefinitely. Throughout the 1870s the commissioners invoked the economic advantages of scenic preservation to coax additional management funds out of a tight-fisted legislature. Similarly, visitation figures buttressed the commission's request for higher levels of support; nearly twenty thousand people came to Yosemite Valley during the decade, up fourfold from the number of visitors between 1864 and 1870.[32]

The effect on the resource was still most apparent in the meadows, where tourists and valley residents alike fed, watered, and rested their horses. Dairy herds and cattle for slaughter were also introduced to the valley. Similarly, the inauguration of regular stage service midway through the 1870s put added pressure on scarce supplies of hay and grass. Residents simply plowed and fenced more of the meadows, sowing them with popular varieties of nonnative grass and grain. As a result, native grasses and wildflowers gradually gave way, retreating to those portions of the valley least used and visited.[33]

With increasing portions of its meadows thus put to use, Yosemite Valley by 1880 was certainly not the park Frederick Law Olmsted had envisioned in 1865. In his opinion, sensitivity to the natural scene was the guiding principle of good management. Anything that compromised the original appearance of Yosemite Valley warranted intense scrutiny simply as a matter of course. It follows that if Olmsted had been asked to decide the future of grazing in the park, his position on the issue would have been clear and outspoken.[34]

Possible comparisons of Yosemite Valley to a farm instead of a preserve convinced the Yosemite Park Commission that something indeed had to be done. But instead of inviting Olmsted back to the park, the commission asked William Hammond Hall, the state engineer, to report on the growing problems of protection and management. Hall claimed to be influenced by Olmsted's work and philosophy; in fact, however, no two people were often farther apart when it came to insisting that the use of public parks yield to the needs of preservation. Hall visited Yosemite Valley in 1881 and filed his report to the commission on May 20, 1882. "No attempt should be made to 'improve' Yosemite Valley," he began, seemingly embracing Olmsted's guiding philosophy. But Hall in fact applied the words *improve* or *improvement* to a long list of public works, "works necessary," he argued, "for the preservation or promotion of the use of the valley." Granted, public works were "by no means *improvements* to the valley"; they were, nonetheless, "*necessary evils,* which *occupation* and *use* bring in their train or force in their advance."[35]

Unlike Olmsted, in other words, Hall accepted increased development of the park as both inevitable and legitimate. Tourism, as the impetus for development, was the unavoidable result of Yosemite's own fame and rising popularity. It followed that although the development of the valley must be controlled, it must still be allowed. Inevitably, the contradictions in Hall's report were serious and inescapable. Given his basic premise, time and again preservation lost while development steadily gained. The issue of structures, for example, elicited the following response: "The only good excuse there can be for putting a house of any kind in the Yosemite Valley is that it will afford a shelter, a convenience, or material comfort of some kind to those who come to view the great natural effects and features of this place." Apparently houses, in Hall's view, were simultaneously frivolous and necessary, on the one hand a distraction yet on the other a prerequisite for a better enjoyment of the park. Hall immediately amended his statement to include "hotels, dwellings, stores, shops, and other structures" as requirements for genteel sight-seeing and amusement. Here again he broke faith with his own preceding statement, offering no "good excuse" why stores and shops in particular were vital park establishments. Instead he returned to his earlier rationale that all structures were "only tolerated features"; accordingly, they "should not be prominently located or conspicuous in themselves." But immediately he followed the qualification with another dramatic contradiction. Suddenly the "ideal house for Yosemite Valley" was both large *and* conspicuous. It "must be of stone," Hall wrote, "its location near the base of the valley walls, with forest trees around and a fine view off in front; its planning spacious, and its construction *massive*" (italics added). Further imagine "a hotel of such character," he wrote, his excitement now obvious, "with a wide portico and a great reception room, fireplaces each as big as an ordinary boudoir, and inside house finish of plain hard wood; outside of stone and tiles; the yard disposed and cultivated to appear as a bit of the natural woodland scenery with its Spring dress on." Only a structure of such magnificence might tempt the visitor "to prolong his stay to enjoy, if nothing else, the fitness of his immediate surroundings as accompaniments to the natural features of the place."[36]

In the space of barely a paragraph, Hall's projected accommodations for Yosemite Valley had mushroomed from houses as "shelter, a convenience, or material comfort" into grandiose buildings obviously intended to become park attractions unto themselves. In these and other instances, he had departed almost completely from his original pronouncement suggesting that buildings should be incidental and as inconspicuous as possible. His hotel especially emerged in his mind's eye as a retreat where visitors, perhaps bored with the scenery, could still appreciate, "if nothing else," the fact that the structure so perfectly blended with its surroundings. By now the very real differences between Olmsted's philosophy and Hall's were dramatically obvious. Olmsted, as a landscape architect, thought first of *protection*. Hall, as an engineer, believed foremost in *construction*.

Now fully committed to promoting Yosemite Valley for greater visitation, the Yosemite Park Commission clearly preferred Hall's 1882 report over Olmsted's original of 1865. Hall included the obligatory statements about protecting park resources; it was simply that his report, unlike Olmsted's, struck a less restrictive balance between preservation and development. The deterioration of the meadows, for example, impressed Hall as just another challenge for his engineering expertise. "The finer forage grasses are being thinned out," he wrote, admitting that overgrazing was contributing to the problem; "the coarser and more robust or hardy grasses and weeds, able to withstand the trampling and cropping, are taking their places." The total area of the meadows had also decreased, "while young thickets of forest or shrub growth are springing up instead." Yet he did not recommend that grazing be eliminated from the meadows nor that annual fires be restored; instead the meadows should "be cleared, perhaps plowed, reformed, and resown." Additional lands suitable for grazing should also "be cleared and brought under cultivation," perhaps "by irrigation as grass meadows" sufficient in extent to overcome "the deficiency in the forage supply."[37] Here again, Olmsted's distinctive blending of enjoyment with discipline was noticeably absent. Hall instead proposed a popular alternative to increased restraint. However restrictive in its own right, his plan for Yosemite Valley intrinsically accommodated more visitation and development.

Adherence to Hall's recommendations for the valley threatened to accelerate the biological changes already in progress. Additional roads, trails, fences, and building sites provided the levels of disturbance so necessary for exotic vegetation to take root. Elsewhere, native grasses were plowed under and more portions of the meadows resown with timothy, Kentucky bluegrass, and other popular alien species. Meanwhile, pines and cedars continued to encroach wherever opportunity afforded, since little except fire and pulling up seedlings by hand had kept these and other trees periodically in check.[38]

As more of the valley closed in, the natural wonders themselves disappeared behind screens of trees. Again Hall's solution was technical rather than biologically informed. Certainly the Yosemite Park Commission "should be safe from censure," he wrote, "if, in opening out the views . . . you apply the axe right freely." Granted "there is much prejudice against cutting down fine trees," he confessed, "but you must look to the ultimate result, and be governed accordingly."[39]

Once more Hall professed to see a bright future; in truth the complexities of park management were largely beyond his grasp. Although Frederick Law Olmsted had greater vision by training and experience, he was given only a brief hearing before his ideas were generally suppressed. No less than in the twentieth century, restraint and discipline in the interest of posterity was not a popular argument in 1865. Hall, in contrast, told the Yosemite Park Commission what it wanted to hear. Visitation could be accommodated and preservation yet advanced. Yosemite Valley could in fact be more things to more people a good deal more of the time. To change the valley while meeting the demand was not to abandon park principles; rather change, in Hall's reassuring words, was both inevitable and predictable. Development of the valley had been forced on the commissioners; they were blameless for succumbing to "necessary evils." Yosemite Valley, as public land, must accommodate the public, including by adding those facilities that appeased popular social tastes. Thus use, rather than the resource, moved ever closer to dominating the park and its future.

❧ National Park

CHAPTER FOUR

A growing awareness of the beauties of the High Sierra, coupled with the appropriation of Yosemite Valley during the 1880s for meeting the needs of tourists, inevitably led to discussion about the desirability of expanding the park of 1864. By itself, however, scenic preservation was not an inducement powerful enough to overcome regional opposition to the plan. Indeed, the opportunity to establish a park entirely in government ownership had been lost even before it was recognized. Motivation sufficient to induce Congress to seriously consider park expansion awaited sources other than preservation interests, most notably the Southern Pacific Railroad and irrigationists in the San Joaquin Valley. Much as irrigators finally were alerted to the problems of protecting major sources of fresh water in the mountains, so the Southern Pacific Railroad had come to recognize the profits that might be realized by promoting tourism throughout the Sierra Nevada. The result of this agitation was not the expansion of the Yosemite Grant of 1864 itself, but rather the establishment of an entirely new preserve surrounding the valley yet retained in federal ownership. Such were the origins of Yosemite National Park, originally set aside by Congress on October 1, 1890, as "reserved forest lands."[1]

The phrase "reserved forest lands" reflected the importance of the original argument that Yosemite National Park was crucial for protecting vulnerable watersheds of the High Sierra. In this manner preservationists wrapped their own esthetic aims around an all-embracing utilitarian cause,

45

one with special appeal to California water, civic, and agricultural groups. The Yosemite Park Commission itself endorsed the proposal in 1881 not only for "the protection of the valley and its rim, the preservation of the water-flow" supplying "a chief element of its grandeur," but also for sustaining "the mines in the foothills, and the great San Joaquin Valley below." Accordingly, at a full meeting of the commission held on March 22, 1881, and subsequently in its biennial reports of 1882 and 1884, the group went on record in full support of the enlargement of the Yosemite Grant to encompass, at a minimum, all of the watersheds feeding into Yosemite Valley proper.[2]

It is therefore not surprising that William Hammond Hall underscored the importance of Yosemite Valley's watersheds in his own report to the commissioners of 1882. He asked, "What is necessary to *preserve* the Yosemite Valley property from deterioration?" and answered, "*First*—The control of the mountain watershed tributary to the valley streams, to prevent the destruction of timber and vegetation generally thereon." Of the 229,000 acres estimated to compose the Merced River watershed, only 30,500 acres were included in that portion of the grant surrounding Yosemite Valley. This left "198,500 acres which drain into the valley" vulnerable to private ownership, particularly "for purposes of sheep and cattle grazing and lumbering. Even now," he noted, "some considerable tracts have been bought up, and the public land surveys are being advanced over the remainder."[3]

At a minimum, Hall recommended expanding the grant to encompass the entire Merced River drainage. Only acquisition of this territory would ensure "efficient preservation of the charms and attractions of the valley itself." If the watersheds above the falls were ever stripped of their timber, "the supply of water, to say the least, will fail much earlier in the season than it now does." The utilitarian benefits of protecting those watersheds were no less important to consider. Specifically, much had been recently published "concerning the effect of deforestation on mountain lands, and the scarcely less disastrous consequences resulting from unregulated sheep grazing over such tracts." Indeed, it would "only require the construction of a railroad up into this region to start the axe in motion at a lively rate." Meanwhile, thousands of sheep were already devastating "the mountain sides every year." Obviously the issue was not merely one of esthetics; in addition, California's economic interests were best served by preserving the

46

state's vulnerable watersheds. Eventually the timber protected in the high country above Yosemite Valley could be carefully harvested and sold by the commission itself, "in place of a few persons being enriched by skimming the cream off from the virgin mountains in their occupation as lumber dealers or wool growers." In this manner, Hall concluded, the commissioners could simultaneously obtain necessary funds for park management while securing "a protective battlement to your valley below."[4]

Hall may not have used the term, but his approach to park expansion was superficially ecological. Had he not repeatedly amended his statements by calling simultaneously for the manipulation of Yosemite Valley and timber cutting in the mountains, his argument would have paralleled that commonly used by modern-day environmentalists. Park boundaries sympathetic to watersheds and animal migration routes, rather than arbitrary squares or rectangles drawn principally around scenic features, have often been the goal of environmental campaigns since the 1960s. Meanwhile, Hall had registered some very persuasive points. Although local opposition to park expansion killed the first congressional bills to address the subject in the early 1880s,[5] support was building among those interests whose concerns were more convincing, especially California irrigators and the Southern Pacific Railroad.

* * *

In John Muir, the individual most associated with Yosemite Valley and the High Sierra, preservation was to find its indefatigable publicist and champion.[6] Politically, Muir joined the preservation movement already in progress. He first saw Yosemite Valley in 1868, four years after it had been set aside by the act of June 30, 1864, and three years after Frederick Law Olmsted had delivered his provocative address to the Yosemite Park Commission. While Muir tended sheep and rambled throughout the backcountry, Congress further debated, and rejected, the outstanding land claims of James Lamon and James Mason Hutchings. Muir was still drawn to the high country rather than politics in 1872, when the United States Supreme Court upheld the Yosemite Park Act by dismissing the liens of valley residents against the grant's property. Similarly, there is no reason to believe that Muir had any influence on the bill establishing Yellowstone National Park, Wyoming. No less than Theodore Roosevelt, who often has been credited with founding the conservation movement itself, John Muir in truth came on the scene when the issue was well advanced. More than a founder of conservation and a committed political activist, Muir helped sustain the movement through his work as a gifted writer, spokesman, and dedicated idealist.

In a similar vein, his first major contribution to Yosemite was one of science rather than of preservation. Conventional geological wisdom, particularly as expressed by Josiah Dwight Whitney of the California Geological Survey, held that the floor of Yosemite Valley had subsided during a series of cataclysmic events. Muir's own investigations in the high country and along Yosemite's rim had definitely convinced him otherwise. Contrary to Whitney's view that Yosemite Valley had dropped away during violent convulsions of the earth's crust, Muir found deposits of glacial silt, striations etched into granite formations, and other evidence suggesting that the valley had been shaped and scoured by successive waves of glaciation. When Clinton L. Merriam, a congressman from New York State who was interested in the same subject, visited Yosemite Valley in 1871, he urged the young naturalist to publish his findings. The encouragement led to Muir's first article, "Yosemite Glaciers," published on December 5, 1871, in the *New York Tribune*.[7]

As was the case when Horace Greeley, the paper's publisher, visited Yosemite Valley in 1859, the *New York Tribune* was still the leading newspaper of its day. For landing his first article in such a prestigious journal Muir could thank Representative Merriam, who submitted the piece on the young man's behalf. Other articles came slowly from his pen; meanwhile, he tramped and botanized the length and breadth of the Sierra Nevada, scaling the heights and picking his way through the canyons he would write about with greater discipline when youth no longer propelled him forward.[8]

Like Horace Greeley, Samuel Bowles, and others who had preceded him, Muir was initially struck by the monumental features of Yosemite Valley, its "noble walls—sculptured into endless variety of domes and gables, spires and battlements and plain mural precipices—all a-tremble with the thunder tones of the falling water."[9] But as a resident of Yosemite Valley between 1869 and 1873, Muir quickly came to appreciate, as had Frederick Law Olmsted, the beauty of its vegetation, apart from its landmarks. Gradually, as a result, his tolerance for the changes made in the valley on behalf of tourism diminished in proportion to their effect. Similarly, he condemned damage to the high country surrounding the park as the work of shepherds and their flocks of "hoofed locusts."[10] Obviously his support for park expansion was building; his first years in Yosemite Valley were simply consumed with personal discovery rather than with politics.

Finally, by the early 1880s the High Sierra was at last being surveyed and thrown open to legal settlement. With the survey of the mountains came the prospect that development would both intensify and diversify as sheepmen were followed, in turn, by settlers and speculators. At least the shepherds had been transients with little interest in owning the high country. The new wave of pioneers not only claimed the land outright but also seemed bent on mining, logging, stream diversion, and similar types of exploitation potentially more threatening to the Yosemite Grant.

Only Congress had the authority to restrict the disposal of the high country, thus serving the best interest of the park; instead, as early as 1881 the Interior Department began offering territory on the perimeter of the Yosemite Grant for sale and settlement. The majority of claims filed were for lumbering and mining; in this fashion tens of thousands of acres of prime timberland fell into private hands between 1881 and the establishment of the national park in October 1890. The national park itself contained approximately sixty thousand acres of inholdings, many in the sugar pine forests bordering the western boundary of the preserve. Thus local opposition to preservation, fueled by speculators and real estate promoters, had successfully stalled park expansion long enough to allow some of the best timber and grazing lands to be designated for exploitation despite inclusion within the park.[11] Prior to 1880 Congress might have established a Yosemite National Park largely free of any outstanding claims to its natural resources. With the opening of those lands to private entry, that possibility had vanished forever.

The passage of the lands surrounding the Yosemite Grant into private ownership occasioned only limited notice among the American people at large. The objects of greatest public concern were still the valley and the big trees. Year by year the valley especially seemed victimized by increased abuse and neglect. Many of its returning visitors, most notably those who had first seen the valley prior to 1870, complained that some of the most breathtaking views of its cliffs and waterfalls had been lost behind screens of encroaching vegetation. In other instances meadows that had previously served as foregrounds for popular vistas had been marred by fencing, grazing, and haphazard construction. The most outspoken critics accused the Yosemite Park Commission of turning Yosemite Valley into a poorly run farm instead of a well-managed public park.[12] Yet none of this controversy focused on the loss of lands previously recommended for inclusion in the preserve. Again the issue was esthetic, and as such its nucleus remained the valley itself.

Meanwhile, the Yosemite Park Commission had been wracked by bitter controversy. In 1880 William Ashburner challenged the right of Governor George C. Perkins to appoint a new slate of commissioners; a new law further limited a commissioner's term of office to only four years. As an original member of the Yosemite Park Commission, Ashburner had no intention of giving up his post. Accordingly, for the second time in less than a decade, a case involving Yosemite made it all the way to the United States Supreme Court. In the interim Ashburner refused to surrender the books of the commission; he relinquished them only when ordered to do so by the Court, which found against him in October 1880.[13]

The commission, for obvious reasons, lost prestige and public confidence. About the only positive outcome of Ashburner's suit was the Supreme Court's reaffirmation of its decision in 1872 that the Yosemite Grant must in fact be managed as a *national* trust. If ever the park was "in any respect diverted from this use," the Court restated, the federal government might be obligated either "to enforce the performance of the conditions contained in the Act of Congress or to vacate the grant. So long as the State keeps the property," the Court concluded, underscoring the point, "it must abide by the stipulation, on the faith of which the transfer of title was made."[14]

As a result of Ashburner's suit, two sets of commissioners and two guardians oversaw the valley between September 1880 and March 1881. Given such an inauspicious start, the new commission struggled to establish its own authority and public confidence. The results were disappointing. By the end of the decade hard feelings against the commission once more ended in heated controversy. In 1885 the commission had granted Charles D. Robinson, a seasonal artist, permission to erect and lease a small studio in the valley. Shortly afterward the privilege was revoked and, Robinson charged, his studio forcibly entered and vandalized by the guardian. Thoroughly outraged, the artist brought twenty-two charges of misconduct against the commissioners, including the destruction of private property, the misappropriation of public funds, and, in general, the violation of the management principles of the Yosemite Park Act of 1864.[15]

In February 1889 the California legislature held hearings on Robinson's accusations. Although majority reports of the senate and assembly exonerated the commissioners, the hearings did suggest that the management of the Yosemite Grant was beset by serious differences of opinion. For example, criticism was particularly sharp against plowing and fencing off the meadows in the valley. Similarly, Robinson and his supporters charged the commission with indiscriminantly cutting and destroying timber.[16]

In retrospect, both charges were convenient subterfuges for people bent on discrediting the commissioners for other reasons, especially for having disallowed special privileges and desired business permits. Charles F. Leidig, for example, the proprietor of Leidig's Hotel, complained that he and his wife had been driven out of business in 1888 by the completion of the Stoneman House, a state-supported hotel capitalized at forty thousand dollars. Furthermore, he charged, the commissioners had denied him and his wife a new five-year lease. Without it, he maintained, he lacked either the security or the inducement necessary to make improvements to his property, improvements that might have enabled him to compete with the new luxury accommodations.[17]

Ultimately, the legislature agreed with the commissioners that the decision either to grant or to withhold leases did not necessarily reflect a mismanagement of the park. More serious were allegations that cutting trees and plowing the meadows had, in Charles D. Robinson's words, done "irreparable damage to the natural beauties of the valley." In defense of the commission, William H. Mills, one of its leading members, reminded the legislature that history and precedent supported both practices. The invasion of trees and underbrush was a matter of public record. Mills had "been astonished," he reported, "to see how rapidly the undergrowth will encroach, where it is not resisted. Left to itself," he concluded, "in my judgment the valley would soon be a very unsightly wilderness." Much the same consideration explained the decision to allow grazing. "We had to have some horses for conveyances; cows had to be there," he stated. "Nobody could get milk unless there were cows." The presence of the animals further explained the need for their restraint. If the fences were removed, the stock would drift throughout the valley, "and you would very soon have your roads injured and made unsightly." Fencing also protected unwary visitors "against stock roaming at large." In short, the issue was not simply one of esthetics; rather the safety and convenience of travelers required that some of the meadows be farmed and be protected by "a good fence." Hay, for example, might cost one hundred dollars per ton if not provided in the valley, where the going rate was between thirty and sixty dollars per ton. "If you had to haul hay a long distance," Mills concluded, justifying his figures, transportation costs alone would "be very high."[18]

Mills's testimony, in retrospect, had a twofold significance. Above all, he deflected Robinson's charges that the commission had acted capriciously and often in haste. Mills painted instead an image of rational planning and foresight. All the more effective, as a result, was his testimony that Native Americans not only had cleared Yosemite Valley historically but also had done so through the use of fire. In his opinion, burning "was a very good method of management." In this manner, by suggesting that the manipulation of Yosemite Valley by the commission derived directly from Native American techniques, Mills effectively built the commission's case for management legitimacy. Equally significant, he argued successfully that visitor conveniences were in fact "needs," requirements no less compelling as justifications for environmental change. Valley modifications necessary to accommodate tourists by lowering costs and increasing comfort might not always be esthetically pleasing; they were nonetheless mandatory to ensure visitation. "I would be very glad if there were no blacksmith's shop in the valley," he confessed, referring to another obvious point of contention. "I would be glad if people could go in on wings." The point was that only stages and carriages offered practical means of transportation. In that case the blacksmith shop, although undeniably "a place of industry," was nonetheless "a necessary evil," something "entirely indispensable" to tourists throughout the valley. "You couldn't get along without it," Mills concluded, reemphasizing his point. "Stages cannot carry people in there and be out of repair."[19]

Sympathy for his point of view suggested how far his argument might be taken. Whenever the comfort or convenience of tourists won acceptance as "needs," it followed that another level of development would be imposed on the park. Originally, tourists had entered Yosemite Valley by foot or on horseback and had camped in the meadows. Gradually the first hotels had been built and opened to the public. As was to be expected, visitors grew in number and filled the new accommodations, leading to further arguments for hotel expansion and development. By 1889 the list of structures in Yosemite Valley was already quite long, including a luxury hotel, the Stoneman House, and a wide variety of other hotels, cabins, stores, studios, and visitor services.[20]

In defense of these and other modifications to the valley, the Yosemite Park Commission generously estimated the floor to be 9,000 acres, of which only 745 acres were meadow or treeless lands formed by overflows of the Merced River. The point again was to deflect the criticism that the best of Yosemite Valley had been appropriated for farming and commercial development. The commission dismissed the charge as nothing but a lie concocted by a "few truthless rascals" bent on destroying public "interest in the Yosemite." In fact, the commission argued, cultivation had "never been tried on more than two hundred acres of the entire floor." The statement ignored the extent of grazing and the effect of valley structures; here too the objective was to silence harsh critical opinion. When John Muir, for example, added his voice to the chorus of criticism, the commissioners' retort was extremely biased and unforgiving. In their view, "the only organized destruction of the valley's forests" had been "attempted many years ago, when the State's primacy was disputed by squatters and John Muir helped run a sawmill." The commission further accused Muir of logging "for commercial purposes," until the mill and its distinguished operator finally had to be "suppressed by the State."[21]

The history of this famous mill had already been well publicized. Constructed and operated by Muir near the base of Yosemite Falls, it had provided the young naturalist with employment beginning in the autumn of 1869. His employer, James Mason Hutchings, needed the finished timber to renovate his buildings and hotel. Muir insisted, however, that fallen trees rather than live ones should be cut. This stipulation had been known throughout the valley. By attacking Muir, the commission simply hoped to undermine his credibility and thereby deflect his charges that the park had been mismanaged.[22] Similarly, Muir's hand had been obvious in publicizing the issue nationwide. In June 1889 Robert Underwood Johnson, associate editor of *Century Magazine,* accompanied Muir on a two-week camping trip to Yosemite and the High Sierra. Muir hoped to enlist Johnson's support in the campaign for the establishment of a national park; the editor, in turn, convinced the naturalist to write articles for *Century Magazine*. Further aroused by the conditions he observed while in Yosemite Valley, Johnson opened the pages of his journal to letters highly critical of the commissioners.[23]

In retrospect, the commissioners did indeed have a case; much of the criticism against felling trees obviously ignored the fact that Yosemite Valley historically had not been thickly forested. Many visitors in 1889 actually complained that too many trees obscured the best views. But the damage had been done; the Yosemite Park Commission had been discredited in the national media. By striking out at Muir, Johnson, and *Century Magazine,* the commissioners did little but contribute to the credibility of their opponents.[24]

In part the establishment of Yosemite National Park was an outgrowth of this controversy. Although the Yosemite Park Commission itself had endorsed every proposal to protect the valley's watersheds, the recent mismanagement charges against the commissioners had cost them public confidence. The objective of preservationists was to retain under federal jurisdiction any new unit surrounding the valley and, if possible, to include the valley and the Mariposa Grove themselves within the larger preserve. However, leaders of the movement, among them John Muir and Robert Underwood Johnson, soon realized that any call for the recession of Yosemite Valley in 1890 would only fuel California's resentment and thereby jeopardize the larger project. Recession could wait for a more opportune political climate. The challenge immediately at hand was to extend protection to vulnerable forests and watersheds above the valley's rim.[25]

Although the full story may never be known, the Southern Pacific Railroad undoubtedly contributed immeasurably to the effort. Yellowstone National Park, promoted since 1883 by the Northern Pacific Railroad, already evinced both the prestige and the passenger traffic awaiting corporate sponsors of national park projects. Railroad officials responsible for land development, especially for the establishment of irrigated farms in California's Central Valley, further grasped the importance of protecting Sierra watersheds. In short, the Southern Pacific Railroad had every reason to be an ally of park and conservation interests. Accordingly, John Muir and Robert Underwood Johnson, facing powerful opposition to their proposal in California and Washington, D.C., logically presented their case for a Yosemite national park to Southern Pacific executives.[26]

On March 18, 1890, Representative William Vandever of Los Angeles, either at the request of the Southern Pacific Railroad or with its blessing, introduced a bill in Congress for the establishment of a national park surrounding Yosemite Valley. The park that was envisioned, however, was not what Muir and Johnson wanted. To the north, for example, both the Tuolumne River watershed and Tenaya Lake had been excluded entirely, in addition to other critical portions of the Merced River drainage itself. All told, the projected park encompassed only 288 square miles. Moreover, the state grant had already been included in the total, meaning that new lands to be protected actually amounted to little more than 230 square miles.[27]

Muir especially was deeply disappointed. "As I have urged over and over again," he wrote Johnson the following May, "the Yosemite Reservation ought to include all the Yosemite fountains." Johnson agreed, appearing on June 2 before the House Committee on Public Lands to argue Muir's case. But neither Muir nor Johnson held the key to prod Congress. Although Muir wrote articles for *Century* extolling the virtues of his plan, he spent much of the summer touring in Alaska. By then the measure seemed dead until the next session of Congress. Yet on September 29 and 30, a substitute bill inspired by Daniel K. Zumwalt, a land agent for the Southern Pacific Railroad and a personal friend of Representative Vandever's, passed the House and Senate with virtually no discussion. More significant, the substitute bill authorized a preserve five times larger than the original, 1,512 square miles of territory exclusive of the existing Yosemite grant. Almost immediately, on October 1, 1890, President Benjamin Harrison signed the measure into law.[28]

The turnabout in Yosemite's fortunes can be laid to several factors. Above all, Southern Pacific officials themselves were committed to a far larger preserve, one sufficient to protect agricultural interests dependent on its watersheds. To be sure, the company strongly endorsed similar programs for many years afterward. Meanwhile, opponents of the project undoubtedly were thrown off guard by phraseology in the bill designating the Yosemite reservation as "reserved forest lands." Here again, the wording was in keeping with the argument that watershed protection, rather than scenic preservation, was in truth the primary motive for establishing a national park. Finally, the bill's introduction during the tumultuous close of the congressional session aided Vandever and his supporters in stifling debate. Regardless, the fortunes of preservation had been very well served. "Even the soulless Southern Pacific R.R. Co.," Muir later confessed, "never counted on for anything good, helped nobly in pushing the bill for this park through Congress." The point was that Yosemite had not been *called* a national park at the time of its establishment. The discrepancy either confused park opponents or, equally probable, convinced them that the project did indeed have some commercial merit after all.[29]

Ostensibly the high country had now been fully protected. In truth, the

Yosemite reservation had some crippling inconsistencies, most notably more than sixty thousand acres of mining, timber, and agricultural claims. Indeed, as preservationists would quickly discover, each claim was a built-in rationale for adjusting the park boundary. On paper, at least, the park was truly impressive. In keeping with John Muir's fondest wish, for example, it included not only the Merced River drainage but also the headwaters of the Tuolumne River watershed in its entirety. Thus the effort begun in 1864 to protect the superlative scenery of Yosemite Valley had expanded to encompass the region as a whole. Granted, the term *ecology* had not been used and indeed was scarcely known. But in the act of October 1, 1890, were the rudiments of future ecological awareness. The challenge now facing preservationists was to keep what they had won. For the future of both park scenery and park biological resources, it was vital that preservationists succeed.

≥ The Commission,

≥ the Cavalry, and the

≥ Natural Resource

In the twenty-six years between the establishment of the Yosemite Grant on June 30, 1864, and the approval of Yosemite National Park on October 1, 1890, debate about the future of Yosemite's resources had been sporadic and inconclusive. With the establishment of the national park, debate was about to intensify. Still retained in state ownership, Yosemite Valley dramatized the phenomenon of a park within a park, inviting constant comparison between the effectiveness of state and of federal control. In keeping with precedent set at Yellowstone in 1886, Secretary of the Interior John W. Noble asked the United States Cavalry to take charge of protection in Yosemite National Park. On May 19, 1891, Captain A. E. Wood, reporting to the secretary of the interior as acting superintendent, set up headquarters at Wawona with a company of troops. In contrast to the Yosemite Park Commission, which so often had been accused of defacing the valley, the United States government appeared resolved that its preserve would not endure similar accusations of management failure and ineptitude.[1]

Much to the enhancement of the cavalry's reputation, the troopers were primarily responsible only for the protection of the park. Expected not only to protect Yosemite Valley but also to develop it for the accommodation of tourists, the Yosemite Park Commission faced a perplexing contradiction. To be sure, arguments that the valley had too many camps and hotels were still some years in the future. Most Californians both expected and understood the commission's emphasis on park improvements and visitor

57

services. However, in those instances when charges of management impropriety in fact presaged resource controversies, during the legislative hearings held in 1889 for example, the duality of the commission's mandate steadily undermined its credibility. Over the long term, the commission was trapped between its roles as developer and as protector. Whatever the commissioners decided about the future of the valley was bound to dissatisfy either commercial or esthetic interests.

The military, on the other hand, held the proverbial high ground. Safely outside Yosemite Valley and its development controversies, the cavalry had more freedom to experiment with matters affecting forests, watersheds, and wildlife conservation. As a science, conservation was barely in its infancy. Data about wildlife, for example, was based primarily on personal observation. What might be called management was mostly trial and error. The point is that the cavalry was allowed the privilege of suggesting some experiments. In the wake of the legislative investigations of 1889, the Yosemite Park Commission rarely convinced anyone but itself that its management was competent and imbued with sincerity.

Of all the discussion that resulted from the charges brought against the commission in 1889, nothing pointed more directly to the emergence of natural resources as a management issue than the sharpening debate about the historical importance of fire. Reporting to the state legislature the following year, Secretary John P. Irish blamed Robert Underwood Johnson for any lingering bitterness aroused by the hearings. As editor of *Century Magazine,* Johnson continued to approve uncomplimentary articles listing "the 'destructive tendencies at work in the Yosemite Valley'. The truth or falsehood of these articles," Irish maintained, "depends upon the original condition of the valley, when first seen by white men, as it came from the hand of Nature and the Indians, who had long since been its guardians." Seen from this perspective, the "entire case" of *Century* was "disproved, and its urgent authors and abettors disgraced." For Yosemite Valley at the time of its discovery "was park-like in its lack of underbrush and small tree growth, with its floor clear under the tall trees, carefully preserved by the expert foresting of the Indians." Yosemite Valley in 1890 contained "one hundred trees, at least, where one grew upon its acquisition by the whites and the expulsion of the Indians." In short, the Yosemite Park Commission could not be accused of cutting down trees where none had originally grown. The problem in Yosemite Valley was not the lack of trees

58

but their presence in unnatural abundance. This was the evidence *Century* "dared not print," he concluded, "because it would prove them to have willfully borne false witness against the management."[2]

Whether or not the commission, further defending its use of fire, simply grasped at anything that may have promoted public sympathy, Irish did, in retrospect, have reason to resent supposition that burning in the valley had been universally destructive. Among the commissioners, none proved more knowledgeable about fire's true significance than William H. Mills, whose resignation from the commission in 1889 further presaged the rapid erosion of its remaining credibility. Not only did he understand the role that burning had played in Yosemite Valley, but he was also among the first to identify the results of fire suppression in the Mariposa Grove of giant sequoias. As he testified in Sacramento, debris accumulating at the base of the big trees "was endangering that forest." Originally the grove had been "burned over in such a way that a little fire did no harm." In recent years, however, "fagots had piled up at the roots of those trees to the depth of four or five feet." Thus a modern fire threatened to "burn those trees up," a tragedy that would only be compounded by the scarcity of giant sequoias. "They belonged to a species which disappeared from the earth hundreds and thousands of years ago," he remarked. Saving the remainder required the periodic removal of "those fagots and the fallen limbs and the bark from around those trees." Otherwise, he concluded, repeating his warning for emphasis, "in some dry season the Mariposa Grove of Big Trees will be burned."[3]

Similarly, the commission's decision to remove trees and underbrush from the valley had been grossly misinterpreted by the measure's opponents. As was the case beneath the giant sequoias, grass and underbrush had been accumulating across the valley floor. If accidentally ignited now, that accumulation would probably burst into "a conflagration" and rapidly turn the whole valley into "a blackened ruin." In either case, Mills contended, the threat struck him as "reasonable," and therefore, from the very start, he had been "in favor of resisting that encroachment of undergrowth."[4]

Mills's reputation, specifically his ties to the Southern Pacific Railroad and the California press, lent special credence to all of his remarks. His observations, moreover, came directly from the field, from weeks of travel and hours of discussion with Sierra Nevada natives and longtime pioneers.

When asked, for example, why fires historically had not burned out the Indians, he noted again that "the accumulation of fagots" undoubtedly was the key. Generally, Native Americans had burned the forest annually, significantly reducing the amount of fuel and litter available to a single fire in any given year. Applied to the giant sequoias of the Mariposa Grove, that principle alone helped explain their survival. "These trees are all blackened," he confessed. "You can see the evidence of past burning through this forest. Many of them are blackened and burned at the roots." But still the trees survived, protected because fires historically had not been life menacing. And such had been the case in Yosemite Valley. "You will see, every now and then," Mills remarked, citing his evidence, "a fallen tree or the trunk of a tree that shows that fires have run through this valley in former times." But that of course had been "when the Indians were Commissioners." Indeed, he concluded, revealing the source of his information without prejudice or embarrassment, "I have always respected the ability of the Indians to manage that valley."[5]

Ironically, Mills's knowledge about the valley and his prescience of proper management techniques were neither recognized nor understood by a majority of conservationists. Most of his contemporaries, among them John Muir, continued to preach that fire should be absolutely excluded from all Sierra forests. Especially in the eyes of nineteenth-century preservationists, the protection of park landscapes called for the strict enforcement of park rules. Invariably, as a result, the cavalry rather than the commission enjoyed preservationists' support. Captain A. E. Wood, for example, in his first annual report as acting superintendent of Yosemite National Park, set a management standard that most preservationists could applaud. "The sheep have been the curse of these mountains," he noted, echoing John Muir's despair about damaging soil erosion caused by "hoofed locusts." Wood further blamed sheep for the disappearance of game, principally bear, deer, grouse, and quail. Sheep trampled birds' nests and separated herds of animals. More alarming, herders set fires in the high country to encourage the growth of grass. "I have effectively stopped such vandalism," he remarked, and again preservationists applauded enthusiastically. As a result, he was convinced that "in a very few years" the national park would once more "be alive with game."[6]

The appeal of cavalry protection was its no-nonsense basis, especially the likelihood that shepherds and other trespassers would be dealt with severely. Shepherds in particular habitually flaunted the park boundary; Captain Wood's solution was indeed most ingenious. Patrols were ordered to separate herders from their sheep; more to the point, men and animals were to be ejected from *opposite* sides of the park, forcing the shepherds to circle back around the entire park boundary in the hopes of eventually reuniting with their flocks. Even under the best of circumstances, reunification required days. Meanwhile, the flock would probably have scattered or been reduced by predation.[7] When preservationists thought of protection, this was the brand of enforcement they had in mind, not the—in their view—lackadaisical or even destructive management practices of the Yosemite Park Commission.

In its defense, the commission returned time and again to William H. Mills's original premise that nothing done for management's sake broke faith with the husbandry of Native Americans. Granted, as the commissioners reported in 1892, "a considerable area of the floor of the valley was cleared of recent underbrush and disfiguring dead trees, and other obstructions to the view." But clearance itself was a technique adopted from the Indians. "The valley originally was a forest park, dotted with open meadows," the commission still argued. "Its Indian owners kept the floor clear of underbrush." Not only was fire carefully used "for this purpose," but also the natives "annually pulled up unnecessary shrubs and trees as soon as they sprouted." It was the absence of trees that "left a free view of the walls, waterfalls, and beauties of the valley." In contrast, allowing nature "her way" only choked "every vista with underbrush," obscuring "many of the finest views" and hastening "the destruction of many fine old trees, especially the oaks, which, when crowded and starved by younger growth, yield to parasites and decay," further increasing "the risk from fire."[8]

Once again the commission's report was biologically sound and historically on target. But the damage to the commission's reputation was deep and irreversible. From now on, whatever the commissioners argued would seem strained and self-serving. The cavalry, in contrast, had won universal respect among preservationists nationwide. Military tenets of strictness and discipline coincided perfectly with preservationists' own assumptions that only rigid standards of protection would save the national parks. "The effectiveness of the War Department in enforcing the laws of Congress has been illustrated in the management of Yosemite National Park," wrote John Muir, for example, in 1895. "The sheep having been rigidly excluded, a luxurient cover has sprung up on the desolate forest floor, fires have been choked before they could do any damage, and hopeful bloom and beauty have taken the place of ashes and dust." Obviously, he concluded, his biases now fully obvious, "one soldier in the woods, armed with authority and a gun, would be more effective in forest preservation than millions of forbidding notices."[9]

* * *

The commission could do nothing right, the army nothing wrong. Indeed, so convinced were preservationists of the army's greater effectiveness that they often overlooked its own management inconsistencies. As acting superintendent of Yosemite National Park, for example, Captain A. E. Wood actually called for the *reduction* of the preserve. His immediate successor, Captain G. H. G. Gale, reported to the secretary of the interior that a large portion of Yosemite National Park was "of practically no value to the sight-seer," nor of any importance "as a conservator of the water supply." As a result he, like Wood, recommended that any commercial districts of little scenic merit be excluded from the park as soon as possible.[10]

The appeal of Gale's report was his promise to continue the strong, uncompromising methods of protection inaugurated by Captain Wood. Accordingly, park defenders like John Muir still refrained from saying anything openly critical of the army and its policies. As long as sheep in particular threatened the high country with invasion, the cavalry's strong-arm tactics of separating sheep from shepherds coincided perfectly with preservationists' overriding objectives.

For much the same reason, preservationists also tended to ignore the cavalry's immersion in the natural resources debate, even though the cavalry arrived at some of the same conclusions about fire that had cost the Yosemite Park Commission so much credibility and support. Under Captain Wood, the cavalry began its management program committed to fighting forest fires, including wildfires ignited by shepherds and occasional bolts of lightning. Wood's successor, however, Captain Gale, sided with the Yosemite Park Commission, noting that fire historically had been of great importance in actually protecting Sierra woodlands. Indeed, Gale remarked, "Examination of this subject leads me to believe that the absolute prevention of fires in these mountains will eventually lead to disastrous results." In the course of a single year, forest litter formed only a thin carpet.

"This burns easily with little heat," he wrote, "and does practically little damage. This fire also destroys, or partially destroys, the fallen timber which it touches, and leaves the ground ready for the next year's growth." Similarly, enough saplings escaped most small fires to replace aging and toppled trees, "and it is not thought," he noted, "that the slight heat of the annual fires will appreciably affect the growth or life of well-grown trees."[11]

In contrast, the suppression of all fires threatened to disrupt the natural cycle. For example, "if the year's droppings are allowed to accumulate," Gale continued in his report, "they will increase until the resulting heat, when they do burn, will destroy everything before it." The buildup of but a few seasons generally resulted in "a vast amount of kindling and solid fuel" that, if ignited, would "convert the forest into a roaring furnace." Granted, shepherds were responsible for the large majority of forest fires; granted too, the herders thoughtlessly destroyed practically "every living thing in the forest within reach of a sheep's teeth." "I will, however," he confessed, "do them the justice to say that they do not kindle all the fires, and that, on the whole, it is a marvel that forest fires are so infrequent." Besides, he concluded, "It is a well-known fact that the Indians burned the forests annually."[12]

In its own defense the Yosemite Park Commission had already argued as much; it was just that the commission, unlike the cavalry, had lost public confidence. Meanwhile, the army was less likely to be seen—and therefore scrutinized—by the average park visitor. Then, as now, the public gravitated to Yosemite Valley; the soldiers patrolled the high country and distant corners of the national park. In short, valley management was far more likely to be criticized. Instances of alleged misconduct, such as stumps and blackened trees, seen in the valley aroused far more concern than did similar examples in the mountains. Simply, the cavalry continued to patrol the proverbial high ground. Management directives above the valley rim were simultaneously clearer and more insulated. For example, Captain Gale might call for burning park forests; however, even if his recommendation did in fact win approval, most park visitors would never see the fires or bear witness to their results.

Rotation procedures among cavalry officers provided the army further insulation from public scrutiny. As a rule the officer in charge of the park served only one or two years. Thus changes in management philosophy evinced by the office of superintendent escaped widespread notoriety. Cap-

63

tain Gale, for instance, a proponent of light burning, was replaced in 1895 by Captain Alexander Rodgers, who did not follow up with a similar recommendation. Rodgers's replacement, Lieutenant Colonel S.B.M. Young, was the next to mention fire, in his report for 1896. But instead of favoring light burning, he roundly condemned it. In his view the accumulation of forest litter significantly retarded damaging water runoff. Annual burning, "as a preventive against forest fires in the dry season," actually destroyed "the natural preservation and regulation of the water supply." For this reason alone, Young concluded, "such measures would be a violation of the spirit of the act of Congress approved October 1, 1890."[13]

On May 22, 1897, Captain Rodgers returned to Wawona for another season as acting superintendent. But again his annual report, submitted the following August, revealed his lingering prejudice against the use of fire. Earlier that summer, he noted, a fire that had threatened the Merced Grove of giant sequoias had been "put out before it could do any harm to these trees."[14] Rodgers did not suggest that several smaller fires might possibly have been of benefit had they burned through the same area.

In 1898 the superintendency of the national park turned over yet again, for the first time going to a civilian, J. W. Zevely (eligible army officers had been called up for service in the Spanish-American War). Under Zevely, Captain Gale's pathbreaking observations about fire were once more in favor. In a word, Zevely agreed that the policy of suppressing every fire was altogether "erroneous." During "conversations had with old mountaineers," themselves "deeply interested" in protecting the forests of the national park, he had also come to appreciate "the consequence" of allowing the forest floor to accumulate too much debris. "The whole mass is highly inflammable," he wrote, underscoring Captain Gale's 1894 report. Accordingly, when fires did ignite it was "next to impossible to control them at all."[15]

Although that conclusion remained controversial, army officers were not openly criticized for any differences of opinion. After 1889 that level of tolerance was rarely extended to the Yosemite Park Commission. However well-intentioned, experimentation in the state park was still liable to meet with someone's strong objection. And of course army recommendations were just that—recommendations only. Officers could not be blamed for making suggestions that they were rarely allowed to try.

Indeed the cavalry had only begun to learn about management options and alternatives. Among army officers as well as state commissioners, knowledge about natural resources was still scattered and rudimentary. Granted, proponents of light burning showed a keen awareness of the issues and, in fact, largely anticipated prescribed burning techniques of the latter twentieth century. But forests were only part of the resource picture as a whole. As yet there had been no comprehensive study of the national park and its resources; manipulation was far more common than scientific understanding. To be sure, the temptation to interfere was the strongest motivation, even if that meant advancing one resource's welfare over that of another.

In other instances, interference seemed benign and noncontroversial. The arrival of the army, for example, coincided with the beginning of extensive fish-stocking throughout the park. Historically, native fish had never lived above four thousand feet in elevation, in short, not higher than the Yosemite and Hetch Hetchy valleys, whose precipitous waterfalls blocked normal migration.[16] In September 1892 the state of California moved in to correct that troubling imbalance, however natural in origin. Thus Captain Wood proudly reported having received "25,000 young rainbow trout" from the "State fish commissioners." "I put 13,000 of them in the small tributaries of the South Fork of the Merced River," he noted, "2,000 in the headwaters of Bridal Veil Creek, 4,000 in the Illilouette Creek above the falls, and 6,000 in Lake Ostrander."[17] With the exception of lower portions of the Merced River, fish had never lived in any of those areas. As a result, Captain Wood had assisted in changing the biological composition of several highland lakes and streams.[18]

Those changes, moreover, were twofold in effect. Not only were trout introduced to pristine waters in the park, but also the number of exotic species represented increased. Only rainbow trout were native to Yosemite National Park. Nevertheless, Captain Wood reported a shipment of twenty thousand New England brook trout, scheduled for distribution by August 1893.[19]

Just two years later, in 1895, the state began operating a fish hatchery in Wawona. Peak production of trout fingerlings averaged five hundred thousand per year. Parties fishing without permits, Lieutenant Colonel S.B.M. Young also reported, were subject to ejection from the park and "loss of their tackle."[20]

Further supported by the hatchery, fish planting by the turn of the century was a well-established practice. In retrospect, agitation for the program was too insistent to ignore. Not only sportsmen but also concessionaires realized fun and profit from more fishing opportunities. Thus Major Benson proclaimed in 1905, "The park is becoming probably the finest fishing grounds in the world."[21] His temptation to overstate was normal procedure; he had been sending cans of fingerlings into every corner of Yosemite, all under the care and protection of his military patrols. Meanwhile no one seemed to mind that Yosemite's lakes were being altered biologically; indeed, who would disagree that a lake without fish was no lake at all?

Only in retrospect did planting fish seem contradictory and manipulative. And by then the practice was too well entrenched to be eradicated. Time and again the same would prove the case in matters affecting wildlife. Much as sportsmen defended their privilege to find fish in Yosemite's lakes, so most neighbors of the national park considered its resources vital to their needs and, consequently, called for similar privileges to hunt, graze cattle, and cut timber as required. Ultimately, the size of the park itself should be substantially reduced. As a gesture of compensation, Californians seriously discussed the possibility of returning Yosemite Valley to federal ownership and control. The point was that the recession of the valley alone would not stop wildlife from ranging outside the national park, especially if much of its territory was eliminated. Once outside the boundary, game would certainly be subject to greater hunting and poaching pressures.

Here again there was growing debate but still little understanding. In essence, resource decisions were beyond the knowledge of the cavalry, the commissioners, or regional politicians. Ultimately, the field of inquiry and debate would have to be broadened, encompassing not only bureaucrats and administrators but also students of natural history. Meanwhile, Congress would determine Yosemite's proper size on the basis of what was known and accepted. The temptation to interfere biologically in the park already foretold that decision. For the moment, a lasting commitment to Yosemite's flora and fauna still seemed years in the future.

Losing Ground

CHAPTER SIX

The uncertainties and inconsistencies of its management aside, Yosemite at the turn of the century was on the verge of unprecedented change. The establishment of the national park a decade earlier had not been greeted with universal acclaim. To be sure, hardly had the greater park been approved when its detractors went on record in favor of significant reductions in its total land area. Predictably, the majority of the opposition came from speculators and developers, especially logging, mining, and real estate interests. As early as 1891 they called for legislation to remove from the park practically all of its sugar pine forests along the boundary to the west, as well as mining and grazing districts to the southeast and southwest.[1] Throughout the 1890s agitation for these adjustments grew in intensity until, in 1905, Congress approved the elimination of 542 square miles of territory from the original park boundary.

From a scenic standpoint the reductions appeared to be inconsequential; by and large the lands removed from the park were at the lower elevations and were well outside its monumental core. In partial compensation for some of the territory eliminated, Congress also extended the boundary northward to encompass an additional 113 square miles of mountainous terrain. The realignment had the most effect on Yosemite's plants and animals. Much of the territory eliminated was important wildlife habitat, lowlands and river valleys that were better suited for breeding and winter refuge. Similarly, the forests lost to the park contained many of its oldest and finest trees. Thus although the national park's grandest scenery had been spared, its effectiveness as a biological preserve had been seriously jeopardized.

Nor had Congress concluded its realignment of the park. As early as 1901 the city of San Francisco had petitioned the federal government for permission to dam the Hetch Hetchy Valley for a municipal water-supply reservoir. In the opinion of preservationists, Hetch Hetchy was nothing less than Yosemite Valley's counterpart. Still, in December 1913 Congress and the president approved San Francisco's request. For the first time the park suffered a significant scenic as well as biological loss. Yosemite at the turn of the century had had great potential for both scenic and biological conservation. Suddenly, in little more than a decade, its future in each category had been compromised by a series of sharp reversals. Preservationists could only conclude the obvious: Yosemite National Park would never be quite the same again.

* * *

"The private landed interests within the boundaries of the park are probably much greater than the Congress knew of when so much area was included within its limits." So Captain A. E. Wood, writing to the secretary of the interior in his first annual report as acting superintendent of Yosemite National Park, set the theme of the boundary controversy for the next fifteen years. Legislation for land withdrawals soon became almost a perennial item on Capitol Hill. H.R. 7872, for example, introduced to Congress in 1894, authorized the secretary of the interior, with the approval of the president, to make any desirable adjustments without further congressional review. "The law establishing this park was passed in 1890, on suspension day," the House Report favoring the bill noted, "without having been previously introduced and considered in committee; hence no opportunity was given the people affected by it to be heard in any effort to modify its boundaries." The result was inclusion within the park of "about 65,000 acres of patented lands and also in the neighborhood of 300 mining claims." And just one of those claims, it had been reported, had already produced "over $3,000,000 in gold."[2]

In Captain Wood's opinion, the problem would be solved if Congress established "natural boundaries" for Yosemite National Park. Mining districts could be removed from the park while still protecting the best timber "and all of the natural wonders, excluding none whatever." The revised park would be smaller but also truer to its original intent. "It excludes no timber," he reiterated, anticipating that his plan might be misinterpreted as an attack on the integrity of the park, especially its watersheds. The point was that his proposal recognized "the only portion of country that furnishes a reason for a national park."[3]

Paradoxically, his recommendation made sense. Hardly had he arrived in Yosemite National Park when his troopers faced the problem of distinguishing between government and private lands. The elimination of all land and mining claims would greatly facilitate a unified management of the preserve. Meanwhile, the issue further testified to Yosemite's ironic origins. Opponents of the national park in Congress had been caught off guard by the reference to its territory as "reserved forest lands." It remained for Secretary of the Interior John W. Noble, whose department Congress entrusted with managing the preserve, to erase the subterfuge by designating all of Yosemite's 1,512 square miles as in fact a national park.[4]

Like Captain Wood, opponents of the national park still argued that its integrity could best be maintained by eliminating those lands requiring the most surveillance. The inconsistency of that proposal was its effect on the resource. If the federal government yielded to exploitation every time something of value was found within the park, it followed that Yosemite would ultimately protect only what no one else wanted. John Muir himself, calling in 1890 for the establishment of a park encompassing the Tuolumne River and Merced River watersheds, used precisely that line of reasoning to plead his point of view. Granted, the watersheds lay "in a compact mass of mountains that are glorious scenery," he wrote. Nevertheless, none of the area was "valuable for any other use than the use of beauty." No other interests would suffer by "this extension of the boundary."[5] Yosemite's opponents now held Muir to his word. The park in fact included timber, mineral, and settlement claims, lands whose elimination would still leave the high country basically intact. Accordingly, resource interests saw no justification for the park to extend appreciably beyond its mountainous heart.

In each of his three reports as acting superintendent, Captain Wood turned to that recommendation as his own administrative theme. In 1892, for example, he surveyed mining claims located in the southwest, southeast, and Mount Gibbs portions of the park, remarking afterward that their isolation alone justified their prompt elimination. "There are no natural

69

curiosities of a destructive character in any of them," he maintained, returning to a basic frontier argument that parks should protect superlative scenery only. "There is nothing in these mining sections that would attract the tourist or wonder-seeker." Rather, each district was located "at an extreme corner of the park," accessible only "by the most fatiguing climbing." Certainly it would be "against public policy" for the government to revoke title to these claims just to "lock them up" in areas of the park that few people would ever get to see. In 1893 he repeated that recommendation with even greater decisiveness. "These mines can not eternally be kept locked up in this park, nor is it good public policy to have them in the park." A national park, he firmly concluded, "should contain nothing but natural curiosities for the preservation of which alone the park was created."[6]

So too Wood's successor, Captain G.H.G. Gale, recommended the excision of the mining districts, which he regarded as "useless for park purposes." Yet in Gale's report were the rudiments of an awareness that parks might in fact serve other important roles. "Quail are decidedly on the increase," he remarked, for instance. Also grouse could "be heard drumming in the woods," and deer signs were "frequent." Bears, panthers, and coyotes were also common "in certain portions of the park and are quite useful coadjutors in maneuvering against the trespassing sheep herder." Indeed, park animals could be "very bold, a pair of panthers having their den within a very short distance from my camp and making their presence known in various ways."[7]

Gradually, Yosemite's potential as a wildlife preserve commanded greater attention in the superintendents' annual reports. In 1896, for example, Lieutenant Colonel S.B.M. Young reported evidence that trappers and market hunters had taken a great deal of game during the winter and spring months. Likewise, tourists had been destroying the nests of breeding birds. "I have refused permits to carry any firearms inside the park boundaries," he wrote, indicating his major effort to stem the wildlife slaughter. Regrettably, firearms were still "occasionally smuggled into the park by campers." In addition, further evidence had been found pointing to "the destruction of fish in spawning beds by shooting and the use of explosives."[8]

Concern about the future of wildlife in part formed the basis of Young's recommendation that absolutely no territory should be taken from the park. Instead he urged the government to acquire title "to all lands within the park boundaries." In this manner he broke completely with his predecessor, Captain A. E. Wood, who had steadfastly maintained that only the elimination of the mining districts would serve the public interest. Young agreed that private lands in the park were very difficult to patrol. "So long as settlers own lands in the park and live thereon trespass can not be entirely prevented," he admitted. And yet, preservation would never be served by reducing the area of the park. Indeed, he concluded, "As John Muir so aptly remarks in the Sierra Club Bulletin, No. 7: 'The smallest reserve, and the first ever heard of, was in the Garden of Eden, and though its boundaries were drawn by the Lord, and embraced only one tree, yet the rules were violated by the only two settlers that were permitted on suffrage to live in it'."[9]

In retrospect, the cavalry was immersed in the natural resources debate gradually taking shape across the nation at large. Young's report indicated that he both read conservation literature and supported strict principles of scenic preservation. In other words, Yosemite's boundary question, like burning, was an important catalyst for disagreement and debate. Here again, the cavalry had become a mirror of more widespread ambivalence, further proof that a working definition of national parks had yet to be resolved.

* * *

Quite by accident, Yosemite National Park at the turn of the century still had much potential as a wildlife preserve. Simply, the park was large enough to provide some semblance of refuge for resident species of animals and birds. It followed that no role of the park, either intended or otherwise, was in greater jeopardy of impairment if mounting pressures for territorial eliminations were successful. In Captain E. F. Willcox, acting superintendent in 1899, wildlife conservation found another of its first and most outspoken champions. "As the game is a source of great pleasure to tourists, it can not be too carefully preserved," he remarked to the secretary of the interior in his annual report. Yosemite was indeed "a grand and beautiful country, abounding in interesting flora and fauna." That too was reason for the park to be "properly surveyed" and maintained, and for "monumental" violation penalties to be established and enforced.[10]

In a similar vein, Lieutenant Colonel Joseph Garrard, acting superintendent, called in 1903 for the "protection and preservation of the game in the forest reserves bordering on the national parks and reservations." In other words, he proposed broadening protection efforts to recognize the movements of park wildlife from one season to the next. In addition to safeguarding animals from poaching within the park, the problem was how to protect wildlife that had been forced outside Yosemite proper by the mountainous terrain. "The animals leave the higher altitudes as soon as snow comes," he noted, "and in the lowlands and meadows about the park fall easy prey to the hunter." Logically, as a result, wildlife conservation had to be extended to encompass all of the government lands surrounding the national park.[11]

Similar to calls for light burning in Yosemite's forests, military summaries of the wildlife problem made biological sense. The key to survival for park animals was protecting their habitat as a whole. In this respect Garrard's successor as acting superintendent, Major John Bigelow, Jr., further observed that the southwestern corner of the national park was especially important as wildlife winter range. Unfortunately, mining and logging interests had long ago targeted this section of the park for complete elimination. "There is no telling where this cutting out, once commenced, would stop," Bigelow remarked, despondent over the entire proposal. He too could only write to the secretary of the interior and plead his case that the flora and fauna of Yosemite National Park were every bit as significant as its scenic resources.[12]

Once again the military had made its review, moving gradually, as in the case of fire, from ambivalence about Yosemite's wildlife to increased knowledge and consensus. But although the army was still free to suggest management options, final approval had to come from Congress or the secretary of the interior. By 1904 a decision regarding Yosemite's boundary was clearly in the offing. On April 28 Congress approved a resolution directing Secretary of the Interior Ethan Allen Hitchcock to examine the boundary question, specifically to determine "what portions of said park are not necessary for park purposes, but can be returned to the public domain." On June 14 Secretary Hitchcock formally announced the creation of a federal boundary commission, composed of Major Hiram Martin Chittenden, U.S. Army Corps of Engineers; Robert Bradford Marshall, a topographer with the U.S. Geological Survey; and Frank Bond, chief of the Drafting Division, U.S. General Land Office. By June 24 the three-member panel had reached Wawona to begin its investigation of Yosemite National Park.[13]

On July 9 the commissioners completed their observations in the field, including a pack trip north to Hetch Hetchy and visits to many of the prominent points of interest in and about Yosemite Valley proper. "The work was then transferred to San Francisco," the commission reported, "where it had been arranged to meet several parties who could not be seen at Wawona or in the valley." Among them was John Muir, who, in the opinion of the commissioners, "represents the best sentiment of the country in favor of preserving the Park." The group also met with state and federal politicians before drafting its final recommendations.[14]

As the author of the draft report, Major Hiram Martin Chittenden brought to his duties considerable knowledge about the national parks. Among his achievements was service in Yellowstone, where his initiative had led to significant road improvements. His book about Yellowstone, published in 1895, was also among the first and most comprehensive surveys of the region. Now, in the instance of Yosemite, he acknowledged the significance of conflicting points of view regarding the readjustment of its boundaries. "There is first an almost universal feeling . . . that the park be not cut down if it is possible to avoid it. On the other hand," he remarked, "the existing situation is such as to lead to continual trouble in the administration of the park." The resolution of that dilemma called for determining the original purpose of Congress in establishing the preserve. Generally, a national park was a "fixed and rigid institution . . . set apart because of some great natural attraction or historic event which it is desired to preserve or commemorate." In all cases affecting economic development, a "more elastic" institution was much preferred. The duty of the commissioners was therefore unmistakable—the elimination from Yosemite National Park of any lands limited in natural wonders but rich in natural resources.[15]

Ultimately, the presence of so many private holdings in the park was even more fundamental to the commission's decision. Landowners had "the right to build roads and in some cases railroads, take out ditches, use a certain amount of timber, drive stock across Government lands, etc." If those privileges were denied, the government virtually compelled claimants "to abandon the development of their property." Obviously such conditions were "very undesirable within a national park." For this reason the commission believed "from the beginning of its work" that all "private holdings should be gotten rid of, so that there shall not remain within the park a single vested private right." Finally, the commission argued, any

73

"sources of temptation" were themselves "a constant menace to the existence of the park, such as mineral lands and other valuable resources." Mineral deposits especially were impossible to protect. Nor would the outright purchase of every claim solve the problem indefinitely; "there would still remain the knowledge of the presence of precious metals in these mountains, and this would form a temptation of the strongest kind to trespass on the reservation and seek to cut it to pieces."[16]

Considering the commission's own stated concern—the *protection* of Yosemite—its recommendation that the government do the cutting beforehand seemed to defy any logical explanation. With that recommendation the commissioners bent to the very forces that they themselves had identified as injurious to Yosemite's integrity and survival. But the congressional resolution authorizing the study left the commissioners no room for expressing their private concerns. They instead were to identify "*what* portions of said park," not *if* those same portions, could easily be returned to the public domain (italics added).[17] In short, the commission's recommendations were predetermined by Congress. Any personal regrets of the commissioners aside, Congress expected them—as government civil servants—to designate which lands in Yosemite could immediately be restored to full commercial use.

All told, Chittenden reported, those lands amounted to 542.88 square miles. Eliminating that area would remove "the greater part of private timber claims," he noted, further reassuring Congress of the commission's dedication and thoroughness. Likewise, "practically all mineral lands" would be excluded, relieving "the park of that never-ending menace to its future existence." Again the irony of his statement was sharp and incredible. The park would be saved, but first one-third of it had to be dismantled. The commission did admit that private holdings could simply be purchased; the problem was that "all private claims would very likely cost as much as $4,000,000, and the mineral lands would still remain a perpetual source of trouble." The commission "therefore decided to recommend the rejection of all that can be spared without serious detriment" to the park, leaving to Congress—at its discretion—whether or not to restore select parcels of private land to government ownership at some time in the future.[18]

In a gesture of compensation, the commission did recommend an extension of the northern boundary to include an additional 113.62 square miles of mountainous terrain. A major objective was guaranteeing protection for the branches of the Tuolumne River watershed. "Already a large portion of its waters is appropriated," the report stated, "and the time may soon come when municipal needs will further draw upon them." In other words, an extension of the boundary northward had its own practical rationale. "There are no patented or mineral lands in this tract," Chittenden remarked. Rather the watershed was "particularly prized by the people of California for the use that it will yet be to the State." Granted, portions of the region possessed "features of great scenic beauty, notably the Hetch Hetchy Valley on the Tuolumne—a second Yosemite—Lake Eleanor, and the Tiltill Valley." Yet "overwhelming sentiment" for protecting this territory derived basically from concern that its watersheds not become contaminated by sheep and cattle grazing. The commission agreed that by extending the northern boundary of the park, "this difficulty will be diminished."[19]

In summary, the report provided an inventory of each of the boundaries of the park, highlighting in considerable detail those portions recommended for exclusion. On the west these sections included all of the timber belt between the Merced and Tuolumne rivers, with the exception of the Merced and Tuolumne groves of giant sequoias. "They are located in the very heart of the great forest," Major Chittenden conceded. The groves nonetheless were small and could easily be retained without jeopardizing the forty thousand acres of private timber claims lying all around them. Indeed the park line had been redrawn "so as to exclude the greater part of these holdings," he reassured Congress. Similarly, the new boundary removed "a considerable amount of mineral land in this section, some of which has mines that have been worked for many years."[20]

Turning to the southwestern corner of the park, the commissioners found "general consent" that all of the territory "as far north as the Merced River is of no value to the park and should not have been included originally." The region encompassed numerous mines that had already turned out "several million dollars' worth of ore." Thus the commission concluded, "From every point of view the park will be better off without this section."[21]

Similarly, for the opposite boundary the commission recommended excluding "all territory east of the great Sierra divide south to Mount Lyell, and thence all east of the San Joaquin–Merced divide to the present south boundary of the park." Here again, the presence of valuable mineral lands justified the deletions. "The scenery is of that grand and permanent character which can not be impaired by the works of man," the report further argued, insisting that the areas eliminated would not be unduly harmed. More to the point, pulling the park line back to the mountain divide provided "an excellent natural boundary which leaves little if any mineral land to the west."[22]

Finally, the commission recommended that the South Fork of the Merced River serve as part of the new southern boundary. While "forming a good line" it conveniently excluded "a portion of the private claims at Wawona," claims the government might otherwise have to purchase. Elsewhere the southern boundary could remain much the same.[23]

Congressional approval of the final report followed swiftly and with only limited discussion. On December 5, 1904, Secretary of the Interior Hitchcock submitted it to Congress; only two months later, on February 7, 1905, President Theodore Roosevelt signed into law the act redrawing the boundaries of Yosemite National Park.[24] The lines determined by Congress were identical to those originally finalized by the boundary commission, suggesting again that its recommendations had been a foregone conclusion.

* * *

To the small but growing preservation community, the act of February 7, 1905, was just another sign of the vulnerability and impermanence of the national park system. Only four years earlier, in February 1901, Congress had also passed the so-called Right-of-Way Act, empowering the secretary of the interior to allow utility corridors across all public lands in the West, including Yosemite, Sequoia, and General Grant national parks.[25] Conceivably, each of the parks might be crisscrossed with acqueducts, tunnels, power lines, and utility poles. To be sure, the act specifically provided for every known form of utility transmission. Thus the portent of the act was dramatically obvious—if ever Yosemite, Sequoia, or General Grant National Park stood in the way of a public utility, that utility, rather than the park in question, would hold the upper hand.

Fearing the worst, preservationists nationwide began marshaling their forces. The formation of the Sierra Club in June 1892 had already proven significant for the future of Yosemite. Throughout the 1890s the club challenged every proposal to reduce the national park; although the act of February 7, 1905, would annul these earlier victories, the club learned important lessons about state and national politics. Its influence was further

II. *The Art of Promotion*

9. Albert Bierstadt, *Lake in Yosemite Valley.* The works of Bierstadt, who first painted Yosemite Valley in 1863, typify the romantic style of nineteenth-century artists. Such idealized depictions upheld the national opinion that the wonders of Yosemite were unparalleled worldwide. Courtesy of the Haggin Museum, Stockton, California.

10. Thomas Hill, *Yosemite Valley.* Hill, like his contemporary, Albert Bierstadt, used artistic license freely, commonly exaggerating the boldness of Yosemite's formations by painting them closer together than they were in actual life. Courtesy of the Rockwell Museum, Corning, New York.

Vol. XIII   MAY 1904   NUMBER I

SUNSET

10 CENTS A COPY
ONE DOLLAR A YEAR

NEW YORK: 349 Broadway
CHICAGO: 193 Clark St.
LONDON: 49 Leadenhall St.

SAN FRANCISCO
CALIFORNIA

11. First published in May 1898 by the Passenger Department of the Southern Pacific Railroad, *Sunset* magazine regularly featured Yosemite Valley in articles, paintings, and photographs. The May 1904 cover, by artist Chris Jorgensen, depicted an Indian woman working a bead loom in front of a Miwok cedar lodge, or u-ma-cha. Half Dome looms in the background. Courtesy of the Lane Publishing Company Archives.

12. Railroad promotion of Yosemite National Park took many suggestive and colorful forms. Posters and brochures, for example, commonly featured Gibson Girls, such as this young woman on skis, ca. 1910. The fanciful imagery aside, note the emerging attention to winter sports as a means of lengthening the normal travel season. Courtesy of the Yosemite National Park Research Library.

13. As an evocative symbol of Yosemite, Half Dome has no equal. Literally scores of commercial artists have featured the landmark. This brochure cover, ca. 1910, is a striking example of the use of Half Dome's special qualities for advertising and promotion. Courtesy of the Yosemite National Park Research Library.

14. Whether natural or artificial, Yosemite's renowned attractions lured advertisers eager to promote their products through the powers of association. In 1920 the Horseshoe Route featured Inspiration Point and the Wawona Tunnel Tree. Courtesy of the Yosemite National Park Research Library.

15. Yosemite Valley's celebrated firefall inspired a most colorful produce label, ca. 1930. Courtesy of the Yosemite National Park Research Library.

FIREFALL
PRODUCE OF U.S.A.
Selected
Quality
PACIFIC
FARM COMPANY
MAIN OFFICE
SAN JOSE, CALIFORNIA

16. Campaigns to market Camp
Curry generally highlighted its
many amusements and diversions,
none of which proved more popular than evening displays of the
firefall. Courtesy of the Yosemite
National Park Research Library.

17. By the early 1930s, concessionaire efforts to identify
Yosemite National Park as a destination resort included special promotions of skating, skiing, and
organized winter sports. Courtesy
of the Yosemite National Park Research Library.

evident in 1904, when the boundary commissioners invited comment from club leaders. John Muir, Joseph N. LeConte, and William E. Colby, composing a special committee authorized to investigate the Yosemite boundary issue, formally responded to that request in a letter dated August 23.[26]

Reluctantly, the three men agreed with the federal park commission that townships two, three, and four south, range nineteen east, comprising 108 square miles of land along the western boundary of the park, ought to be withdrawn and added to the Sierra Forest Reserve. The club had been swayed by knowledge of the fact that so many private holdings existed in this area. Otherwise the club opposed additional withdrawals as "too great an encroachment upon the wonderful scenic features." For example, no changes should be made along the northern and southern boundaries, with the exception of slight adjustments required by the elimination of township four south, range nineteen east. Similarly, the committee urged "that no territory" be withdrawn to the east. Rather Muir and his associates asked for the *addition* of 72 square miles to the eastern boundary—all of township two south, range twenty-six east, and the western halves of township one north, range twenty-five east, and township four south, range twenty-seven east. "We make this recommendation for the following reasons," the men concluded. "The park is not sufficiently protected on the east . . . from the invasions of sheep and other private interests, the territory mentioned includes very few private holdings and, finally, it embraces many scenic features of such importance and of so remarkable a nature that they should be made a part of the national park."[27]

Predictably, the boundary commissioners rejected all but the Sierra Club's endorsement of boundary eliminations in the timber belt to the west. Indeed, the commission argued, Muir, LeConte, and Colby simply could not have been aware of the reasoning behind its decision to place the eastern boundary of the park along "the crest of the mountains." Again the basis for that decision was economic reality. "Valuable mineral lands will be excluded," the commission noted. "The extension of the boundaries, as proposed by the Sierra Club, would include the Tioga mines, a large number of private holdings, and the mining town of Mammoth." Their presence in the park would only lead to "new complications in the east," problems little different from those the commission had "sought to get rid of in the west." The club's chief concern, protection of the scenery, would not be served by merely extending the boundary. The scenery itself was "on too large a scale." Besides, the territory lost to the park would still be retained by the government "in a forest reserve."[28]

But the Sierra Club had come to realize the sense of false security in that argument. Government ownership was no longer the crux of the issue; rather the debate hinged on emerging distinctions between federal forests and parks. The commissioners themselves admitted that a forest reserve was "a creature of Executive proclamation, pursuant to a general act of Congress." The law in question was the Forest Reserve Act of 1891, which gave the president unilateral authority to designate "forest reservations" on the public domain. It followed that any president might simply invoke "the same process" to change a forest reserve or have it "annulled altogether." Similarly, the secretary of the interior had "wide latitude" to grant a variety "of privileges on the reserved lands, such as the right to open up mines, cut timber, take out ditches, graze cattle, build roads, etc." In short, the commission conceded, although a forest reserve provided "sufficient protection to save timber lands from destruction," it also simultaneously encouraged "the proper development of many of their natural resources."[29] And that was just the issue—what levels of exploitation were undeniably "proper"? On the other hand, national parks generally were not open to any form of resource development, not even development regulated by federal officials. Thus the Sierra Club could find little reassurance in statements that territory lost to Yosemite National Park nonetheless would remain in government ownership.

However the commission had argued its case, the irony of its report was still inescapable: to protect Yosemite from development, first the commission would throw out of the national park everything subject to development. Members of the commission, most notably Hiram Martin Chittenden, defended that contradiction to the bitter end. "It was the purpose of our Commission," he wrote Robert Underwood Johnson, for example, "to eliminate from that Park everything that might form a strong inducement from outsiders to attack the reservation." Certainly, Chittenden thought, Johnson would agree that those motives were sincere. After all, he concluded, pleading his own sense of helplessness, "If there are gold mines in a public reservation there is simply no use in trying to prevent their development."[30]

Regardless, the damage had been done. "Game seems to be gradually on the decrease," Major H. C. Benson, acting superintendent, reported to the secretary of the interior on September 30, 1906. "The park as originally constituted . . . [had] extended on the south and west well into the low country, reaching the plains on the extreme southwest." As a result, national-park lands had provided "a winter resort for game between the high Sierras and the low plains"; most important, game seldom had gone "beyond the borders and was therefore fairly secure." But all that had changed. The act of February 7, 1905, by eliminating the timber belt and most private claims, had excluded from the park "all land lying lower than 5,000 feet . . . with the exception of the Yosemite Valley itself." What that fact portended for game was already apparent. In winter, migrating animals were forced out of the high country onto lands recently excluded from the park. But although those territories had historically been wildlife range, any semblance of protection had obviously been dropped. Game "grown fairly tame" while in the park seemed to be an easy target for unsportsmenlike hunters seeking only "large bags."[31]

As Benson further noted, reduction of the park had not come to a close with the act of February 7, 1905. Yet another excision, approved on June 11, 1906, eliminated an additional sixteen square miles of territory on the southwest boundary, ostensibly to allow railroad access into the park between Wawona and Yosemite Valley but also—and more to the point—to facilitate logging operations beginning on private lands along both sides of the Wawona Road. As one of the few military superintendents to serve in his post for more than a single season, Benson was able to observe the cumulative effect those boundary adjustments had on park wildlife. Thus in 1908 he repeated: "Game is on the decrease. Each reduction of the park has cut off another portion of the winter resort of game." Growing numbers of "so-called hunters" were simply lying in wait beside springs and along game trails, "shooting every animal that is unfortunate enough to cross the boundary to get water." Even so, the solution he had first proposed in 1905 still seemed radical indeed. If allowed ten thousand dollars to erect fifty miles of barbed-wire fence across the Merced River watershed, he intended to force animals and hunters to stay on their respective sides of the new park boundary.[32]

Yosemite had been spared, but the price seemed crippling. Fully one-third of its original area had been lost to mining, logging, grazing, and utility access. Granted, a scientific awareness of natural resources was yet to

79

be realized; certainly none of the military superintendents, despite their wide travels in the park, had compiled what might be accepted today as base-line data about natural environments. Basically, knowledge about plants and animals stemmed from personal observation and commonsense reasoning. For example, even if Major Benson did not count wildlife populations fully and systematically, he did observe that certain species, such as deer, seemed hard hit by the reductions in their former winter range.

The future of those lands was also becoming clear. Those in government ownership passed into the control of the U.S. Forest Service, a new federal agency approved only one week prior to the park adjustment act of February 7, 1905. Motivated by a deep conviction that natural resources existed solely for human benefit, Forest Service leaders reaffirmed that lands adjacent to Yosemite National Park would be opened to many forms of commercial development.[33] Given both that management philosophy and the size of park reductions, friends of Yosemite seemed more than justified in harboring further apprehension about the fate of its forests, watersheds, and wildlife populations.

* * *

Barely a few years separated the reduction of Yosemite National Park from the next blow to fall on its natural resources. A short distance within its northwest boundary as recently aligned, roughly twenty miles north by northwest of Yosemite Valley proper, lay Hetch Hetchy, considered by early publicists to rival Yosemite Valley itself. But unlike its distinguished counterpart, Hetch Hetchy enjoyed only a sprinkling of visitors. To be sure, the absence of roads and hotels in Hetch Hetchy preserved many of the wilderness charms already sacrificed in Yosemite, including untrammeled meadows and carpets of wildflowers. Yet the lack of visitors also had its drawback. By the turn of the century, Yosemite Valley was known to millions of Americans, whereas Hetch Hetchy's knowledgeable following numbered but a few thousand.

As early as the 1880s the city of San Francisco had begun scouring the High Sierra to find a suitable source for a permanent fresh-water supply. Obviously a reservoir in Yosemite Valley—already protected as a park— was out of the question. Hetch Hetchy, on the other hand, had several compelling advantages, including limited awareness of its natural features. Granted, Hetch Hetchy rivaled Yosemite Valley, if on a somewhat reduced scale. Granted too, in 1890 Hetch Hetchy itself was included within Yosemite National Park. Still, the floor of Hetch Hetchy was already in private hands. The decision was made: San Francisco would ask for Hetch Hetchy as its reservoir site.

What San Francisco had not foreseen was the growing ranks and influence of the preservation movement. Among members of the Sierra Club in particular, Hetch Hetchy quickly passed from obscurity into regional prominence. Accordingly, San Francisco's initial petition in 1901, to dam the Tuolumne River at the valley's outlet, ran into a storm of opposition. Sympathies within the Interior Department itself lay with preservation; in 1903 Secretary Ethan Allen Hitchcock officially denied a dam permit as "not in keeping with the public interest."[34]

Eventually, of course, Hitchcock could be overruled. And indeed in 1908 his successor, James A. Garfield, finally awarded San Francisco its permit to dam the Hetch Hetchy Valley. Led by the Sierra Club, preservationists carried their battle to Congress, but the outcome was swayed from the start by utilitarian points of view. Simply, the reservoir was practical and apparently needed. Besides, Yosemite Valley had already been protected, and Hetch Hetchy was touted as its rival rather than its replacement. The argument was very basic: If the United States had two Yosemites, could not the lesser be dammed? By wide majorities in both houses of Congress, Garfield's permit was ultimately upheld, and on December 19, 1913, President Woodrow Wilson affixed his signature to the act allowing San Francisco full rights to the Hetch Hetchy Valley.[35]

So often and exhaustively has this story been told that historians have ignored its overriding significance. Essentially, much like the realignment of Yosemite's boundaries in 1905, the outcome of the Hetch Hetchy controversy was a foregone conclusion. The federal park commission had noted in 1904 that the readjustment of the national-park boundary did not "exclude the very valuable water resources"; fortunately, all were "capable of a use which will enhance the beauty of the park and serve the public as well." Put another way, water development need not detract from the beauty of Yosemite. The commission resurrected the long-standing argument that dams in the high country could protect the spectacle of park waterfalls during the dry summer months while further contributing to municipal water supplies. With reservoirs, the best of both scenery and utility could be enhanced, adding "beautiful lakes to the landscape," main-

81

taining "the cataracts throughout the season," and, finally, conserving "the water for the people below."[36]

In the end, the loss of Hetch Hetchy was another example of the victimization of Yosemite by its own utility. Perhaps increased knowledge of its plants and animals, coupled with scientific evidence corroborating the requirements for survival, could have swayed a few proponents of development to reconsider their stance. Even so, that argument was in the future. Meanwhile, Yosemite National Park had both its defenders and its prophets, most notably the fledgling Sierra Club and its president, John Muir. But even Sierra Club leaders were prone to disagree and, occasionally, to contradict the emerging opinion that national parks ought to embrace other resources besides scenic wonders. Beyond that consensus, what preservationists needed most—more knowledge and more numbers—they simply did not have. Yosemite under those circumstances had done well just to escape without further losses. That fact, at least, was some reason for comfort as the dark cloud of Hetch Hetchy settled over the entire national park movement.

❧ *Changing of the Guard*

As the loss of the Hetch Hetchy Valley in 1913 further testified, the earlier reduction of Yosemite National Park had done nothing to resolve the issue of park integrity. About the only thing preservationists still had to cheer about was California's agreement in 1905 to return Yosemite Valley and the Mariposa Grove to the federal government. Congress formally accepted both tracts the following year; the agency responsible for protection was also quickly identified. For the first time since its arrival at Wawona in 1891, the cavalry was put in charge of both the high country and Yosemite Valley. With the transfer of army headquarters from Wawona to the valley in the summer of 1906, preservationists looked forward to a new era for the park, characterized, above all, by military efficiency and unified management.

Yet as the cavalry soon discovered, the management of Yosemite Valley called for more than patrols and the ejection of trespassers. For fifteen years that distinct but limited role had meshed ideally with the needs of the high country and with military tradition. Suddenly the cavalry was ordered to fill the void left in Yosemite Valley by the abolishment of the state park commission. As a result, the army found itself dealing not only with shepherds and poachers but also with valley residents, tourists, and park concessionaires. Clearly the requirements and expectations of management had multiplied severalfold. In the high country, cavalry authority had gone basically unchallenged. In the valley, on the other hand, people conditioned by forty years of management give-and-take expected more say in the overall operation of the park.

83

Concessionaires, visitors, preservationists, politicians—all required considerably more of the acting superintendent's time and attention. Resource management alone called for a greater variety of decisions. For example, sighting a bear or a mountain lion in the high country was likely to raise excitement and perhaps even a demand that the animal be killed. Still, generally there was less concern in the backcountry about visitors' safety. In Yosemite Valley the presence of wildlife in close proximity to residents and visitors evoked not only excitement but also occasionally fear. Such concerns were often baseless, but that was not the point. Simply, what the cavalry decided seemed more immediate and visible. In the high country, sightings of so-called dangerous animals might in fact be ignored. In the valley, the luxury of decision making in isolation had been largely stripped away.

It followed that the question would be asked yet again: Was army management for the park any more appropriate or desirable than the previous custodial arrangement with the state of California? The answer came in 1914 when civilian rangers replaced the troopers and the cavalry era drew abruptly to a close. The search for management unity now turned to Congress and to the expected authorization of the National Park Service. Another milestone in the history of Yosemite National Park was about to be realized.

* * *

The retrocession of Yosemite Valley to the federal government closed one period of management debate and opened yet another. Advocates of the transfer, among them the Sierra Club and the Southern Pacific Railroad, looked forward to the advantages of unified control.[1] "The state commissioners have done as well as could be expected," the Sierra Club's board of directors remarked in a special letter to Congress. Diplomatically, the Sierra Club dropped any direct reference to the commission's alleged corruption and management ineptitude. Instead the board emphasized the commissioners' struggles with the state. "They receive no salary," the club stated, for example. "All the time they give to the affairs of Yosemite Valley must be sacrificed from the time devoted to their regular vocations." Moreover, the commission's budget was a "paltry ten or fifteen thousand dollars annually." And it was "with difficulty" that the commission had convinced the legislature to appropriate even that amount. "The State commissioners are entitled to praise for what they have accomplished in the face of such adverse conditions," the club therefore admitted, seeming to ignore the earlier criticism of some of its distinguished members. Nevertheless, the underlying problem remained unresolved: "The State is unable to properly care for Yosemite Valley."[2]

Shrewdly, the Sierra Club's definition of "proper" care included projects intended to promote tourism. To be sure, federal ownership of Yosemite Valley would allow the "construction of the best roads, bridges, and trails," the club stated emphatically in its letter to Congress. "Ample hotel accommodations of the best quality would be provided. A telephone system for the entire park to guard against forest fires would be inaugurated." Similarly, the system of toll roads approaching the park—so despised by tourists—could "be abolished, and in all probability a splendid boulevard constructed up the Merced Canyon, which would reduce the time and expense of travel one-half and greatly increase the comfort." In fact, better roads and hotels probably "would attract immense numbers of tourists from all parts of the world," people presently discouraged only "by the arduous nature of the trip and the lack of accommodation."[3]

Leading opponents of recession, among them concessionaires and local developers, took precisely the opposite stance, suggesting that the state was more amenable to all forms of commercial enterprise. Another argument underscored the potential injury to California's pride and reputation if Yosemite Valley reverted to federal control on the strength of earlier charges against the state park commissioners.[4] Given these objections, the strategy of the Sierra Club was indeed most effective. Of course, the club undoubtedly heeded suggestions from the Southern Pacific Railroad, whose own interests in tourism and passenger traffic would be far better served by federal appropriations for valley improvements. Indeed, as early as January 5, 1905, John Muir appealed directly to Edward H. Harriman, whose railroad empire included not only the Southern Pacific but also the Union Pacific and Illinois Central lines. Unquestionably, Harriman's influence with the California legislature effected the approval in 1905 of the state's transfer bill. Muir, greatly pleased, appealed to Harriman a second time in 1906, requesting assistance in winning congressional acceptance of the state's intended gift. "I will certainly do anything I can to help your Yosemite Recession Bill," Harriman wrote Muir on April 16, 1906.[5] And once again the industrialist was as good as his word. His request that a vote be taken was speedily honored, thereby freeing the bill from the threat of a lengthy deadlock. Accordingly, on June 11, 1906, President Theodore Roosevelt signed H.J. 118, a joint resolution of the House and Senate accepting California's act to reconvey Yosemite Valley and the Mariposa Grove.[6]

As yet, little had been said about natural resources; the Sierra Club, for one, seemed to retain its long-standing confidence in military efficiency, promising that "perfect order would prevail, no matter how great the number of visitors," just as soon as army protection was extended to the valley.[7] On an ominous note, however, an amendment to the resolution accepting Yosemite Valley was the instrument for a second reduction of Yosemite National Park. That second reduction, it will be recalled, cost the national park another 10,480 acres, adding slightly over sixteen and a third square miles to the 542 taken out the previous year. In short, another important gain had been offset by another significant loss. The monumental core of Yosemite National Park might have had greater security, but resource issues affecting forests and wildlife were still basically unresolved.

Not to be discouraged, Major H. C. Benson, acting superintendent, continued to press for the recognition of wildlife problems in the park. Indeed, wildlife conditions were uppermost on his mind that summer of 1906 as he moved park headquarters from Wawona to Yosemite Valley. As he had already observed, the boundary adjustments of 1905 had seriously disrupted the park's original wildlife range. More to his amazement, conditions even in Yosemite Valley seemed entirely out of hand. "The Yosemite Valley itself has, during recent years, been a death trap to all game that was unfortunate enough to enter it," he reported. "Practically every person living in the valley kept a rifle, shotgun, and revolver, and any animal or bird . . . was immediately pursued by the entire contingent, and either captured or killed." In fact, he concluded, his words still tinged with amazement, "A bear pen constructed about three years ago was found by me within 400 yards of the Sentinel Hotel."[8]

An incident early in September dramatized Benson's point. As he reported, "Two bears entered the valley, causing great consternation among those people who had been living here for some time." Everyone "seemed to think that these bears should at once be pursued and driven out." His sympathies obviously lay with the bears. "It is hoped that within a short time game will learn that the valley is a safe retreat and not a death trap," he concluded. Toward that end he recommended year-round protection of the park, further underscoring the futility of seasonal patrols. "Immediately upon the withdrawal of the troops from the park it is overrun with pot hunters, and these same men often remain throughout the entire winter, killing and trapping all the game in their vicinity."[9]

In retrospect, Benson was among the first to identify the foundations of wildlife management in national parks. Contemporary thinking focused on Yosemite's grand scenery. A good many people in awe of the park's waterfalls and cliffs had practically no regard for its wildlife populations, especially for animals believed to pose danger to residents and visitors. In Benson's view, at least, national parks should be sanctuaries for both people and wildlife. The problem was that national parks had not been established on biological principles but rather, far more basic, in celebration of the grandeur of the American scene.

Another problem was psychological. Unlike scenery, wildlife was capable of arousing the deepest fears and emotions. The California grizzly was extinct in Yosemite; the species still causing so much excitement was the black bear, *Ursus americanus*. This bear not only was historically more common but also was considerably less dangerous. Even so, most Americans visiting Yosemite at the turn of the century would not have been swayed by the argument that their ignorance of such distinctions was setting the stage for wildlife problems well into the future.

Much as the extermination of the buffalo became a symbol of America's vanishing frontier, so bears were to become symbolic of national-park wildlife and its needs. At the turn of the century, bears in Yellowstone delighted tourists; attracting the animals required little more than scattering food and garbage around camps and hotels.[10] In Yosemite the wildlife picture in 1900 was somewhat less dramatic. There, to reemphasize, the grizzly was already extinct; decades of illegal poaching and grazing had taken their toll of other wildlife species as well. "To see Bear or Deer, or any other animal life at times required days of travel," Gabriel Sovulewski, one of the earliest civilian rangers, recalled in 1936. Simply, the animals "were killed on sight." Traps also "were plentiful" for both large and small game. Further corroborating Major Benson's observations, he reported, "I found Bear traps on the floor of Yosemite Valley as late as 1906," even "after the Valley was ceded back to the United States and became part of the national park." As a result, he concluded, "It was several years before the wild animals became friendly and were not afraid to face men, women, and children on the floor of the Valley."[11]

What Sovulewski failed to mention in 1936 was his initial advocacy of the elimination of the bear population. "It is not necessary for me to call your attention to the question of bears in the valley," he wrote Benson's successor, Major William W. Forsyth, on November 11, 1910. No doubt the major had already received "many complaints." The "bear question" nonetheless was "very serious"; therefore, "if possible, some action should be taken to rid the valley of their presence." In Sovulewski's opinion the matter had come down to a choice "between campers and bears." More specific, "if the bears remain here," he warned, "camping in Yosemite Valley will be a very serious proposition."[12]

Typically, Sovulewski had not distinguished between normal bear behavior and that induced by lack of human knowledge. Always the problem was bears, not people. In that vein Mack A. Erwin of Selma, California, an advertising representative for several park concessionaires, also took "the liberty" to give Major Forsyth "the facts," opening his letter of complaint by noting that he, his wife, and four children had already suffered two encounters with Yosemite's notorious "beasts." The first occurred the night of August 19. As the Erwins slept, "three grown bears pillaged the camp and took everything in the shape of edibles." Erwin awoke to find the bears walking around his sleeping children, "all," he added for emphasis, "under the age of 5 years." The following evening he built a large campfire and lit a kerosene lantern, hoping these "would bluff the bears." Only then did he walk to the village, leaving his family behind in camp. The ruse was a failure. Just minutes after he had left, "the five bears came marching up and before Mrs. E. was aware they were within 20 feet of where she was washing the dishes. Seeing her, the two large ones reared up and gave a mad growl—showing defiance." Although his wife quickly gathered up the children and immediately fled the area, "before she had gotten 30 yards away," Erwin remarked, "the bears had climbed upon the table and they remained until they cleaned the camp."[13]

At last he acknowledged that tourists who fed bears "might in part be responsible for the presence of the beasts." Open refuse in the garbage pits also seemed enough "to induce any bear to make his nightly calls." Erwin confessed, "That alone would bring them down into the valley." Still he did not admit his own complicity in the problem; his observations of human carelessness ended where his campsite began. "The last experience leads me to believe that the bears are a menace to life and at all times they are a source of annoyance," he wrote, again ignoring that food left in the open explained the bears' raid on his camp. "I cannot get my family to go back to the Park to camp and I have heard dozens of others say the same." Nor would the situation improve. "Until the bears are either *killed* or *caged* there will be a constant decrease in private camping." The rights and safety of park visitors came first. "Sleeping in the open is the most attractive health feature that this Valley affords," he explained, "and the presence of the bears forbids this!"[14]

A less destructive prohibition that would allow bears and people to coexist—banning food left out in the open around buildings and campsites—still eluded Erwin and his contemporaries, including Major Forsyth. In both his annual and monthly reports he too left open the possibility that some of the bears might have to be destroyed. For example, he wrote the secretary of the interior on November 4, 1910, justifying that point of view, "It is, in my judgment, a matter of time only, when some frightful disaster will occur on one of the high trails due to some riding party meeting a bear." Forsyth could just imagine the horror of horses and mules tumbling "over the cliff." He therefore asked for authority "to hunt the bears out of the Valley using shot guns loaded with very small shot." "In this connection," he concluded, further revealing the power of public opinion, "a copy of a letter from Mr. Mack A. Erwin, Selma, California, is enclosed."[15]

Although painful, the method outlined by Major Forsyth at least avoided killing the bears outright. But again the enormity of his request was swallowed by emotion. As long as people considered bears a threat to life and limb, any sign of an animal's real or imagined aggressiveness was bound to occasion a deadly response. Just two years later, for example, Forsyth presented evidence suggesting that his program failed to distinguish between bears acting aggressively and those reacting in self-defense. Ranger Gaylar, assigned to pepper the animals with buckshot, reported that he had killed "perhaps eight or ten bears" in his own self-defense. Under the circumstances, of course, it would have been impossible to determine whether the bears really meant anyone any harm or had simply lashed out at Gaylar's own aggressiveness.[16]

Undoubtedly Ranger Gaylar had overreacted; his response was nonetheless in keeping with current perceptions. Opinions about wildlife were still largely influenced by frontier myths and emotions. Obviously lacking was scientific knowledge of animal behavior. Certainly any conviction that

89

bears also had a right to live unmolested in the Yosemite environment had yet to win an effective minority of converts. Extending the concept of sanctuary from scenery to wildlife was just beginning in national parks. And even as that process gained momentum not every species received equal consideration. The temptation was much too strong to judge animals in human terms, to distinguish between "good" and "bad" species as well as between individual animals displaying "moral" or "immoral" behavior.

The result in Yosemite was the persecution of any animal or species of wildlife believed to jeopardize visitor enjoyment of the park. The list included black bears, mountain lions, coyotes, and rattlesnakes. Fur-bearing animals were also trapped and hunted for their skins. Understandably, biologists would look back on the period as one of ignorance and tragedy. But of course park managers viewed the situation through entirely different eyes. The long-term tragedy was the compounding of emotions, the persistence of prejudice against wildlife even in the face of emerging scientific awareness. Greater knowledge of wildlife behavior did not immediately lead to greater human tolerance. Especially in the case of confrontations between animals and people, the burden of guilt almost always fell on the animals. More than any other gulf between common sense and prejudice, this double standard—that only the animals could do wrong—would have to be bridged if parks were indeed to become refuges for both wildlife and people.

* * *

Wildlife aside, the priority of park management was accommodating more visitors. Still at issue throughout the period was the *level* of accommodation. A keen awareness of the process by which temptations became "needs" had led in 1865 to Frederick Law Olmsted's singular warning not to allow anything into Yosemite Valley that might distract visitors from their natural surroundings. Subsequently, the California commissioners learned by bitter trial and error how easily preferences among visitors could evolve from luxuries into needs. Simply, taste became necessity. In Olmsted's view, succumbing to that argument would be management's worst failure, for the park would be undermined by compromise after compromise, each an imposition on the resource rather than a legitimate social need.

As a group, concessionaires obviously had the most to win from labeling wants as needs and, it followed, more to lose from an impairment of such labeling. All that visitors really needed, namely nourishment and a place to sleep, was basic to the range of services most concessionaires hoped to provide. Profit was in luxuries, especially those easily transported and saleable at a premium, including postcards, candy, and small souvenirs. Alcoholic beverages also met sales criteria perfectly. Thus it was small wonder that the consumption and sale of beer, wine, and liquor served as a telling symbol of the ploys used to justify every park compromise as a pressing social need.

Unlike food and shelter, liquor was something everyone could certainly live without. Yet reporting to Secretary of the Interior John W. Noble just after the establishment of Yosemite National Park, Charles D. Robinson, the same local artist who had brought charges of misconduct against the Yosemite Park Commission, defended alcohol as both a legitimate sales item and a necessity. "I would state that there has always been a bar of some description attached to the various hotels," his letter began. Entering the valley, the visitor passed, in succession, "a licensed bar at the store of A. Cavagnaro," another "at the Barnard Hotel attached to the hotel building," and still another "at the Stoneman House in a separate building distant from the main hotel building between 400 and 500 feet." The detached structure "also kept a general store and a billiard room." On trails leading out of the valley the thirsty traveler could find refreshment "at Snow's Hotel or Casa Nevada at the base of the Nevada fall," and "also a bar at McCauley's Glacier Point hotel at the summit of Glacier Point."[17]

On the question of the need for these bars Robinson was most emphatic. "Up to the present time," he maintained, "the bars attached to the hotels have been found almost indispensible for the use of guests." The need obviously was greatest "upon first ascending from the Valley floor." At those "great altitudes," where visitors first encountered "extremely dry and rarified air," many experienced "sensations of faintness and sometimes of slight heart failure or great difficulty in breathing." For these reasons, Robinson noted, "stimulants" were "absolutely necessary at these summit hotels." The need applied to "many women" as well as most men, who there discovered "for the first time in their lives, perhaps, symptoms of heart disease." Accordingly Robinson decided, "Remedies in the shape of stimulants must be immediately at hand." Alcoholic beverages were no less welcome, "if not equally necessary," on the visitor's return to the valley floor. The problem again was the number of people "unused to such unwonted exertion" as was required for these trips in the high country "of intolerable severity." Robinson's conclusions thus seemed inescapable: "In the confines of the New National Park, if it be ever opened to public travel, I think that the presence of liquors will be absolutely necessary and their absence attended with positive danger."[18]

Having concluded that liquor equaled safety, Robinson's argument bridged the remaining gap between credibility and absurdity. Liquor suddenly became a requirement for the *protection* of the visitor. Of course the argument was ridiculous; tourists were more likely to kill themselves by intoxication than by gasping for breath in rarified air. The point is that simply repeating the argument gave it a hint of plausibility. From there, the power of precedent was on Robinson's side. The longer visitors enjoyed alcoholic beverages in the park, the harder it would be to deny them the privilege.

The pattern, once established, was most difficult to break. Whatever the project, once qualified as essential it was likely to win support. In that vein the commission concluded its own forty-two-year administration with efforts to control flooding and erosion by confining the Merced River to a single valley channel. Such a feat, the commissioners confidently reported as early as 1892, was "by no means beyond the resources of engineering science and practical construction." In due course intelligent management would "curb the stream in floodtime and preserve the groves and meadows from the damage which it now inflicts at will." This, coupled with the clearance of encroaching vegetation, would finally deliver Yosemite Valley "from the two capital dangers of fire and water which have heretofore menaced it."[19]

The transfer of management authority from the commission to the cavalry did nothing to erode arguments that protecting human lives and property justified the further manipulation of natural resources. Once begun, the development of the park had become self-fulfilling. Those advocating change need only twist their arguments from obvious expressions of individual preference into all-embracing statements of common social need. Protection, in contrast, called for discipline and restraint, for resisting inevitable tendencies to define everything as either useful or profitable. Those were the standards Frederick Law Olmsted had espoused; they were not yet, however, turn-of-the-century standards for the majority of Yosemite's managers, visitors, and leading concessionaires.

* * *

With David A. Curry, the outspoken founder and original proprietor of Yosemite Valley's Camp Curry, the promotion of tastes as needs came sharply into focus. In 1899 Curry and his wife, Jennie, both Indiana schoolteachers, placed several tents on the valley floor just beneath Glacier Point. Such were the humble but breathtaking beginnings of the Currys' summer camp. Through personal and professional contacts, including an earlier transportation venture in Yellowstone National Park, they attracted nearly three hundred guests in the first season. Indeed, by the end of the summer their number of tents had nearly quadrupled.[20] Little more evidence was required to convince the Currys that their initiative, experience, and eye for location had combined to provide them with a lucrative opportunity.

The Currys, moreover, knew how and what to advertise. Most notably, they quickly revived the firefall, the celebrated evening cascade of glowing embers pushed over the cliff at Glacier Point. Ever afterward associated with Camp Curry and its founders, the spectacle in fact dated back to one Fourth of July in the early 1870s when James McCauley, owner of the Four-Mile Trail from the valley to Glacier Point, decided to entertain valley spectators. Others had approached him with a plan to throw fireworks off the cliff; McCauley reciprocated with a scheme of his own, announcing his intention to build a large fire and push the flaming embers over the precipice. At least fifteen hundred feet of sheer granite fell away from Glacier Point to the first ledges down below; people in the valley would enjoy unobstructed views of the entire cascade, accompanied by the booming reverberations of the detonating fireworks.[21]

As the Currys soon recognized, the location of their camp directly beneath Glacier Point invited periodic revivals of the firefall as a drawing card for patronage. Occasionally guests were asked for contributions and a worker was dispatched up the cliff to prepare the pile of firewood and, on cue from Camp Curry, to send the burning embers on their brief but spectacular journey into the abyss. In addition to attracting guests, the firefall stymied the competition. How indeed could other camps and hotels emulate the Currys' spellbinding stunt? Ever mindful of their competition, the Currys assumed financial responsibility for the firefall in order to sponsor it nightly throughout the summer months.[22]

The Currys, it may be argued, now had everything they could have wished for—superior location, grateful guests, and the promise of repeat business for years and years to come. Yet the outward appearance of Camp Curry as just a small family enterprise was an illusion they fostered as carefully as the firefall. In truth the Currys were driven to success in every sense of the American Dream. Expansion was the objective of any entrepreneur; to accept the status quo was in effect to admit one's failure. The strategy of park concessions dictated constantly importuning park management to allow operations to be enlarged from season to season. Growth was the objective and the Currys played the game masterfully. The stipulation that the government would establish national parks but turn them over to private enterprise for the development of visitor services was rarely defended with greater conviction than by David Curry.

Outspoken, determined, and some would say ruthless, he rapidly alienated every park superintendent with whom he had to deal. Indeed, hardly had military supervision come to Yosemite Valley when Curry and Major H. C. Benson were already at odds. On July 11, 1907, for example, Benson reported to Secretary of the Interior James A. Garfield that "J. B. Cook and David A. Curry, business lessees of Yosemite and Curry camps respectively," had submitted letters "relative to the increasing of facilities for the accommodation of guests." In Benson's opinion Camp Curry had already exceeded its capacity; further expansion, in other words, seemed totally unjustified. "It will be noted that Mr. Curry claims his present capacity to be 318," Benson wrote. However, it appeared he maintained that number only at great discomfort to his guests. Sanitary facilities especially were "exceedingly bad." Specifically, only ten toilets served the 318 people Curry claimed he could accommodate. His cesspool also was "very small, not properly constructed and very unsanitary." Simply, to raise the capacity of his camp during periods of peak demand, Curry resorted to separating "men and wives, putting all men in one tent and the women in another, where they are packed in like sardines." In truth his capacity was closer to "about 175." At least Benson was "of the opinion that the accommodations should be of such a nature that people would be able to have separate beds and separate tents if they desire it."[23]

But sanitary problems would only worsen if expansion was approved. Secretary Garfield agreed, and on August 1 ordered M. O. Leighton, the chief hydrographer of the U.S. Geological Survey, to make a full investigation. Just three weeks later Leighton strongly advised against further expansion unless Camp Curry was moved to a more suitable location. "The present site has now been in use nine years," he remarked. A projected increase from 250 to 500 guests per day would intolerably strain the primitive methods of waste disposal currently in use. "There are on the borders of the camp troublesome accumulations of garbage and other organic matter," Leighton further noted, specifying the exact nature of his and Major Benson's concerns. Certainly uncovered garbage and untreated human wastes could not be considered anything but "a menace to the health of the persons patronizing the camp."[24]

In Curry's defense, pollution problems were widespread throughout Yosemite Valley.[25] Nor did the push for expansion of visitor services come from park concessionaires alone. Originally the California commissioners, and now the Department of the Interior as well, were also eager to accommodate more tourists in the valley. Curry was often singled out because he was so visible and abrasive. Rather than admit his own part in the park's evolving problems, he constantly shifted blame onto management authorities. Here again, not until he faced losing Camp Curry's enviable location did he finally agree to improvements in its waste disposal systems. But, to reemphasize, Curry was not motivated by a deep sense of responsibility to his guests. Even in the present location, he finally conceded, Camp Curry would be prohibited from further expansion until it was purified. The depth of his frustration—and his priorities—showed through in his response. "I have told thousands of tourists that it is the finest camp ground God ever made," he complained in a letter to the secretary of the interior, bitterly objecting to Leighton's recommendation that Camp Curry still be moved. "Its present location affords the best show ground for avalanches of fire from Glacier Point, and Curry's stentorian voice, both of which have become advertising features in its present location."[26]

Even more to the point, he openly accused park officials of trying to drive him out. The accusation was bound to win the enmity of the superintendent and his staff, who in turn saw Curry's insubordination as the product of his greed. In a report dated October 6, 1908, Major Benson went so far as to describe him as "a detriment to the Valley, as he is constantly complaining of conditions that exist, imagining that everybody is imbued with the single idea of annoying him and preventing him from making money." In truth the only problem was Curry himself. "He stirs up discontent in his camp against the existing order of affairs," Benson wrote, noting Curry's habit of lambasting park officials during evening displays of the firefall and at other public gatherings. Similarly, Curry falsely accused his competitors of disrupting his operation. Thus Benson felt obligated to

95

be blunt in his own right. "He has now been in the Valley for ten years and has reaped a good harvest, and in my opinion, the Valley would be very much better off without his presence in the future."[27]

Yet *public* opinion, Curry realized, was far more important than Benson's. Accordingly, each time the Department of the Interior suggested that Camp Curry be relocated, its proprietor took his case directly to Congress and the press. In the end, his array of printed circulars, newspaper advertisements, letters to the editor, and personal correspondence to leading politicians proved highly effective, not only for these current issues but also for several others that were to follow. With the exception of a multiple-year lease, Curry ultimately won practically everything that he had initially been refused, including the right to expand both his camp and its visitor services.[28]

Thus Curry symbolized the growing influence that concessionaires wielded over the development of the park. The key to expansion, Curry demonstrated, was not to take "no" for an answer. Whatever its drawbacks, persistence paid off. "I asked for studio privileges at Camp Curry for the present year," he wrote on September 21, 1911, for example, "which were not granted. I now renew my request." Shrewdly, he justified this pure convenience as a *necessity* for visitors, as another pressing social need. "Camp Curry is distant more than a mile from all the studios at present," he noted. "It requires too much exertion for 3800 guests, staying an average of six or seven days each, to walk more than two miles every time they wish some little thing from a studio." For instance, requiring "tourists to walk over two miles for a barber," he complained, "for soft drinks or ice cream, for cigars, for newspapers, for fresh fruit, or for studio privileges, is to curtail 50 to 75 percent of their desires in all those lines."[29]

Curry's underlying motive had at last been revealed. Rather than protect his guests from overexertion, he simply hoped to steal more business from existing competitors. Nor did he seem in the least concerned that those smaller concessionaires currently specializing in selling the items that he had enumerated might, because of his request, lose most of their business to Camp Curry. "The establishment of a studio at Camp Curry would damage very little the present studio concessions," he argued, offering no evidence whatsoever in support of his claim. Instead he reemphasized his camp's isolation, acknowledging only in passing that studio privileges "would increase my own receipts."[30]

Thus did Curry's formula—ask and ask again—lead incrementally and steadily toward expansion of his camp. From every standpoint of business his formula was sound; for park legislation, it masked a troubling inconsistency. For whom and for what were national parks intended? If private entrepreneurs controlled all visitor services, was not expansion for the sake of greater profit the logical outcome? Why should David Curry be blamed for promoting his interests? More fundamentally, the flaw was in park legislation. In effect, Congress had authorized competitive management units. Even though concessionaires were regulated by the government, the fact remained that they would never relent. Any government weakness, it followed, in turn would lead to concessionaires' greater strength. Curry graphically depicted how to manipulate that arrangement. To use the vernacular, the squeaky wheel got the grease.

In that regard, nothing more angered park officials than Curry's constant willingness to go over their heads by appealing directly to the secretary of the interior, the Congress, and the public at large. On February 4, 1913, for example, he complained bitterly to Representative John E. Raker of California that park management had absolutely no understanding of why he should be "entitled to normal business security." "We certainly appreciate your efforts in our behalf lately," he began his letter, "though I fear we shall not get our desires. We, as business men, would like to be treated like business men. We are more like mendicants who ask and are refused without being vouchsafed any reason." Similarly, a one-page printed circular dated April 10, 1914, implored the reader, "as a friend of Camp Curry," to write Secretary of the Interior Franklin K. Lane, "asking his favorable consideration of questions now pending, concerning the concession of the Curry Camping Company," and also to write the reader's congressman, "asking him to cooperate with his fellow Congressman, Hon. J. E. Raker, who represents the Yosemite district, in presenting to the favorable consideration of Mr. Lane the claims of the Curry Camping Company."[31]

Above all, Curry vehemently objected to the firefall's abolishment, for which, he claimed, "no reason had been given." The Interior Department's edict, handed down on March 3, suggested only that the firefall might be a hazard. "You realize the pleasure and amusement caused by the fire fall to Camp Curry's guests and other Yosemite tourists," Curry wrote in protest. "Camp Curry wants the fire fall restored." The remainder of the circular enumerated his long-standing grievance: He too should be allowed to sell postcards, fruit, candy, guidebooks, magazines, maps, fishing tackle, and photographs. Similarly, he still insisted that Camp Curry be awarded a multiple-year lease. "I am starting for Washington at once and hope a letter from you will go forward immediately," he concluded, "lending your support to as many of these propositions as you believe are worthy."[32]

Public opinion, Curry realized, was a powerful ally, at times even stronger and more influential than park management itself. It was said, for example, that the abolishment of the firefall in 1914 was intended solely to punish him for his ridicule of park authority.[33] Even so, the decision did little to dampen his militancy. He simply found all the more reason to mimic James Mason Hutchings, portraying his camp as just another small family business and himself as a businessman who was being unreasonably harassed by government bureaucrats. Meanwhile, whatever the grievance, the key to courting public opinion was to state that whatever the public wanted was in fact a crying need. "Candies are as immediate necessities for the ladies as cigars are for gentlemen," Curry therefore argued in his printed circular. "Camp Curry wants the right to sell fruits and candies as well as the other necessities which are allowed."[34]

The argument was not to end there. Rather, Curry and other concessionaires solidified their positions in the park, time and again resorting to "need" as justification for a widening range of projects and services, from the sale of small items like candy and cigars to the expenditures for larger capital investments like auditoriums and swimming pools. Each "need", when introduced, invariably took on a life of its own. The guest who found candy and swimming pools one year expected similar luxuries on the next visit. The possibility that one or more might undermine the purposes for which the park supposedly had been established seemed to elude even government officials. The issue of park control still begged for resolution, not only to strike a working balance for accommodations and services but also to ensure that increased development would not overwhelm the natural scene.

The military, it was finally recognized, was not appropriate to that task. For one thing, military regulation of civilians in peacetime was probably illegal; in either case, protection was no longer a simple matter of standing between poachers and resources. David A. Curry was only one example of the growing number of individuals seeking to exploit the park legally. As management duties multiplied in political and social complexity—and as park visitation dramatically increased—it seemed less and less desirable that the military should intervene in wholly civilian matters.

A final consideration was military prestige. The army's original mission—to protect the high country's forests and meadows—had been simple and pure. Finally involved in the civilian intrigue so common to Yosemite Valley, the army was frequently portrayed as just another government bureaucracy. Inevitably, tensions between civilians and military superintendents steadily multiplied. So too, the motives and convictions of the common soldier were increasingly called into question.[35] The outcome was inevitable; in 1914 civilian rangers replaced the military throughout Yosemite National Park, and the era of army administration came abruptly to a close.

The arrival of the civilian rangers presaged the establishment of the National Park Service, approved by Congress and the president on August 25, 1916. Preservationists' hopes had at last been realized; for the first time, national parks had an agency of their own to oversee the protection and enhancement of their natural resources. That ideal, at least, was winning acceptance as the sole priority of park management. But in Yosemite, especially in the confines of the valley, there was still good reason to doubt whether that ideal could withstand unforgiving realities.

❧ *University of the Wilderness*

CHAPTER EIGHT

Predictably, the transition from military to Park Service management had little immediate effect on resource policy in Yosemite. Appearances to the contrary, continuity far outweighed change in the identification and protection of plants and animals. Pressure for redirection came from outside the Park Service. University scientists and educators often pointed the way toward responsible management, especially for natural resources. Otherwise, precedent was still a force too powerful to dislodge. Long before the arrival of the National Park Service, the infrastructure of Yosemite had assumed a life all its own. Even if the option had been seriously considered at the time, relocating buildings, roads, and maintenance facilities outside the park would have aroused a great deal of opposition. Tradition was on the side of visitation and development. It therefore came as no surprise to a small minority of critics that the Park Service itself was strongly committed to those priorities.

Among concerned reformers, few would contribute more than the faculty and graduate students associated with the Museum of Vertebrate Zoology of the University of California at Berkeley. In their estimation, Yosemite National Park provided outstanding opportunities for the study and promotion of the natural sciences. As one result, the relationship between Berkeley and Yosemite gradually transcended the linkage of California's most famous natural landmark with what was to be recognized as the state's leading university. The association further heralded increased emphasis throughout the national park system on the protection and enhancement of biological resources. The key disappointment among university scientists was the reluctance of park officials to acknowledge this responsibility consistently and with conviction. At least new directives seemed in the offing, prompting scientists and park managers alike to proclaim the national parks as America's "outdoor universities."[1]

* * *

If the protection of biological resources had been a more prominent factor in the establishment of Yosemite National Park, its identification as an outdoor laboratory for the study of the natural sciences might not have clashed repeatedly with the entrenched preconceptions that visitors were of first importance and resources a distant second. The entire built environment of Yosemite Valley in particular, from roads and bridges to camps and hotels, was structured to accommodate growing numbers of tourists. The completion of the Yosemite Valley Railroad in 1907, coupled with the opening of the valley to automobiles in 1913, guaranteed that greater numbers of visitors would arrive. The railroad itself came only to El Portal, thirteen miles west of Yosemite Valley proper. Yet the distance was easily bridged by stagecoach and later motor coach. Indeed, the completion of the railroad simply exerted pressure on the federal government to improve the existing roadway from El Portal up to the valley through the Merced River Canyon. These improvements, in turn, prompted increased awareness of the ease of admitting automobiles beyond the park entrance. Although that debate was sharp, its resolution was never seriously in doubt. By 1913 the horseless carriage had joined the stagecoach and wagon as another legitimate claimant to the valley floor.[2]

Replacing the military management the following year, civilian administrators simply took up where army superintendents had left off in calling for improved accommodations to keep pace with the growing number of visitors. The new administration was especially sensitive to upper-class patrons, for whom rustic accommodations on the order of Camp Curry seemed entirely inappropriate. Gradually momentum was building for the construction of a true luxury hotel to provide wealthy guests with something more attractive. Since the loss of the Stoneman House to fire in 1896, the supply of hotel rooms in the valley had not kept up with the demand. Justifying the movement of investors away from hotels, concessionaires argued that maintaining larger buildings was becoming too expensive, especially because the Interior Department tended to award mostly short-term leases. The shorter the lease, the less opportunities concessionaires had to recover construction costs.[3] Or so the argument went. In either case, concessionaires could obviously see the advantage of longer leasing arrangements. The point still being ignored was that the urge to accommodate every class of visitor had nothing whatsoever to do with protecting the park. In reality, more development steadily contributed to the erosion of the wilderness base. Especially in the case of park visitors and wildlife, inevitable confrontations led to more calls for extermination of the animals rather than insistence on stricter rules of conduct governing visitor behavior.

Restrictions on visitation in the interest of resource management remained the farthest idea from anyone's mind. To the contrary, even preservationists, ever aware of the loss of Hetch Hetchy to the city of San Francisco, considered greater numbers of tourists to be the salvation of the park.[4] Likewise, the transition from military to civilian authority in the valley did nothing to temper the ambitions of its leading concessionaires, most notably David A. Curry. On February 6, 1915, for example, Curry applied directly to Secretary of the Interior Franklin K. Lane not only for permission to sell fruit, photographic supplies, bread, and pastries but also for "the right to establish pool tables and a bowling alley in Camp Curry during the coming season." As in previous requests, he forcefully argued that simply the size of his camp justified his asking for all of these privileges. "Camp Curry will have more capacity this season than all the other combined hostelries in the Valley," he noted, "and should therefore be complete in itself for taking care of the public." Again he reasoned that whatever the public wanted somehow ought to be provided. "It makes a tired camper angry at the authorities to ask for bread or pastry or kodak supplies," he wrote, returning to that familiar theme. "Besides," he added, "they are angry at the hotel man for not being up-to-date."[5]

The strategy for Curry, like most other concessionaires, was to continue to insist that luxuries were needs. Anything even a few people simply desired suddenly became something no one could live without. Public opinion, Curry shrewdly realized, became that much harder to defy. Every year the objective was the same—to petition government authorities for as many new services as possible. Although some would be denied, others would always be approved. Eventually a concessionaire might wind up with everything he had asked for. Meanwhile, he had increased not only his opportunity for profit but also, and no less important, his overall influence in dealing with park management.

In Curry's case, the Department of the Interior still tried to bridle his ambition by refusing to grant him more than an annual permit. Curry, however, was not that easily intimidated. If a request was denied, he simply renewed it. If the department rejected it a second or third time, he took his complaint directly to the public, bending the ear of sympathetic guests and politicians about the unfairness and duplicity of government policy. In short, whatever the department refused it could expect to see again. Thus Curry kept pressing his case and, on November 20, 1915, again won approval for a majority of his outstanding requests, including many previously denied. The list included the rights to all of the following: a bowling alley; billiard and pool tables; the operation of a motion-picture projector and a stereopticon; the sale of fruit, bread, pastry, and tobacco; permission to charge for dancing; and the sale of music and records published by the company.[6] Once more the lesson of the moment was not quickly forgotten. Whatever the issue, the concessionaire's best weapons for dealing with the government were persistence, perseverance, and determination.

Yosemite, in retrospect, had come to another major crossroads. The question now literally begged to be asked: What potential effect would pandering to tourists have on the long-term integrity of the park and its resources? Obviously concessionaires had no incentive to raise this issue; for them the natural features of the park were just something more to be sold. As a group they had already bitterly complained that the Department of the Interior did little to make Yosemite more enticing year-round. "Yosemite Concessions in general are money makers for about two months in the season," David Curry wrote Secretary Lane in September 1916, "and for the rest of the time, they might as well take money from one pocket and put it in the other and allege that this was a money making process."[7]

Profit stability required a much longer tourist season. "Please allow me to suggest further attractions," Curry remarked, "that would absolutely extend the season to six months." Golf courses headed his list; next in priority was the reestablishment of the firefall, still, in his opinion, the best "advertising stunt" ever conceived for bringing business to the park. Similarly, he endorsed the long-standing proposal that Yosemite Creek above Yosemite Falls be dammed, allowing floodgates to control its volume throughout the dry summer months "in such quantity as to show Yosemite tourists what Yosemite Falls are." His stationery itself was highly revealing of his biases; prominent beside his letterhead was a picture captioned as follows: "Tennis and Croquet at Camp Curry."[8]

Curry wasted no time petitioning the department to adopt his profit-making schemes; even as he wrote Secretary Lane he had submitted a formal request for permission "to establish a nine-hole golf course in the meadow adjacent to Camp Curry." Even more boldly, he further asked "to maintain in connection with its baths a masseur and massage department," whose prices, of course, would be regulated by government authorities. That concession nonetheless rang hollow, for on October 2 he vigorously protested revoking the company's license to take trout from park streams and lakes. Any insinuation that the fish were becoming scarce was simply untrue. "There are many lakes twenty-five to forty miles from the Valley," he wrote, "that are so overstocked that the fish are actually starving to death." If the government would designate Camp Curry a lake all its own, he personally guaranteed that its stock would be maintained "up to the right standard—that is, to the point of efficiency where trout could be produced to as great numbers as the feed provided. Or I could assume artificial feeding," he concluded, finally dropping all semblance of concern for the fish as something worth seeing rather than selling, "for I would be interested in providing trout for a thousand people during about forty days of the season . . . and for a smaller number during the rest of a five or six month season."[9]

In this instance, at least, he never got the chance to press his point, for on April 30, 1917, he died, a victim of diabetes. Yet his heirs, and especially his wife, proved every bit as forceful in protecting and expanding Camp Curry's interests. So too concessionaires throughout the park continued to benefit from David Curry's formula for success—in all dealings with the government never take "no" for an answer. Dramatic increases in visitation further strengthened every operator's position. At the time of Curry's death, between twenty-five and thirty thousand visitors were entering the park annually, a fivefold increase in only fifteen years.[10]

Invariably, every effort to prepare for growth muted any conviction that preservation for its own sake should be management's top priority. Far more often, public awareness about protection was molded by writers, scholars, and activists outside government ranks. Yosemite's attraction for university scientists in particular was the many opportunities it still provided for field investigation. Scientists, as a result, swiftly moved to the forefront of protection efforts by suggesting various methods for sustaining the park's plant and wildlife populations. A far greater challenge was to convince the Park Service to adopt those suggestions. Thus time and again scientists found themselves repeating the familiar warning that only more sensitive management would ensure the welfare of Yosemite's biological resources.

* * *

In Joseph Grinnell, the director of the Museum of Vertebrate Zoology of the University of California at Berkeley, scientists found an indefatigable champion of park protection and research. The son of a government physician, Grinnell was born on February 27, 1877, at Fort Sill, Oklahoma, where his father administered to plains Indians living on the reservation. When young Joseph was seven the family moved to California, settling east of Los Angeles in the suburb of Pasadena. Southern California in the 1880s still had much open space, allowing Grinnell to pursue his boyhood interest in the study of birds. Ornithology continued to be his passion while he completed high school and college in Pasadena, then entered Stanford for graduate study in the biological sciences. In 1908, at only thirty-one years of age, he was appointed director of the state university's new Museum of Vertebrate Zoology, which was just taking shape across San Francisco Bay in the college town of Berkeley.[11]

Even as Grinnell began his new duties, Yosemite National Park was a major topic of discussion throughout the university. Many prominent leaders of the Sierra Club were Bay Area educators and business associates. As further testimony to Yosemite's popularity, publicity agents for the Santa Fe, Southern Pacific, and Yosemite Valley railroads timed slick promotions of the park to coincide with the opening of each climbing and hiking season. Growing debate about the Hetch Hetchy reservoir only added to the standard fare of articles and advertisements concerning Yosemite travel. If Hetch Hetchy was in fact dammed, the water would flow into the Bay Area's leading city. Accordingly, the controversy inspired scores of articles, with the result that Yosemite National Park as a whole did not escape further revelations about its many attractions.

More than scenery, the lure of Yosemite for Joseph Grinnell was the opportunity it afforded to study plants and animals in their natural surroundings. Even at the turn of the century, California landscapes were fast disappearing, and with them any hope of reconstructing all of their original biological intricacies. Increasingly it appeared that only the larger national parks, among them Yosemite, would provide some semblance of protection for what remained of the state's varied flora and fauna. Elsewhere the future for rare and endangered plants and animals did not seem to be as bright. A few biologists, for example, already suspected that the California condor was in trouble. In fact, as early as 1912 Grinnell was asked whether he believed the great bird would eventually become extinct in the wild.[12]

At the time, he was optimistic the condor would survive. Yet he realized how much that opinion relied on speculation. In truth, scientists still knew very little about the California landscape. In the interest of filling in one of those gaps, on October 7, 1914, he informed Secretary of the Interior Franklin K. Lane of preparations to undertake "a Natural History Survey, under the auspices of the University of California Museum of Vertebrate Zoology, along a line through Yosemite from Merced Falls to Mono Lake." Thus Grinnell formally announced his research interests in Yosemite, little realizing that the endeavor in its many stages would consume much of his time and energy during the next ten years. Indeed, as he further noted in the prospectus accompanying his letter, the objectives of the survey were detailed and comprehensive. He planned to identify all the mammals, birds, and reptiles in the area to be explored and determine their distribution, habits, and ecological relationships, "in other words," as Grinnell concluded, "their natural history." No less important, all of the data was to be compiled in a "permanent published record, in a form to be attractive to the public, both lay and scientific."[13]

His reassurance that the survey's findings would be shared with the general public, and not just with research specialists having a similar background and training, was far more than an attempt to court the favor of Secretary Lane. Rather, Grinnell insisted throughout his life that conservation would be advanced only if knowledge about the issues was broadly disseminated. Although peer review was important, knowledge must have a purpose above and beyond the confined intellectual discourse so common among university scholars. "The Yosemite National Park is visited by thousands of people each year," he noted in his prospectus, further justifying the survey and its objectives in this vein. Undoubtedly "a certain proportion" of those visitors "would find an account of its natural history of immediate service as a source of information concerning the animal life encountered." Likewise, a "natural history of so famous a region . . . would doubtless prove of wide acceptance also among people not privileged to visit this National Park but who have a general interest in the out-of-doors." To date, practically nothing had "appeared in print concerning the birds of the region," and almost nothing regarding "the mammals and reptiles." For this reason alone, "a detailed comparative faunal study of the central Sierra Nevada on both of its slopes would be a highly desirable consummation." Such a study, he concluded with boldness and confidence, "would fill in the gap now existing in our knowledge of the vertebrates of California."[14]

Thus Grinnell further reassured his sponsors and colleagues that whatever his commitment to general education, his primary goal was still original research. Although that research had considerable value for the lay public, he fully intended to maintain its scientific credibility. Regrettably, that objective would not be accomplished without having some effect on the park. Scientific accuracy required study in the laboratory as well as in the field. Consequently, Grinnell also asked Secretary Lane for permission to set traps "and use shotguns within the boundaries of the Yosemite National Park, solely for the collecting of specimens of birds, mammals and reptiles, within moderation, as may be required for scientific use."[15]

That request was denied when one of Lane's subordinates refused to grant Grinnell permission to undertake the survey itself. Grinnell therefore appealed directly to the secretary. Once more his letter revealed not only the depth of his commitment to scholarship and public education but also, and equally important, his ties to influential Californians who might offer their support. "The enclosed letter from the Sierra Club shows that this organization is in hearty sympathy with the aims of my proposed work," he noted. "In fact, it has agreed to publish a popular version of the results of the undertaking." In considering that opportunity alone, Grinnell could only repeat his "great disappointment" that an application "for purely scientific purposes has been denied." Perhaps the nature of that objective had not been well defined. "Let it be understood that no *game* animals whatsoever would be disturbed by myself or any authorized assistant," he wrote by way of clarification. "The greatest interest attaches to the obscure or little known rodents, carnivores, insectivores, small birds and reptiles," all of which required laboratory study and, accordingly, the use of traps and "small-bore shotguns within the Park limits."[16]

Characteristically, Grinnell wasted no time while waiting for Lane's reply. On November 11 he had already informed Gabriel Sovulewski, the park supervisor, that he and his assistants would "at once begin work from El Portal down." In other words, they would concentrate on the territory due west of the park. A month later Grinnell returned to Berkeley to find Secretary Lane's letter of November 25 authorizing, exactly as the professor had requested, a waiver of the restriction against trapping and shooting in Yosemite "so as to permit of one scientific study of life in the park." Grinnell was elated. "I greatly appreciate the attitude you have taken in this matter," he replied on December 14, "and feel assured that you will find no reason to regret the favorable action of your Department." Work within the park itself would start up immediately; "in fact, my address for the coming month will be Yosemite, California," he proudly announced. "I have already visited the Valley twice this fall, and am pleased to report a spirit of cordial cooperation on the part of everyone in the Valley, notably Mr. Gabriel Sovulewski, Supervisor, and Mr. O. R. Prien, Chief Ranger."[17] Thus he subtly but unmistakably reassured Secretary Lane that any further obligations to government authority would also be carefully identified and formally acknowledged.

His authorization finally in hand, Grinnell literally immersed himself in research and fieldwork, returning only briefly to his desk in Berkeley to keep up with correspondence and administrative chores. He enjoyed, in short, all of the advantages of the scholar—time, support, and freedom from bureaucracy. His work habits, in turn, were reflective of that freedom. Day after day in the field afforded numerous opportunities for study and reflection. It was research pure and simple, and research of the type so envied by people forced to answer to authority. Unlike most civil servants, Grinnell had a unique opportunity to cut through the standard prejudices about Yosemite and its resources. And cut through them he did, in the process further educating himself about the kinds of bureaucratic limitations that had solidified prejudice in the first place.

Among those limitations, he came to realize, was a veiled but distinct mistrust of anything authoritative or academic. The scholar's freedom of independent judgment was a bureaucratic nightmare. In his usual cooperative spirit, Grinnell wrote Stephen T. Mather, Franklin Lane's new assistant secretary: "It might give standing [to the Yosemite study] if the Department of the Interior would formally request a report from me bearing on the general problem of the treatment of wild animals in the Yosemite National Park. This I would willingly furnish, and it might prove to contain information of general bearing on Park problems elsewhere." Grinnell had no idea how much government officials feared the term *problem*. Mather, in either case, did not rise to the bait. With characteristic caution he replied only to acknowledge that "a broadgauge survey like this should develop some very interesting and valuable facts." He asked for a copy of those findings but not, as Grinnell had offered, for a special report regarding the *treatment* of wildlife in Yosemite. Privately, Mather contributed one hundred dollars to the completion of the park's natural history; publicly, however, he kept official distance. Since 1911, every bill introduced on Capitol Hill for the establishment of a national park service had ended in failure. With that goal still months if not years away from realization, it was no time for Mather even to suggest that the management of the national parks was anything less than ideal.[18]

More to any bureaucrat's liking was Grinnell's preliminary report, filed January 13, 1916, which enumerated the total days spent in the field and listed the items collected. "The first stage in the undertaking has been completed," he proudly declared. Work had been especially intense during the summer and fall of 1915; all told, seven zoologists had spent 770 days in the field, 202 of those spent by Grinnell. Specimens collected totaled 3,539, representing 315 species of mammals, birds, reptiles, and amphibians. More than 1,600 pages of field notes had been written, "descriptive of habits, appearance in life, voice, and manner of occurrence of the various animals encountered." Another 567 photographs had been taken, "chiefly of birds and mammals"; similarly, reconnaissance maps had been prepared, "showing distribution by life-zones." As planned, everything had been deposited in the University of California Museum of Vertebrate Zoology. He further reported that it was "now, therefore, the property of the State." As a result, compilation of the data could finally begin. But he added, "At least a solid year of work in the Museum yet remains before we can expect to have the reports ready for publication."[19]

Three reports in all were planned, the first "a technical paper on the systematic status and relationship of the lesser known vertebrate species of the region"; the second "a scientific treatise" on research problems regarding animal distribution; and the third "a semi-popular account, in book form, of the natural history of the birds, mammals, reptiles, and amphibians of the Yosemite region, to be illustrated, and to include a discussion of animal life as an asset of National Parks."[20] This, the field guide, was dearest to Grinnell's heart, not only because he intended it to open the eyes of park visitors but also because, as he now more diplomatically suggested, he hoped it would serve as a philosophical pillar for the protection of wildlife as an *asset* of the national parks.

The book, Grinnell realized, would take years to complete. In the meantime he was eager to publish his thoughts about park wildlife and its importance to the general public. On September 15, 1916, only three weeks after congressional approval of the National Park Service, he and his assistant, Tracy I. Storer, noted with pride the appearance of their article, "Animal Life as an Asset of National Parks," in *Science* magazine. Grinnell and Storer argued that national parks had advantages deserving wider notice; among these, "the study of natural history" was listed as high in priority. Broadly defined, nature study was one of the purest forms of outdoor recreation. "In this respect a national and a city park are wholly different," they maintained. "A city park is of necessity artificial, in the beginning at least when the landscape is planned and laid out; but a national park is at its inception entirely natural, and is generally thereafter kept fairly immune from human interference. Herein lies the feature of supreme value in national parks," they concluded. "They furnish samples of the earth as it was before the advent of the white man."[21]

But of course that assertion was only wishful thinking. Yosemite National Park itself had been extensively modified by grazing, logging, hunting, and fire suppression. Nonnative grasses and weeds had been widely introduced; feared animals like the grizzly bear were already extinct. In truth, Grinnell and Storer were simply trying to make a point. Although national park landscapes had been altered, they alone offered some hope for protecting biological diversity, especially given the far greater modification the countryside as a whole had undergone. Simply for that reason, similar attempts "to modify the appearance of a national park by laying out straight roads, constructing artificial lakes, trimming trees, clearing brush, draining marshes, or other such devices," were, in their opinion, "in the worst of bad taste."[22]

The reasons for their outspoken assessment were both biological and esthetic. "Even down timber," they noted, "is an essential factor in upholding the balance of animal life, for fallen and decaying logs provide homes for wild rats and mice of various kinds, and these in their turn support many carnivorous birds and mammals, such as hawks, owls, foxes and martens." Similarly, no undergrowth should be removed other than what was "absolutely necessary," for again many birds and mammals used thickets as "protective havens" from their enemies. The removal of such cover would "inevitably decrease the native animal life." Of related concern, equal "vigilance should be used to exclude all non-native species from the parks, even though they be non-predaceous," for these would only upset "the finely adjusted balance already established between the native animal life and the food supply."[23]

Granted, phrases like *finely adjusted balance* veiled the uncomfortable reality that so many of those relationships were already out of sync. Grinnell and Storer themselves injected the ominous admission that nowhere was park wildlife receiving the protection it deserved. "It goes almost without saying," they declared, for example, "that the administration should strictly prohibit the hunting and trapping of any wild animals within park limits." Exceptions should be made only for the collection of specimens "for scientific purposes by authorized representatives of public institutions," and this only in recognition of the fact that scientific knowledge might resolve wildlife problems. Otherwise, hunting and trapping in national parks were totally out of place.[24]

Native predators, it followed, were no less worthy of protection. "As a rule predaceous animals should be left unmolested and allowed to retain their primitive relation to the rest of the fauna, even though this may entail a considerable annual levy on the animals forming their prey." No other declaration propelled Grinnell and Storer farther ahead of their time. "The rule that predaceous animals be safeguarded admits of occasional exceptions," the scientists conceded, somewhat softening their earlier statement. "Caution, however, should be exercised in doing so, and no step taken to diminish the number of . . . predators, except on the best of grounds."[25]

Ideally, all of these goals would be pursued in the interest of public education. "As the settlement of the country progresses," they remarked, "and the original aspect of nature is altered, the national parks will probably be the only areas remaining unspoiled for scientific study." Indeed, it seemed all the more imperative "that provision be made in every large national park for a trained resident naturalist who, as a member of the park staff, would look after the interests of the animal life of the region and aid in making it known to the public." There it was again—dramatic evidence of Grinnell's twofold commitment to science and public education. Of course science had first priority. The naturalist's "main duty would be to familiarize himself through intensive study with the natural conditions and interrelations of the park fauna, and to make practical recommendations for their maintenance." And maintenance *did* include predators. "Plans to decrease the number of *any* of the predatory species would be carried out only with his sanction and under his direction" (italics added).[26]

Those tasks accomplished, the naturalist would devote the remainder of his time to public education, through "popularly styled illustrated leaflets and newspaper articles . . . and by lectures and demonstrations at central camps." In this manner the naturalist would not only advance conservation but also "help awaken people to a livelier interest in wild life, and to a healthy and intelligent curiosity about things of nature." The scientists concluded from personal observation, "Our experience has persuaded us that the average camper in the mountains is hungry for information about the animal life he encounters." Simply a few suggestions for study were usually "sufficient to make him eager to acquire his natural history at first-hand, with the result that the recreative value of his few days or weeks in the open is greatly enhanced."[27]

✳ ✳ ✳

The origins of park interpretation have so often been credited to others—most notably Stephen T. Mather, the first director of the National Park Service—that interpretation's far greater debt to Joseph Grinnell has been either discounted or forgotten.[28] Literally from the moment of its founding, the Museum of Vertebrate Zoology sponsored lectures that were intended for general audiences and that touched on a wide variety of natural history topics. Those lectures were fundamental to Grinnell's evolving campaign to educate the public about wildlife and conservation. Logically, as a result, his work in Yosemite became an extension of that earlier effort, the culmination of which was his article in *Science* magazine calling for a systematic approach to public education in the largest national parks. His fondest hopes were to be realized in 1920, when Yosemite became the first national park to establish an official program of field interpretation.

To reemphasize, interpretation stood apart by virtue of its attempt to reach the general public. Formalized instruction in the national parks could be traced back as far as August 1870, when the Berkeley geologist Joseph

LeConte took a party of his students on a summer field trip through Yosemite. By the turn of the century, other university scholars and teachers were following his lead, involving their classes in a variety of summer courses directly associated with national park areas.[29] But the public was not invited to join these original field studies. Grinnell hoped to reach average park visitors, those individuals, as he noted, who had no interest in formal research but who nonetheless, finding their curiosity aroused, wished to learn something more about the natural history of their surroundings.

Until the appearance of Grinnell and Storer's article in *Science,* Interior Department officials had expressed little or no interest in a program of that type. Even when Stephen T. Mather wrote Grinnell to acknowledge having seen the publication, he said only, "It contains much material which will be valuable to us in our plans for the parks." Mather said nothing specific about public education. More to the point, Grinnell also received a letter of congratulations from C. M. Goethe, a prominant land developer in Sacramento, California. Goethe had first written the professor in January 1909 to inquire about the museum's series of public lectures on local zoology. Over the years their correspondence increased; in the process, each discovered the other's commitment to outdoor education. A devout nationalist and social activist, Goethe saw the back-to-nature movement as a prerequisite for the survival of Western civilization. More modestly and less stridently, Grinnell simply wished to keep the public informed about conservation issues and California ecology.[30]

Beyond that difference in their emphases, Grinnell and Goethe felt much the same about the value of learning in the out-of-doors. "I have never forgotten the talk that we had in our home years ago," Goethe wrote, "when we discussed nature study in general and your remark to the effect that scientific men were so busy with extending the frontiers of their research that they did not always recognize a responsibility to the great mass of the unscientific." *Science* magazine itself, he complained, had such a limited circulation. "I receive the Scientific Monthly but only seldom see Science." For that reason he would have missed "Animal Life as an Asset of National Parks" had it not been for Grinnell's thoughtfulness in sending him an offprint. "The question arises in my mind," Goethe therefore concluded, "how can we give this wider publicity?"[31]

Grinnell, of course, had already taken the initiative through the Museum of Vertebrate Zoology. For years he had encouraged his brightest students to be active in conservation efforts, especially the statewide campaign for the enactment and enforcement of strict game-protection laws. The Extension Department of the University of California provided another avenue for reaching the general public. A course entitled "Birds of California," for example, drew twenty-seven students in September 1916. "Included in the class," reported its instructor, Dr. Harold C. Bryant, "were three well-known physicians of San Francisco, and their wives; two well-known business men, several teachers, and a number of other notables of San Francisco society." This proof of his program's influence was enough to encourage Grinnell to carry on with his plans. "I will be glad to incorporate the main facts into my report to the President for the current year," he replied to Bryant with thanks, then added a note of praise. "There is no one else in the University, or in the state, for that matter, to subserve the function you have chosen."[32]

In Grinnell's estimation, the experience gained at Berkeley begged for swift adoption by the national parks. The challenge was to convince the Park Service of the merits of inaugurating a program of public instruction. Shrewdly, Grinnell furthered that campaign by reporting not only the progress of his research but also how that research might be applied for specific lay audiences. On September 1, 1917, for example, he reassured Stephen T. Mather that with fieldwork on the Yosemite project having been satisfactorily completed, he would now be turning more attention to his "most important" objective—preparing "the 'popular' account of the natural history" of the park. As promised, he and coauthor Tracy Storer intended to provide Yosemite "with a most thorough and . . . generally useful handbook of natural history yet put out, either in America or abroad." Although the actual writing would take a good deal of time, the professor remained confident that the final product would be well worth the effort.[33]

In correspondence with Horace M. Albright, Mather's chief assistant, Grinnell continued to press his case for park interpretation. "I feel convinced that the National Park Service has an important function to perform in the spreading of a knowledge of general natural history," he wrote Albright in September 1918. Ideally, the Park Service would come to appreciate its unique position for reaching "an important class of people at a time when they are willing and anxious to get such information." He looked "forward to the time . . . when each National Park will provide each visitor, gratis, a manual of the local natural history—a good deal more comprehensive than the brief lists now appearing in your 'Circulars of Information'."[34]

Grinnell realized, of course, that America's entry into World War I had upset everyone's plans, including his own. Work on the Yosemite natural history was basically at a standstill while Tracy Storer completed his military obligation. The return of Grinnell's energetic colleague following the war rejuvenated Grinnell and his interest in Yosemite National Park. On March 27, 1919, he wrote Enos Mills, the distinguished Colorado conservationist, that the University of California, "in cooperation with Mr. Albright" of the National Park Service, had "planned for the coming summer an extension lecture course in Yosemite Valley, applying the 'laboratory out-of-doors' idea." In addition, the Park Service intended "to establish at its headquarters in Yosemite a Museum illustrating the local natural history." In that endeavor Grinnell was "most especially interested." The museum would provide "an incentive and guide to visitors to go out of doors and hunt up the animals, *alive*, in their natural surroundings." Just imagine, he concluded, a museum that "would *not* be merely a morgue!"[35]

Characteristically, Grinnell took no credit for himself but rather praised Mather and Albright for their support and enthusiasm. The idea was nevertheless Grinnell's. On June 6, 1919, he again wrote to Mather, suggesting that the program in Yosemite was still incomplete. A recent visit to Yosemite had made him even more keenly aware "of the possibilities of making better use of the natural history assets of the Park." Specifically, he still had in mind "a natural history leader or guide," who would "be available for service at the several public camps of the Valley, particularly those with the largest registration, such as Camp Curry." The guide should have "the highest standing as a biologist," be of a "pleasing personality," and be "a facile and polished speaker." It followed that "he should *not* be a casual pick-up, of unpolished language and manner." The leader or guide would "give twenty minute evening talks on local natural history—birds, mammals, reptiles, fishes, forests, flowers—perhaps two or even three such talks could be given at different centers in one evening." It could further be arranged for the guide "to take out 'bird classes' forenoons."[36]

As Grinnell envisioned the position, the "resident Park Naturalist" would be a full-fledged member of the National Park Service "administrative staff, to hold office in the Valley from May 15 to September one."

Competition for the appointment would be nationwide, not only to guar-antee "the most far-reaching results" but also "to secure the approval of the best educated classes in the country." The professor believed the best candidates would be found in leading universities. "Simply to illustrate the type of man needed," he concluded, "I would name, as eminently qualified, Professor J. O. Synder, of Stanford University; Dr. Loye Holmes Miller, of the State Normal School, Los Angeles; Dr. Harold C. Bryant, of the University of California; and Mr. Tracy I. Storer, of the University of California, and also of the Museum of Vertebrate Zoology."[37]

Here again, in Grinnell's letter, may be found the real origins of park interpretation. Although Mather seemed to be more supportive, he re-mained noncommittal. "This will acknowledge your letter of June 6," he wrote, "with the interesting suggestion you have made of having a natural history leader or guide available in Yosemite Park during the summer season." Mather agreed that "it certainly would be a splendid thing" and further conceded "that at the present time much information is only fur-nished in a more or less haphazard way." Yet he would still have to take the matter up with Assistant Director Albright. Possibly, certain "legal restric-tions would be placed on such an appointment." In either case, it was "quite likely that the proposition would have to receive the consent of the Civil Service Commission."[38]

Instead of waiting for the Park Service to make up its mind, Grinnell, with C. M. Goethe and others interested in the project, worked to place talented interpreters at different locations. That summer, for example, Harold C. Bryant and Loye Holmes Miller gave lectures and nature walks at Lake Tahoe, California, generally under arrangements with Fallen Leaf Lodge. On July 19, Bryant wrote Grinnell to inform him that Mather had stopped by. "He stated the nature guide proposition had gone through," Bryant noted. "He wanted me to go to Yosemite immediately under civil service appointment." But of course Bryant was already committed and had to turn Mather down. "I certainly hope that the matter does not drop there," Grinnell replied, obviously disappointed but fully sympathetic. "The main thing is to get a precedent set."[39]

Fortunately, Grinnell need not have worried. Mather's offer to both Bryant and Miller held until the following year, when they and two other naturalists, Ansel F. Hall and Enid Michael, officially inaugurated park interpretation in Yosemite Valley. "Am getting a fine start," Bryant reported to Grinnell early in June. "There is plenty of interest. Could keep several guides busy. Have great difficulty in limiting the classes. Started with 20 this morning and ended with 27."[40] No words could have been sweeter music to Joseph Grinnell's ears.

Neither he nor Tracy Storer needed further incentive to redouble efforts to complete the Yosemite natural history. Between 1920 and its publication in 1924, the bulk of Grinnell's correspondence once again addressed his fervent hope that the book would reach the widest possible audience. He explored, for example, the possibility that the Park Service might agree to sponsor the volume. The expense, Mather concluded, was simply too prohibitive. With mild reluctance Grinnell settled for the University of California Press, taking some comfort in its promise to push the book "in every way feasible," including extensive advertising and free distribution of two hundred review and complimentary copies.[41]

One of the first books off the press went to Stephen T. Mather. "You may have forgotten all about it," Grinnell began his letter introducing the volume, "but way back in 1915 you contributed a sum of money to this Department of the University of California . . . to defray the expense of a natural history survey of the Yosemite region." The book had just been published, he said, and would arrive under separate cover. "In it we try to set forth our findings in a way that will attract and hold the interest of the ordinary run of intelligent laymen," he wrote, still underscoring its wider purpose and themes. Indeed the book emphasized, "over and over again," how national parks served the public by protecting "original conditions as regards living things." For that reason alone, he and Tracy Storer hoped that *Animal Life in the Yosemite* would "find wide distribution among the best class of visitors, not only in Yosemite, but in others of our National Parks." He asked, "Whatever you can do, officially or otherwise, toward placing the volume before the public, will help to secure the wide use of the book that we desire."[42]

The key to the future of national parks was public knowledge and awareness. In Grinnell's case, his courage to break the shackles of academic insularity lay precisely in that conviction—the scientist's role was not just to train future scientists but also to make certain that knowledge had direction and purpose. Ultimately, every American, not just park administrators and scientists, would have something to say about the future of national parks. General information, it followed, was more important than specialized data for ensuring that parks and their biological resources would in fact survive. Specialized knowledge could even be a drawback, especially in dealing with decision makers who were somehow threatened by new information. Obviously Grinnell knew far more about the national parks than did the vast majority of government officials. He therefore diligently avoided any hint of seeking praise but rather, in the interest of maintaining his effectiveness, gladly allowed others to take full credit for any of his accomplishments, even for those ideas so clearly his own.[43]

One of those ideas was park interpretation. However, instead of worrying about who received credit for its inception, Grinnell sought to use interpretation as his springboard to a public understanding of the parks. Invariably, the informed park visitor would be more curious *and* protective, and therefore more likely to insist on sound management practices. In effect, Grinnell had convinced the Park Service to reach and inform its potential critics. Likewise, he continued to seed park interpretation with his most capable colleagues and students, further assuring himself internal access to Park Service management circles. Eventually, he realized, his former pupils and friends themselves would rise up those management ladders, making changes, it stood to reason, where change *really* counted.

Above all, Grinnell cemented the relationship between national parks and American education. Symbolically, the marriage between Berkeley and Yosemite was but a small indication of the linkages yet to come. Rarely was it said, but already the University of California was part of park tradition. Stephen Mather and Horace Albright, the two names most closely associated with the founding years of the National Park Service, were themselves Berkeley alumni. In instances of strain or disagreement, Grinnell could always count on the fact that pride in their university and its personnel would result, at the very least, in a hearing for his suggestions. And so to Berkeley professors, students, and alumni went the honor of founding Yosemite's "university of the wilderness." From its graduates, Grinnell now looked forward to the evolution of a new public consciousness of the importance of national parks as refuges for biological diversity.

❧ The Science of Sanctuary

As Joseph Grinnell realized, a consistent and rational policy of natural resources management in national parks would be far more difficult to effect than outdoor education. Resources meant science, and scientific information that might influence management decisions was constantly evolving. In university circles, change was the rule. However in most bureaucracies, the National Park Services included, deep-seated prejudices were not as quickly erased just by new ways of thinking. Yosemite again served as a telling example. Despite Grinnell and Tracy Storer's plea in 1916 to respect biological relationships in national parks, the Park Service still permitted its rangers to hunt and trap Yosemite's wildlife for personal profit. Initially Grinnell had resigned himself to the practice and in fact had used it to good advantage, purchasing skeletons, skins, and carcasses for the Museum of Vertebrate Zoology and its research collections. But that use was limited and strictly for science. The possible extinction of certain species of fur-bearing animals in the park convinced him that trapping for its own sake was not only wrong but untenable. "I believe it would be in the interests of . . . the Yosemite National Park as a wild life refuge," he therefore wrote the superintendent on July 8, 1920, "if all trapping of wild animals were henceforth absolutely prohibited."[1]

As a scientist Grinnell was already suspect; as a critic he multiplied his problem severalfold. The protection of predators ran contrary to every existing policy of eradicating those animals from the national parks. The burden of proof was his; he had to convince the Park Service bureaucracy that his reasons were compelling. Meanwhile, the National Park Service showed far less interest in science and far more concern about accommodating visitors. Yet Grinnell was still determined to bring about change. The establishment of Yosemite's interpretive program reassured him that the rudiments of biological awareness were finally in place. He now set about the difficult and time-consuming task of bridging the gap between scientific research and Park Service application of that research directly in the field.

∗ ∗ ∗

Grinnell's basic premise in his article in *Science*—that national parks should be managed as islands of biological diversity—already clashed with preconceived notions that the parks' constituency was much too small. Almost from the moment of its inception, the National Park Service had waged an intensive campaign intended solely to attract more visitors to national park areas. Washington B. Lewis, appointed superintendent of Yosemite on March 3, 1916, testified, in microcosm, to the significance of that effort. Like every superintendent managing a major park facility, Lewis devoted most of his time to matters affecting Yosemite's physical plant, especially its roads, bridges, buildings, and concessions. Days spent outside the park generally were taken up by meetings with railroad executives, chamber of commerce officials, politicians, and journalists—anyone, in other words, whose position and influence might help boost visitation. Conversely, whenever those same individuals toured Yosemite, again it usually fell to the superintendent to meet and entertain them.[2]

Invariably, the best testimony that a superintendent could offer to his success was a demonstration that visitation to his park was constantly on the rise. No other statistic was more compelling proof to anyone associated with a national park as a business or political opportunity. Local chambers of commerce in particular were delighted to see hard evidence for the argument that national parks were indeed beneficial to their surrounding communities. Merced and Fresno, among other bustling towns in the San Joaquin Valley, already looked to Yosemite National Park as a source of tourist revenues. As the western terminus of the Yosemite Valley Railroad, Merced especially had taken full advantage of the boom in Yosemite travel that had begun with the completion of the railway in 1907. Park-bound passengers from both the Santa Fe and Southern Pacific railroads changed trains in Merced. Even if that stopover required only one or two hours, the town was host every year to thousands of potential customers whose one and only reason for passing through in the first place was Merced's strategic importance as the gateway to Yosemite National Park.[3]

Predictably, communities that were denied an opportunity for rail access to Yosemite eagerly supported the construction of better highways. Ever mindful of the automobile's skyrocketing popularity, the Park Service planned for a future when cars would dominate travel to all major parks. As early as 1916, visitation to Yosemite by car slightly exceeded the number of people arriving by rail, 14,527 as opposed to 14,251.[4] Afterward the push for better roads to the park accelerated annually, culminating in 1926 with the completion of the All-Year Highway between Yosemite Valley and Merced. Passenger travel on the Yosemite Valley Railroad plummeted virtually overnight.[5] More significant, however, park visitation soared, reaching an all-time high of 490,430 people for the fiscal travel year ending September 30, 1927, up nearly 1,700 percent from the average visitation figures of only ten or twelve years earlier.[6]

Once more, it followed, management decisions affecting Yosemite National Park were strongly dictated by such numbers. Especially in Yosemite Valley, there was little scientific evidence to gauge what effect tens of thousands of new visitors annually would have on vegetation and wildlife. At best, planning was reactive. That was the circumstance Grinnell and his students sought to change, not only by demonstrating that park planning could be more rational and predictable but also by insisting that natural resources should always be part of the planning equation.

As ever, the scientists' competition was traditional park values, above all the belief that national parks were set aside primarily for human recreation. The growing problems with that philosophy aside, the Park Service heralded every increase in visitation as another convincing example of management success. Grinnell remained confident that visitors would gradually come to appreciate, through education, the biological importance of the park. Meanwhile, instructing Park Service officials themselves in scientific principles seemed crucial to redirecting latent management priorities. Thus with the same optimism and conviction that underlay his campaign for park interpretation, Grinnell adopted as his personal crusade every effort to infuse the National Park Service with a far greater sensitivity to biological resources.

* * *

Inevitably, Grinnell's research of the natural history of Yosemite National Park motivated his immersion in its resource and management issues. Ideally, the park would be a sanctuary for endangered plants and animals. In 1915, for example, he proposed that breeding pairs of the California beaver—believed to be threatened with extinction—might find suitable refuge in Yosemite National Park. The project was disallowed by Stephen T. Mather, but not before Grinnell had learned some valuable lessons on biology and politics. In his anxiety to save the beavers he had proposed their introduction into Yosemite Valley itself, even before he could say with certainty that they would not materially interfere with vegetation or stream-flow. Although the animals might be saved, what other park resources might be affected in the process? In a rare moment of indecisiveness, Grinnell did not have an answer, at least not one with sufficient credibility to satisfy government officials. The scientist had learned his lesson. In any attempt to move government, one's research must be definitive.[7] Also as a result of this incident, he came to realize that good science did not always flow from good intentions. The reintroduction of exotic or long since extirpated species into national parks might only threaten the existing biological relationships. It followed that if Yosemite was to be a refuge, then animals already living there should have first priority. Likewise, no species' welfare should purposely be advanced over that of another.

As early as 1915, in an exchange with Robert Sterling Yard, special assistant to Stephen T. Mather, Grinnell revealed how rapidly those principles had evolved. Yard proposed that the population of gray squirrels in Yosemite Valley be reduced. Would the professor agree to write "a very brief article on this subject" that Yard could submit to newspapers nationwide? "This should not be perhaps more than four or five hundred words long," he indicated, "and should state the facts with unmistakable authority." And those "facts" seemed to be as follows: "The destruction of the natural balance of life due to the disappearance of the squirrels' natural enemies should be brought out very clearly and particular emphasis should be laid upon the theory that squirrels feed on birds' eggs and thus make of the beautiful Yosemite a songless forest."[8]

Yard obviously intended to use Grinnell's article as a bureaucratic shield. "Otherwise," he admitted, "news of the destruction of squirrels in the Yosemite would be altogether misunderstood," resulting in "unjust criticism" of the Interior Department. "I must insist," Grinnell replied, elevating science above politics, "that the amount of actual data as yet in hand concerning the gray squirrels is not sufficient to warrant any such emphatic statements against it." Perhaps by the conclusion of his fieldwork in Yosemite "something" more substantive would have been found. "We must have the *facts*," he declared emphatically, then added an even more significant revelation. "My field experience already this summer is bringing about revision of opinion in a number of other respects, and it may modify decidedly my 'theories' as well as the impressions of others in regard to the extreme perniciousness of the gray squirrel."[9]

Neither Grinnell nor Yard could have foreseen that just five years later, in a strange twist of irony, a devastating epidemic would practically wipe out Yosemite's gray squirrel population. Virtually overnight, debate about their abundance turned into universal concern about their chances for recovery. Meanwhile, Grinnell had long since made a convincing case for rethinking existing prejudices about squirrels as *enemies* of birds. A more scientific and less emotionally charged terminology held that birds and squirrels might compete at times for the same sources of food. "I am sure I do not wish to bring any unmerited punishment upon the gray squirrel," Yard confessed, acknowledging his enjoyment of its presence at his "home place in New Jersey." Granted too, the birds apparently were not being harmed. There simply was "a fairly prevalent belief all over the United States," he argued, still defending his prejudice, "that squirrels destroy birds' eggs." As a result, whatever the professor found would undoubtedly "prove most interesting and valuable."[10]

The key point in Grinnell's argument was the need to separate emotion from scientific research. Because gray squirrels were native to Yosemite they undoubtedly belonged there. Their toll on other species in the park had invariably been accounted for in the existing biological equation. If any animal could in fact be labeled an "enemy" or a "nuisance," more likely that animal had been thoughtlessly or accidentally introduced. "We would urge the rigid exclusion of domestic dogs and cats from national parks," he and Tracy Storer argued by way of example. Cats especially could "not be trusted, however well fed they may have been at home, to let birds alone." Allowing cats to revert to the feral state simply risked adding "one more predator to the original fauna," thus tending "to disturb the original balance, by making the maintenance of a normal bird population difficult or impossible."[11]

Much as terms such as *normal* and *original* indicated the depth of Grinnell's commitment to protecting all species of wildlife, so also was his sincerity nowhere more evident than in his defense of native predators. The long-held view of predators as enemies of national parks was partially suggestive of Grinnell's initial ambivalence. At the very least, predator reduction programs in Yosemite National Park provided an abundant source of specimens for his research and museum. Park rangers found the arrangement equally attractive as a means of earning additional income. Grinnell cautioned, however, that the museum could accept only unblemished specimens. "It is very important that animals be killed without breaking the skulls," he therefore remarked in a letter to Ranger Forest S. Townsley. "A broken skull is almost useless." Otherwise, the museum would reimburse Townsley "$2.00 each for as many as four entire coyotes (sent unskinned just as you catch them); 4 Lynx Cats at $2.00; 2 Gray Foxes at $1.25; 2 Red Foxes at $4.00; 1 Fisher at $8.00; 2 Martens at $5.00; 1 Wolverine at $15.00"; and five weasels at fifty cents each. It was "understood," of course, that animals would be trapped only with the permission of the chief ranger. "It may be that you will only be authorized to kill such animals as are believed to be a nuisance in the Park, such as coyotes. At any rate, make sure of this," he declared, "before trapping for anything."[12]

Townsley quickly set his lines, reporting to Grinnell on January 28, 1915, that the skulls of one female coyote and two male skunks had already been shipped. "I caught the coyote and largest skunk near Cascade Falls, altitude about 3500 ft.," he noted. "The smaller skunk was caught near Mirror Lake, altitude about 4000 ft." That the ranger had so carefully followed instructions merited an obvious hint of praise from the meticulous scientist. "The information you transmitted concerning the coyote and skunk skulls has been received and recorded on the labels and in our catalogs," Grinnell replied. "This renders the specimens you have contributed of greatest value to us in our natural history work."[13]

On February 19 Ranger Townsley wrote again to confirm the shipment of a coyote "caught near Mirror Lake, elevation 4100 ft." Just two weeks later he reported the shipment of another Mirror Lake coyote and "the skull of a male Lynx cat, also feet of same." Grinnell acknowledged his receipt of the original coyote with a reminder that he was looking for the bigger mountain variety. "To make the situation clear, let me repeat that we cannot pay more than $2.50 each for any of the common coyotes. I certainly hope you get some of the other things that we need," he concluded, "and as I listed to you before."[14]

Always the scientist, Grinnell defended the right of any legitimate scholar to collect specimens for research, even in national parks. Parks, for obvious reasons, were a most important source. But with that possible use of their fauna aside, he began to argue the distinction between trapping limited numbers of animals strictly for science and frivolously trapping wildlife solely as a means of supplementing salaries, which was obviously the case in Yosemite National Park. In that regard Townsley's letters were both informative and troubling. "Coyotes, Lions, bob-cats seem to be very much on the decrease," he reported to Grinnell on October 22, 1916, for example. "We trapped and shot about 50 coyotes last winter and you already know what J. Bruce did to lions out this way." Praise for Jay Bruce, the state lion-hunter, was just another example of the government's official prejudice toward predatory animals.[15]

Grinnell's doubts about that policy had already been suggested in *Science* magazine, but he said nothing to Townsley. Still, it was evident that his conclusions had pretty much jelled: With the exception of a few animals removed strictly for scientific research, no species of wildlife—not even predators—ought to be purposely eradicated from the national parks. And so he argued once again, this time even more forcefully, on July 8, 1920. Writing to Superintendent Washington B. Lewis, he called for an absolute ban on all trapping in Yosemite. "I am inclined to be in entire accord with your views on the matter," Lewis replied. He would, however, have to discuss the issue "with Mr. Mather and others in the Park Service before taking any definite action." Grinnell realized that this qualification did not bode well for his plan. "I shall be glad to know what the result of the discussion of the matter with Mr. Mather will be," he responded. Then he repeated Lewis's words: "I certainly hope it leads to definite action."[16]

Wisely, Grinnell left Lewis a bit of room to maneuver. In his reply to the superintendent, Grinnell qualified his statement. "I should say: protect every sort of animal life in National Parks—*except* mountain lions and rattlesnakes!" In part the qualification revealed lingering vestiges of Grinnell's true ambivalence; in part it was simply a concession to political reality. Although mountain lions and rattlesnakes filled biological roles of their own, park visitors in general did not support the protection of species they so feared and misunderstood. As yet the public seemed to favor eradicating those animals from national parks. For the moment, winning protection for species threatened with outright extinction—"namely," Grinnell indicated, "marten, fisher, wolverine, red fox and the like"—seemed far more important than risking everything in support of animals so strongly associated with human prejudice and emotions.[17]

Meanwhile, Grinnell kept subtle pressure on the National Park Service, writing to Lewis the following month to ask how many fur-bearing animals each ranger had trapped in Yosemite the previous season. "I do not propose to make use of this data in any way to the dis-interests of yourself or the rangers in question," he remarked, reassuring the superintendent that his motives were purely scientific. "These statistics would simply indicate the possible product of the area in question, in terms of furs." But of course those statistics *would* further reveal the kinds and total number of animals in fact being killed. The welfare of predators especially was still uppermost in his mind. "I hope you have gotten in touch with Mr. Mather by this time," he concluded, "and gotten his views with regard to the absolute protection of carnivorous animals in Yosemite Park, save for mountain lions and, possibly, coyotes."[18]

Whether or not it was intentional, Grinnell's afterthought about coyotes relaxed Lewis's guard. Back came the inventory the professor had requested, along with the superintendent's acknowledgment of Grinnell's apparent sympathy for eradicating coyotes. "Reports from the Rangers seem to indicate an increase in the number of coyotes in the Park," Lewis wrote, still totally unaware of Grinnell's true feelings. Thus Lewis was also "inclined to think that for the protection of the deer, trapping of these animals should be continued."[19]

Grinnell's prompt and unqualified reply must have taken the superintendent by surprise. He did not in fact agree with further trapping for coyotes. Instead he questioned whether the animals could indeed be trapped effectively "without at the same time catching numbers of the other carnivores which it is desirable to protect." Besides, with deer naturally on the increase was it not logical "to expect a commensurate increase in their natural enemies? And is not this state of affairs the perfectly normal thing? In other words," he concluded, "would it not be best to let nature take its course?"[20]

Possible exceptions to the rule should be perfectly obvious, such as the occasionally dangerous animal that needed to be killed. Indeed Grinnell was never one to support absolute protection for individual animals. Otherwise he was constantly troubled by what appeared to be purposeful and expedient relaxations of park philosophy. "It would seem to me," he further confided to Lewis, "that national parks should comprise pieces of the country in which natural conditions are to be left altogether undisturbed by man. The greatest value of parks from both a scientific and recreational standpoint will thereby be conserved."[21]

Much as that conviction helped realize his ambitions for public education in the parks, so it sustained him in his dual campaign to eliminate trapping and to recognize the role of predators. From the outset, his scientific arguments on both endeavors ran exactly opposite to government policy. To be sure, since its establishment the National Park Service had worked ceaselessly to eliminate predators from all major parks. Accordingly, the director's annual reports noted proudly year to year that the largest species, among them wolves, mountain lions, coyotes, and bobcats, were everywhere in decline. Ironically, the director's statement about predator control for the fiscal year ending July 1, 1920, appeared in the *Annual Report* directly beneath a paragraph praising Joseph Grinnell and Tracy Storer for their educational work in Yosemite. "The hunting of predatory animals by our ranger forces within the various parks," Director Mather declared, "is carried on annually with great diligence and good results." Indeed he concluded, "A very gratifying increase in deer and other species that always suffer through the depradations of mountain lion, wolves, and other 'killers' has been observed."[22]

Here again, the depth of Grinnell's patience was very much in evidence. Although the callousness in Mather's statement invited an indignant response, Grinnell was never one to place combat before education. As always, he preferred the role of conscience and advisor; criticism for its own sake was often pointless and ineffective. Even among bureaucrats, he realized, learning was basically incremental. In the long run, patience was the key to every educator's success. The challenge was to persuade the Park Service without demeaning its management or its motives. Grinnell may have wished for much faster results; professionally he realized why those results were often so elusive. Instead he took confidence in the power of knowledge. At least if the Park Service was receptive to new ideas, ultimately the decisions of its leadership should reflect that new awareness.

Persuasion, in other words, was much to be preferred over self-righteous indignation. Grinnell wrote literally thousands of letters, memos, and notes to park officials; in each he was careful never to badger or accuse, but always to advance new ideas solely as food for thought. "It seems to me," another of his letters argued softly in this vein, "that while the lakes and waterfalls

127

and forests each and together tend to stimulate the senses and the mind to pleasurable excitement, the animal life, provided interest in it is once aroused, undoubtedly constitutes a much more subtle and alluring objective." Granted, the natural history of wildlife was "only one of the channels of reaching" the park-going public, "but it happens to be," he closed with both emphasis and diplomacy, "the one that looms importantly in my own mind."[23]

As always, Yosemite was his proving ground for testing those ideas. That was only logical; the park was closest to Berkeley and dearest to his heart. He also maintained throughout his life that California provided enough subject matter for any natural scientist. Like the state, Yosemite was so enticing by virtue of its size, which assured a broader diversity of objects for study. And predators must always be a part of that biological legacy, Grinnell declared, his conviction still growing. As further proof of his sincerity, by 1927 he had abandoned even his qualification that mountain lions might be controlled. "I wish to repeat my belief," he thus wrote E. P. Leavitt, acting superintendent of Yosemite National Park, "that it is wrong to kill mountain lions within Yosemite, or within any other of our National Parks of large area. They *belong* there, as part of the perfectly normal, native fauna, to the presence of which the population of other native animals such as the deer is adjusted."[24] At the very least, no one could accuse Grinnell of being inconsistent. His resolve was unshaken. Any interference, even to eliminate mountain lions, was bound to have unforeseen consequences for Yosemite's ecology.

Another object lesson in the need to avoid interference was the case of the missing California gray squirrel. As late as 1914 Grinnell and Tracy Storer had estimated that four thousand animals lived in and near the valley; by 1921 that entire population had apparently fallen victim to an epidemic of skin mites, or scabies. "Of course there *must* be *some* Gray Squirrels left," Grinnell argued the following year. "The rate at which they 'come back' will be interesting to determine." Eventually, he elaborated, survivors of the epidemic elsewhere in the Sierra Nevada should find their way to Yosemite Valley and allow for the natural restoration of the former population. Meanwhile, he was further intrigued by reports that the disappearance of the squirrels had led to an increase in nut-eating birds. "Nature apparently abhors a vacuum," he concluded enthusiastically. "If one ecologic type of animal disappears another promptly takes its place."[25]

128

Ten years earlier Grinnell might have thought otherwise; in 1915, it will be recalled, he had strongly promoted introducing beaver to Yosemite Valley. But now he was convinced that such introductions were in error, especially when the species in question had developed in separate and distinct areas remote from the park. The Park Service, however, was still uncertain what its policy should be and, like most bureaucracies, kept swinging from one extreme to the other. In May 1925 Superintendent Lewis called Grinnell from Yosemite and suggested that gray squirrels be transplanted from the California coast. "I do not think it wise," Grinnell replied, following up their conversation with his usual tact. Simply put, the two species were different. "Even if the transplanted form should thrive," he argued, "it would inevitably result then in taking the place of the native squirrel." The smart choice was patience. "Even though your native squirrel is now scarce, almost to the point of extermination," Grinnell admitted, "it is my belief that it will 'come back'." Individual squirrels had already been sighted in the park. "It will only be a matter of a few years before they get back to normal status," he reassured Lewis, then closed with what had become his unqualified philosophy. "And it is much the best plan to conserve and encourage the *native* fauna, especially in a National Park."[26]

Although Superintendent Lewis left open the possibility of bringing gray squirrels to Yosemite from nearby Sequoia National Park, Grinnell's argument was convincing, and no exotic animals were introduced. Much as Grinnell had predicted, the native population gradually recovered, until finally, by World War II, gray squirrels in the valley were no longer a rarity. Grinnell achieved another significant breakthrough in November 1925, when W. B. Lewis finally banned all trapping in the park. "I have just learned of your official action," Grinnell wrote him enthusiastically. "This is mighty good news to me, for I believe that you have acted in the best interests of the Park, as regards its best use." Of course the people most affected by the ban would object "for a time," but those objections would gradually "die out." Meanwhile, Grinnell hoped the precedent would catch on in other national parks, "to the end that no native animals in them will be any longer considered as 'vermin,' to be continually harassed." Nor could he resist another opportunity to close philosophically. "The old phrase, 'let nature take its course,' applies rightly to National Parks, if to no other areas in our land."[27]

Here again, Grinnell's weapon had been soft-spoken but uncompromising repetition. If the right thing was said often enough, it would be heard eventually. The ban against trapping had been ten years in the making and was, to be certain, very unpopular among the rangers most affected. "But time is ever a mitigator," Grinnell further confided to one young admirer in Yosemite, the naturalist Carl P. Russell, "and I feel sure that in due time, the situation will become a matter of course and be accepted as the best way to conserve animal life as a whole, for the uses for which National Parks were established." To Stephen T. Mather went a similar admonition. "I hope that Superintendent Lewis's action will be duplicated in our other National Parks. There is no such thing as 'vermin' among the animals comprising the native life within park areas."[28]

Grinnell obviously was winning converts; the question was whether government officials as a whole would be convinced before predators were totally eliminated from most western parks. The answer proved to be no, at least for wolves, mountain lions, and other so-called dangerous species. Some predators drifted back into the parks from surrounding wilderness areas or survived in scattered remnants within the parks themselves. But other species, especially wolves, were apparently lost forever. "I cannot concur in the recommendation that it is wrong to kill mountain lions in Yosemite," E. P. Leavitt, acting superintendent, wrote Director Mather in response to Grinnell's views, "but feel that they should be killed so as to limit their numbers sufficiently to give reasonable protection to the park deer, which are more desirable."[29] And Leavitt's bias against predators was only one example of the deep-seated prejudice that still permeated the National Park Service. Grinnell's reluctant pupils, it appeared, still had much to learn.

     * * *

In all management there is inconsistency; nor, Grinnell realized, were government officials solely responsible for favoring some species of wildlife over others considered less desirable. Rather, that temptation appeared to be universal. Even well-meaning friends of Yosemite never lacked for suggestions and schemes, and among them the introduction of exotic animals remained high in priority. The addition of the adjective *endangered* was also certain to arouse the requisite amount of public and official sympathy. A notable example was the proposed introduction to Yosemite Valley of a herd of Tule elk, a species native to the San Joaquin Valley but not to Yosemite itself. At most, the animals may have climbed into the Sierra Nevada foothills a thousand feet or so. The elk did face extinction, having lost their lowland habitat to human encroachment. Activists, as a result, were searching for suitable locations to place remnants of the herd. One of those activists, M. Hall McAllister, fixed his attention on Yosemite National Park.

An affiliate of the California Academy of Sciences in San Francisco, McAllister wrote Stephen Mather in December 1918, urging him to consider placing Tule elk in Yosemite Valley proper. "A herd of these beautiful animals," McAllister later wrote, further adding to his argument, "which game writers unquestionably give the title 'The King of all Deer,' will prove a great attraction and surely add to the appearance of the meadows bordering the highway." Nor would McAllister stop there. "It would seem to me most laudable to restore the Yosemite to its pristine glory of years ago and have grizzly and black bear among the talus, elk and deer on the meadows, beaver and mink in the streams, and mountain lion and mountain sheep on the cliffs." But that left the problem of keeping the animals where they supposedly belonged. McAllister proposed fencing; fortunately, he maintained, the elk or deer paddocks "could be so large or camouflaged so the animals would not know that they were controlled."[30]

Mather referred McAllister's correspondence to Superintendent Lewis for review. He replied, "I am unqualifiedly in favor of any such a movement that will increase the variety of attractions to the visitor to the park." Lewis further believed that Yosemite had been at "one time a native home of the California Elk."[31] He was mistaken, but that was not the point. McAllister's credibility rested on the conviction that visitors would enjoy seeing the animals. The Park Service was in a race for more visitors, and anything that might stimulate visitation was bound to be compelling.

Understandably, Joseph Grinnell disapproved "because of the fact," as Lewis reported back to Washington, "that contrary to the general belief, the California elk was never a native of this particular section." Lewis further remarked, "Professor Grinnell not only doubts that they would survive at this high altitude and the climatic conditions of Yosemite, but also doubts the advisability of attempting to stock the Valley with animals other than those indigenous to this section." Lewis advised further discussion, including a consultation with Dr. T. S. Palmer, chief of the Biological Survey of the U.S. Department of Agriculture. "I beg to say that the proposition seems to narrow down to two questions," Palmer replied. "Is it practicable, and is it worth while?"[32]

The answer to the first was a qualified yes. Palmer appreciated "fully the objections mentioned by Dr. Grinnell that the elk is not indigenous to the valley, and that it belongs to a lower life zone and does not naturally range in the mountains." However, he was given to understand that no one was proposing a full-fledged introduction "in a wild state." More to the point, the elk were intended as "a small exhibit herd" for visitors, a herd maintained "more or less" under "artificial conditions." Accordingly, if the animals' preferences and needs were fully considered, such as by locating their enclosure to receive as much sunlight as possible throughout the winter months, then undoubtedly the herd would not be in jeopardy.[33]

Regarding the worth of the exhibit, there could not be any question. "Next to the Buffalo," Palmer maintained, "the Elk is of more interest to the general public than any other kind of native big game." The California elk in particular was a stirring example of American conservation. "These and other facts, particularly the part taken by the California Academy of Sciences in securing the reestablishment of the species, should be brought to the attention of visitors by appropriate labels on the enclosure, by notices on the Yosemite publications, and otherwise." Indeed, it was "highly appropriate that the exhibit should be made in Yosemite Valley where it will be seen by visitors from all parts of the world." In this fashion the enclosure might also serve as "an object lesson illustrating the great work which the National Park Service is doing for the conservation of Wild Life." In short, Palmer hoped McAllister's "generous offer" would be approved.[34]

It was, in retrospect, too much good publicity for the Park Service to pass it up. By 1921 the herd—originally numbering twelve animals—had been established in Cook's Meadow. All told, the paddock enclosed twenty-eight acres. Although Grinnell obviously was disappointed, he remained diplomatic, objecting only to the result and not to the spirit of the enterprise. As the decade drew to a close the Park Service itself began having second thoughts. "A difficult administrative situation is developing in Yosemite," reported Ansel F. Hall, chief naturalist, in 1928, "on account of the comparatively large area set aside several years ago as an elk paddock." And even that was too small. Simply, no one had foreseen the herd's abundant growth rate, now averaging 25 percent annually, which presented "a continually growing problem in the matter of the necessary care."[35]

The decision in 1933 to relocate the herd to a refuge in the Owens Valley, east of the Sierra Nevada, marked another satisfying victory for

Joseph Grinnell. "You cannot over-estimate my personal satisfaction," he wrote Charles Goff Thomson, Superintendent Lewis's successor, "that the transfer of the elk out of Yosemite Valley was so successfully accomplished." Grinnell had further praise for those handling the enterprise, noting in a letter to Arno B. Cammerer, director of the Park Service, that everyone involved displayed "a high grade of ingenuity and knowledge of animal behavior." That again was Grinnell, always balancing informed criticism with genuine compliment. Nor could he resist another moment of reflection and interpretation. "I have always myself held the opinion that a National Park is not the place in which to maintain any sorts of animals in captivity. It is the free-living native wild animal life that the Park gives such rich opportunity for seeing and studying."[36]

One final inconsistency therefore merited Grinnell's skepticism and displeasure—the establishment and maintenance of the Yosemite Valley "zoo." The facility began inauspiciously in 1918 with the display of three orphaned lion cubs. Soon afterward a bear cub was added to the exhibit; at best, the zoo was an unattractive assortment of enclosures and cages. To Colonel John R. White, superintendent of Sequoia National Park, Grinnell confided his reaction of distaste and dismay. "I am particularly glad that you agree with me that any sort of zoo has no place whatsoever in a National Park," he wrote. "I, too, hate like anything to see wild animals in cages." To kill an animal outright was one thing, "but I am burdened with guilt," he confessed, "if I ever attempt to place under captivity any wild creature."[37]

Grinnell made that point formally at the superintendents' conference of 1928. "It is the chipmunk, the squirrel, the deer, the bear, *out-of-doors*," he declared emphatically to the gathering of park officials, "that the visitor must be directed to seek, for his own best enjoyment—his own good." Generally, animals in captivity were "unhappy, unnatural, . . . more or less diseased," and "relatively *un*interesting as objectives of study." Rather, "the free, unfettered, wild animals out-of-doors, behaving normally," proved "most thrilling to the beholder, and far and away the most instructive." Granted, zoos had their place "in a crowded city, for benefit of people who cannot reach the open spaces." A national park, on the other hand, should not be artificial, for it already provided a "zoological park in the widest and best sense."[38]

Again, someone with less understanding of bureaucracy might have lost patience. Grinnell persisted, however, and finally, in November 1932, the

133

Yosemite zoo was abolished. Even so it ended on another note of irony. With the approval of Park Service Director Horace M. Albright, the three remaining lions were killed and two of the pelts sent back to the California State Fish and Game Commission. In that manner the state's lion-hunter, Jay Bruce, was finally able to collect on the bounties that he had previously forfeited by donating those animals to Yosemite in the first place.[39]

By now it was nearly twenty years since Joseph Grinnell had first taken an active interest in the study and management of Yosemite National Park. Although he borrowed occasionally from colleagues and students—debts he repeatedly and carefully acknowledged—no other scientist came close to the hours that he spent writing, cajoling, and educating park officials. If the Park Service had a conscience, it was Joseph Grinnell. From the abolishment of trapping in Yosemite to the removal of its zoo and exotic Tule elk, no one figured more prominently in laying down sound principles of biological regulation, principles whose wisdom had relevance far beyond the boundaries of Yosemite.

Consistently Grinnell had put his faith in education and research. Only the best training, he believed, would motivate both park officials and the general public to respond to their natural surroundings with insight and sensitivity. But even education, of course, could accomplish only so much. In truth, many people openly resented being told how to act, especially when preservation somehow seemed to impinge on their enjoyment of the park. Administrators too were susceptible to expedience and prejudice. Simply, too many actors were competing for attention on Yosemite's grand stage. Accordingly, even as Grinnell laid down his science of sanctuary, it remained to be seen whether all of the forces that had been historically adverse to preservation could indeed be reversed or at least better controlled.

❧ Sanctuary on Trial

CHAPTER TEN

For Yosemite the 1920s and 1930s were a most important cross-roads. Led by Joseph Grinnell, scientists were challenging long-held beliefs, above all that the park, in the final analysis, was meant for recreation. Rather, Yosemite should be seen as a great open-air classroom, a sanctuary where every native resource, from the smallest plant to the largest predator, would be protected and studied in its natural environment. Up against that ideal were the traditional park values of increased access, development, and economic self-interest. Government officials and concessionaires alike still measured their success by the level of visitation. That left the problem of how to deal with a growing number of visitors whose interest in the landscape was easily disrupted or distracted. Park features were wonderful but not consistently entertaining, especially after dark. What else should be provided for the visitor's diversion and amusement?

Like earlier prophets, particularly John Muir and Frederick Law Olmsted, Joseph Grinnell defined entertainment as the study of ecology. Evenings would be spent attending lectures and campfire programs. Yet most visitors, concessionaires argued, wanted something more to do. Besides, the whole of Yosemite was practically uninhabited, allowing plenty of room for sanctuary outside developed areas. But the rate of change still concerned perceptive scientists; just how long would even that wilderness stay remote and inaccessible? Yosemite had become so much a part of California's mobile culture—so much a magnet for the tourist and the automobile—

135

that inroads throughout the high country itself no longer seemed improbable.

* * *

As in Yellowstone and other large parks, the black bears in Yosemite were an early barometer of the tension between resource management and development pressures. Although encounters between bears and visitors had already occurred, it was not until the 1920s that the problem became acute. Previously the majority of bears had been hunted or chased out of the valley; even government soldiers and civilian rangers had killed bears on occasion. Dogs were also used to keep the animals away from residences and camps. Finally, under the National Park Service, government officials began to understand the basics of normal bear behavior. The number of animals in Yosemite Valley was found to be greatest in the fall, when sources of natural foods in the high country were all but depleted. Bears also were attracted to the valley by the visitors' food and garbage, the latter conveniently made available in Yosemite's open dumps and pits.[1]

Normally bears were scarce until late August or early September, in short, until well past the peak of the regular tourist season. But even that began to change as sources of food increased. In addition, visitors began looking for the bears. Amusement replaced fear of the bears as people delighted in their antics. The cliffs were immovable, but park animals were alive. Writing Stephen Mather in May 1924, for example, one visitor confessed, "The tameness of the deer, bear, and birds is the greatest attraction of them all." Indeed literally "thousands of people annually" were coming to Yosemite Valley just for the pleasure of feeding "bears sweets from their own hands at their feeding grounds," in other words, at the government garbage dumps, already known as the "Bear Pits" among valley residents and visitors.[2]

The ramifications of open garbage were not lost on Stephen Mather. "Isn't it about time," he immediately wrote Superintendent W. B. Lewis, "that we worked around toward some plan for the incineration of garbage as the true solution?" Otherwise, confrontations between visitors and bears seemed only inevitable, since "it is possible that too many bears may be attracted to the Valley, where they may become a nuisance to the campers."[3]

Although the proposal made sense, other sources of food and garbage—including the campsites themselves—still would have attracted large numbers of bears. Logistically the problem was coming sharply into focus; as long as the number of visitors increased, totally separating people from bears would be next to impossible. Meanwhile, a combination of biases undermined even modest suggestions for making the attempt. Simply, visitors wanted to see bears, and the Park Service—ever conscious that more visitors spelled its own success and survival as a federal agency—was not about to cool a romance the public so firmly endorsed.

Rather, the Park Service openly encouraged it. And this was not the first time visitors had been entertained through resource manipulation. But bears, as potentially dangerous animals, were obviously in a different category than fenced or caged mountain lions, rattlesnakes, ground squirrels, or Tule elk. There was, nonetheless, a widespread conviction that bears could be controlled and still provide entertainment for thousands of visitors. Accordingly, as early as 1924 the Yosemite National Park Company, the Curry Company's leading competitor, received permission to spread crankcase drainings from its buses over the government garbage dumps in an effort to break bears of their habit of frequenting those pits. But the intent was not to stop bears from eating garbage; the real motive was to force the animals over to new feeding platforms just erected by the concessionaire. "It seems to me," wrote one irate visitor, "that the object of the Company's action is to secure patronage for their [evening entertainment]. If the creatures are hungry the little food put out will attract them."[4]

In a lengthy report to Stephen Mather, Superintendent Lewis carefully explained that no one intended permanent harm to the bears. However, the accusations of concerned park visitors—that the Park Service had openly allowed its dumps to be polluted with oil—were also fully confirmed. "Up until about two years ago," Lewis remarked, "bears were just about as scarce in Yosemite Valley as deer." Even now bears customarily did not appear in the valley until late in the season. "For many years," he continued, "they did all their feeding at the garbage pits at night and it was only with the greatest difficulty that tourists going to the pits after dark were enabled to get a glimpse of a bear." And that, Lewis argued, was indeed most unfortunate, for with a greater number of bears frequenting the valley, "and a decrease in their timidity," they had in fact become "an increasing source of interest to visitors to the park."[5]

Because the garbage pits were "accessible only by rough and narrow roads," and also because "the stench of burning garbage was not particularly pleasing" to visitors, Lewis had listened to the overtures of the

Yosemite National Park Company. Its proposal called for providing "a feeding place somewhere near the Village" where bears could be given "clean" and "sanitary" garbage. Lewis himself "was not particularly keen" that the government build the facility; then, in 1923, "the Company suggested that they experiment with the thing themselves, which I allowed them to do. They put a feeding platform near the river bank about a mile below Yosemite Lodge on the north side of the river and erected a couple of electric flood lights." Next the concessionaire experimented with ways to bait bears "until they got into the habit of coming to feed at a regular hour in the evening." Once the animals were responding on cue, the company began running its motor stages "nightly to a point on the river bank on the opposite side of the river and directly opposite the feeding platform." The floodlights "were turned on, and the people were given an opportunity to watch the bears for fifteen or twenty minutes."[6]

The motive, Lewis admitted, was company profit. "This finally became one of the scheduled trips of the Company and was patronized quite extensively." Buses ran from both Yosemite Lodge and Camp Curry. "A charge of $.50 was made for the trip, money refunded if no bears were seen." It followed that the concessionaire had a strong incentive for bears to be present. Of course, private motorists paid nothing for the privilege of using the same facility. Nor did it "detract from the garbage pits them-selves," since later in the year the pits also "were patronized day and night by hundreds of motorists."[7]

Competition was far more likely at the beginning of the season, when bears in Yosemite Valley normally were not as active. Consequently, around May 1, 1924, the company manager had approached Lewis and asked "permission for the Company, in order to get the bear show started, to burn garbage with oil for a few days in order to try to drive, some of the bears at least, up to their regular feeding platform." Lewis had approved. "Unfortu-nately," he confessed, "instead of confining this to a few days they kept it up for three or four weeks and it was only stopped when I got a protest some two weeks ago." In other words, he had bent to company pressure until his own complicity had been revealed. Still, he maintained that the protesters tended "to exaggerate the situation materially." In fact the experiment had failed. Burning garbage with oil had not resulted "in driving the bears to the feeding platform as was expected." As proof, the company had discon-tinued its trips "until later in the season," when bears "just naturally" became more plentiful. "Like most of these protests," Lewis concluded, still defending his concurrence in the matter, the issue had "two sides." He saw nothing to justify either the "elimination of the bear show" or its modification "in any way."[8]

In retrospect, Lewis's stand marked another retreat from preservation, as well as the beginning of Yosemite's perennial bear problem. Whichever had come first—public pressure to see bears or the Park Service's decision to openly encourage that activity—the fact remained that the animals were being trained, in effect, to behave unpredictably and abnormally. Like any wild animal offered a secure source of food, bears had quickly responded to the availability of garbage in Yosemite Valley. Suddenly even Lewis saw the problem that was developing. If the large government dump in the lower end of the valley was closed, the withdrawal of the bears' food supply might "force them more than ever into the public camping area." In that case, even though the installation of three new incinerators had just been approved, it might still "be necessary" to resort to artificial feeding "in the lower end of the Valley, separating and delivering clean garbage for that purpose."[9]

In the pursuit of one objective—public enjoyment of the bears—the Park Service had suddenly confronted a host of unforeseen problems, problems whose resolution was made all the more complicated not only by increasing levels of visitation but also by the knowledge that bear shows were profitable. In the pattern of David Curry, the Yosemite National Park Company had shrewdly found a way to turn a spontaneous park tradition into a formalized paid event. Lewis himself subconsciously acknowledged the distinction. "I recall how people used to sit for hours, quietly, in the dark, waiting for a bear to appear in order that they might turn their spotlights on him and get a glimpse of him as he dashed away in the timber."[10] All at once the sense of anticipation, the quiet, and the spontaneity were gone. No longer was the visitor's patience either a virtue or a necessity. For just fifty cents and a money-back guarantee, bears would magically appear at the concessionaire's feeding platform, not only in greater numbers but also on time.

In its eagerness to maximize visitation, the Park Service had not thought through the contradictions of feeding bears *anything*. In addition, what were the consequences of allowing a concessionaire to profit by that activity, even if it was later found to be in the animals' best interest? The Yosemite National Park Company had a stake not only in the activity but also in the facility the company had provided. In other words, reminiscent of David Curry's appropriation and popularization of the firefall, the Yosemite National Park Company had extracted a park tradition, and the control of that tradition, from government officials. Henceforth any reversal of that decision would be easier said than done. Much as the firefall, abolished by the Interior Department in 1913, was restored to Glacier Point just four years later, the feeding platform would have to be discontinued over the objections of its investors and supporters, who predictably would defend its legitimacy on those very grounds—precedent and cost. Similarly, the longer the platform was used, the more the public would accept it and, in time, simply conclude that feeding bears was a hallowed park tradition.

* * *

As a group, park naturalists held the most reservations about wildlife policy in Yosemite. Many, after all, were students, friends, or colleagues of Professor Joseph Grinnell's. They tended, as a result, to bring to their positions his uncompromising conviction that national parks should be refuges of biological diversity. Recreation should be spontaneous and nondisruptive, imbued with an appreciation for what the natural world by itself had to offer. The Park Service should be concerned less with entertainment and more with education and preservation. Park officials were not responsible for "making things happen"; rather, the visitor was responsible for accepting parks for what they were. At the very least, parks could not be everything to both visitors and natural resources without risking the consequence of mixed priorities and seriously eroding the resource.

Those who trusted Professor Grinnell as a chief proponent of that philosophy increasingly took him into their confidence or asked him for advice. To reemphasize, many who came to him in this fashion were long-time colleagues or former students. In October 1927, for example, the issue of bears evoked a plea for greater caution from Carl P. Russell, Yosemite's park naturalist. A master's degree recipient from the University of Michigan in 1917 (he would obtain his Ph.D. there in 1932), Russell had come to Yosemite in 1923 as a summer field naturalist. His promotion to park naturalist led invariably to correspondence with Grinnell, whom Russell came to admire for his unremitting good advice. Yet in a draft position paper just brought to the naturalist's attention, Grinnell had argued that although every *species* of native wildlife ought to be protected in national

III. *Visitation and Development*

18. John Muir accompanied this most important visitor, President Theodore Roosevelt, through Yosemite in May 1903. The men pose on Glacier Point. Courtesy of the Yosemite National Park Research Library.

19. As the founders of Camp Curry in 1899, David Curry (standing, white tie) and Jennie Curry (seated, white dress) projected a wholesome family image. Nevertheless, both, as committed businesspeople, were often accused of putting personal interests ahead of the welfare of Yosemite. Courtesy of Shirley Sargent.

20. On September 15, 1915, an employee of the Curry Company folded this photograph and included it in a letter to President Woodrow Wilson. He accused David Curry's chief competitor, D. J. Desmond, of serving alcoholic beverages to minors at Desmond's Camp Yosemite. "We see in this picture a baby," the employee wrote, "barely out of its cradle, with an empty glass setting in front of it; we also see in the background a typical representative of Satan pouring out his vile decoction." Actually, Curry had planned the letter and picture himself, hoping to discredit the Desmond enterprise. Courtesy of the National Archives and Records Service.

21. Turning their backs to Yosemite Falls, guests swim and listen to live music at Yosemite Lodge, summer 1926. The Yosemite Park and Curry Company vigorously promoted every such diversion from the natural scene, hoping that more amusements would entice patrons to lengthen their stay. Courtesy of the Yosemite National Park Research Library.

22. Indian Field Days, 1925. Yosemite Superintendent Washington B. Lewis poses with Chief Lemee (Chris Brown), while a large crowd gathers along the racetrack in the background. First held in 1916, Indian Field Days won Park Service endorsement as a means of boosting Yosemite visitation. Courtesy of the Yosemite National Park Research Library.

23. Frederick Law Olmsted, Jr.,
ca. 1920, just a few years before he
accepted an invitation to serve on
the Yosemite National Park Board
of Expert Advisers. Taking up
where his father left off in 1865,
he further condemned purely commercial or artificial pursuits in
Yosemite Valley, among them Indian Field Days. Courtesy of the
National Park Service, Frederick
Law Olmsted National Historic
Site.

24. Government regulations imposed during the late 1920s and
1930s finally banned automobiles
and campers from using open
meadows. The overflow crowd
shown here camps in Stoneman
Meadow, May 29, 1927. Courtesy
of the Yosemite National Park Research Library.

25. The larger Yosemite's visitation, the more concessionaires, travel clubs, local business people, and government officials insisted on modernizing park facilities, especially roads. A steam shovel operated by the Bureau of Public Roads scoops paving materials directly from the Merced River in Yosemite Valley, ca. 1930. Courtesy of the Yosemite National Park Research Library.

26. The new bridge across Wildcat Creek on the Big Oak Flat Road, photographed December 2, 1939. Courtesy of the Yosemite National Park Research Library.

27. The ecological damage of road building in Yosemite was generally overlooked. Esthetic damage, however, could sometimes be masked or repaired. Here workers with the Civilian Conservation Corps paint the scarred rock face above the west portal of the new Wawona Tunnel, August 24, 1933. Courtesy of the Yosemite National Park Research Library.

parks, reducing the population of those animals known to be causing problems might still be acceptable. "Don't, for the love of Mike," Russell replied in strict confidence, "let such a suggestion regarding disposition of Yosemite *bears* come from your office. With such a leverage certain ones of our officials will do a splendid job of eliminating the bear nuisance!" Already there was "plenty of tendency to drive out and kill the Yosemite Valley animals." Proponents of eradication were still looking for any excuse. "A word from an authority in your position," Russell therefore warned, "would bring on a grand slaughter, I fear."[11]

Even more troubling, the Park Service seemed indifferent to a permanent solution. "Almost alone," Russell noted, "I've stood for non-molestation of bears." The way to reduce their so-called depredations was not to kill more animals; rather, the solution was to insist on greater responsibility from both residents and visitors. Simply, human carelessness was supplying bears with too many artificial sources of food. "Right now we are dumping no garbage in out-of-door cans," he reported, identifying one method of reducing those sources. "Each household has been supplied, or will be supplied, with small sanitary cans to be held inside and dumped each morning when the garbage wagon calls." Granted, garbage that had not been incinerated still wound up in the dumps. "But at any rate bears are not bothering camps and houses as they were." As long as garbage could "be supplied at the old dumps every year," he therefore concluded, "I think no serious damage will be done by bears."[12]

In another noteworthy departure from standard management biases, Russell blamed people for most bear-inflicted injuries. At the least, it seemed inconsistent to kill so many bears for actions aided and abetted by human interference. "I don't feel that we are justified in killing a third of the bears now in Yosemite Valley, nor even a half dozen," he remarked in this vein. Recently, for example, a female bear with cubs had been singled out as "a menace to visitors by sending a score to the hospital with minor scratches and bites." Presuming she would be killed, he concluded emphatically that he would prefer "to place the responsibility upon the foolish visitors who insist on feeding her, and her cubs, from their hands. She injured no one who left her alone."[13]

Grinnell's response left little doubt that Russell had made his point. "I have your letter of October 7 before me," the professor wrote, "with its vigorous and *logical* defense of the bear." He would, accordingly, defer to

Russell's judgment, "as based on an intimate personal knowledge of the situation—including its human factor." The draft recommendations in question would immediately be revised and only then sent as an "Open Letter" to the park superintendent, "for whatever possible good it may do."[14]

Russell, it may be said, was also ahead of his time. Even Joseph Grinnell was not yet prepared to argue that wildlife had certain rights transcending human perceptions of animals and their worth. What Russell seemed to be saying was that bears did have rights, at least that of behaving as any parent, human or otherwise, would in the protection of its young. Was it asking too much of park visitors *not* to approach a female bear and her cubs? Even more to the point, why exterminate bears but not punish people? Whose behavior, after all, was truly abnormal? "I have yet to be molested in any way by a Yosemite bear," Russell stated, further elaborating on his defense. Rather, the blame for such encounters usually lay on the other side. Bears kept getting into trouble because *humans* were careless. "I put no bacon in my screened porch," he remarked, offering another prime example of an everyday stupidity. As a result, he was not in the least surprised that no bear gave his porch "a second sniff."[15]

Russell's common sense aside, bear management in Yosemite for the next fifty years was a constant juggling act between periods of occasional leniency and ones of vigorous control. Control at best was interference, resulting mainly in capturing bears and transporting the animals to remote portions of the park. At worst, large numbers of bears were killed under the rubric of public safety. "Something has to be done," Superintendent C. G. Thomson pleaded to Grinnell in 1929. That spring alone, more than thirty people had been injured, "and some serious damage had been done to automobiles by marauding bears." The situation in Thomson's view further justified borrowing two dogs "to help us discourage the bears from remaining at Happy Isles, Camp Curry, the Lodge, and similar living and circulation areas." Otherwise, he confessed, the solution was simply "to shoot the offending bears" and be done with the entire problem once and for all.[16]

Thomson did not approve what he called "that lazy method"; on the other hand, he too was a victim of pejorative language. Bears were "marauding," "offending," "dangerous," or "troublesome." "Of course, our responsibility is to the visitors," he argued, further revealing his rationale for stepping up bear-control measures.[17] And to Carl P. Russell that was just the point: What really was accomplished by controlling only bears? What about insisting that park visitors be responsible as well? After all, if the public encouraged bears to behave abnormally, the penalty was just a reprimand, but if bears injured visitors in the process, the penalty was often death.

Like wildlife issues in general, the question of bear management in Yosemite had considerably sharpened because changes in the park had been so rapid and dramatic. Those changes, moreover, were both physical and philosophical. Physically, Yosemite by the late 1920s averaged nearly a half-million visitors a year. The Park Service greeted each visitor as a measure of success, proof that the American public wanted and supported its national parks. But more visitation also brought more problems, ranging from minor infractions and weekend overcrowding to a plethora of issues not as easily resolved. Simply, the park's physical plant was undergoing greater and greater strain. And just as the government moved in to correct the situation, giving priority, for example, to better roads and accommodations, along came a new awareness of park ecology and its needs.

The issue had been sharpened. Where did human responsibility toward the resource begin and end? More specific, were parks to accommodate increasing crowds of visitors apparently at the expense of everything else?

* * *

As Yosemite's history testified, commitments to the protection of natural resources tended to be considerably weakened the closer those resources lay to existing or planned development. Put another way, protection of an area was always least controversial the more remote that area was from the demands of civilization. That irony of conservation was perfectly mirrored in Yosemite Valley, where those favoring greater development already commonly invoked the argument that wilderness enthusiasts had the rest of the park (that is, the high country) practically all to themselves. Preservationists dismissed the argument exactly for what it was, a seductive invitation to accept only what no one else wanted. In their view the challenge was to mitigate every change, to bring people and resources together even in Yosemite Valley without constantly succumbing to human frivolities at the environment's expense.

That mandate aside, record visitation throughout the 1920s presaged another rush to modernize and expand park facilities. Charles W. Michael, Yosemite's assistant postmaster and an amateur ornithologist, was among those who complained bitterly that the valley was being overrun. "Yosemite Valley is getting to be an awful place," he wrote Joseph Grinnell in July 1927. "We have had crowds all season and right now the camps are very much crowded. The air is filled with smoke, dust, and the smell of gasoline." The following summer Michael's report was very much the same. "I am tired of the constant whizz of automobiles," he confessed. Fall in the valley was far more peaceful and "lovely." Unfortunately, "sooner or later" the public at large would also "get wise to this fact and then there will be no rest at all for those who like peace and quiet."[18]

Least among them, it appeared, was the National Park Service, for whom the "whizz" of automobiles was the sweet sound of success. Also to attract visitors, the Park Service encouraged an annual rodeo, better known in Yosemite circles as Indian Field Days. The idea was first suggested in 1916 by the Desmond Park Company, the forerunner of the Yosemite National Park Company and originator of the bear-feeding show. The company asked local Indians to a barbecue in the valley; in return, tourists were entertained with dances and were invited to purchase native crafts, "which," Superintendent Lewis later reported, "did not sell particularly well."[19] Admittedly, the entire event was a disappointment and was therefore discontinued.

In 1920, however, Indian Field Days was revived, this time as a full-fledged rodeo complete with horse-bucking, pony races, and mounted tugs-of-war. Subsequently the three-day festival was cut back to two days; still, the number of Indians and visitors participating had steadily grown. "Accordingly," Superintendent Lewis was finally pleased to report, "we feel here that this thing is becoming quite an event and is beginning to draw visitors to the park. It is generally held about the first week in August," he further observed, "after the heavy flow of travel has stopped and undoubtedly has had some effect on the prolongation of our heavier travel season." The Yosemite National Park Company was delighted, having further suggested "creating an Indian village here in the Valley." Apparently the objective was to "charge an entrance admission to the evening dances and Pow-wows that would be given." Here Lewis himself cautioned that he might draw the line, noting the danger of creating "side shows of all kinds to which admission would be charged." Meanwhile, Indian Field Days had certainly served its purpose—the attraction of more visitors to Yosemite National Park.[20]

144

Indian Field Days, the firefall, the bear show—the list of such activities was obviously growing. But again, each was promotional. None contributed to the preservation of the environment. All, moreover, had been inspired by concessionaires, further suggesting that profit rather than park ecology was the true object of concern.

So too the Park Service went along and, it could be argued, enthusiastically approved. Indeed, when talk finally did get back to regulation, the government seemed far more worried about visitor services than the environment. In Yosemite the tide of visitation had led to growing concern about the quality and quantity of all types of accommodations. For years the two largest competitors, the Yosemite National Park Company and Curry Camping Company, had thrown charge and countercharge at each other about unfair business practices.[21] Each company, it appeared, had found a ready-made excuse for any alleged failure to meet the public's needs.

The government had finally heard enough. In 1925 Secretary of the Interior Hubert Work insisted that the companies merge and pool their facilities; henceforth they would be awarded a virtual monopoly of all accommodations and sales. Theoretically, regulation from the Park Service's perspective would be easier and more direct. Similarly, the Yosemite Park and Curry Company, as the new organization would be called, would have far more capital to invest in major construction projects.[22]

Just two years later, for example, on July 14, 1927, the Yosemite Park and Curry Company opened the opulent Ahwahnee Hotel, thereby realizing a thirty-year dream for true luxury accommodations on the floor of Yosemite Valley. Structurally the Ahwahnee was a shadow from the past, grand testimony to the period when only wealthy Americans could afford to visit the national parks.[23] Symbolically, however, it was dramatic witness to the new management structure. Increasingly, concessionaires spoke in terms of their *partnership* with park officials. The implication was obvious—both were after the same results. Legally the National Park Service was in absolute control of Yosemite; in practical matters, however, the Yosemite Park and Curry Company was becoming more and more influential. The establishment of the legal monopoly did more than consolidate leasing privileges; it further consolidated and enhanced the concessionaire's business and political base.

The question again was simple: What would happen if opposing wills clashed, especially if the quest for profits seemed contradictory to the needs of preservation? In that instance might not the Park Service itself be at a great disadvantage, having aided, in effect, the development of a powerful management structure alongside its own?

Although the potential for conflict of interest was practically everywhere, the extent to which park resources might in fact be compromised was still most dramatically visible in calls for controlling bears. As visitor complaints about bears steadily mounted so did the Yosemite Park and Curry Company's concern that the animals were driving away business. "It is literally true," wrote the company president Donald Tresidder on September 30, 1927, "that the Curry Housekeeping Camp was forced to close this Fall at least two weeks earlier than contemplated because of the fact that our guests simply would not endure the bear nuisance." Company estimates of revenue losses totaled "hundreds of dollars weekly through guests who enter the Park contemplating a stay of from one to two weeks but who leave within a day or two, owing to the fact that they spend their nights defending their property against the bears and dare not leave their camps during the daytime for the same reason." Nor did the problem end there. "For example," he further reported, "at Camp Curry cars have been partially demolished by bears in their attempts to get candy or other sweetstuffs locked in the machines." And in at least one instance, an "outraged guest, who had his sedan almost torn to pieces," demanded payment for damages from the Yosemite Park and Curry Company and threatened a lawsuit.[24]

Simply removing foodstuffs from peoples' cars had not thwarted the animals in the least, "because guests who took boxes of candy or food to their tents . . . returned from meals to find suitcases torn open and, in two instances, found not only their clothes and effects destroyed but the tents themselves completely demolished." And the situation was no different in company housing. "Night after night," Tresidder remarked, "our employees are forced to stand guard." One camper had finally "evolved the scheme of throwing a rope over an overhanging limb and pulling the food out of the bears' reach." But only the preceding night a bear had "climbed out on this limb, broke it down," and proceeded to run off with the food. The guest then "thought it was the company's duty to give him and his wife meals at the cafeteria, in view of the destruction of his property."[25]

Everywhere, in short, the situation was much the same—guests were leaving the valley prematurely "because of their fear of bears." Even people who normally stayed between one and three months were cutting back their visits by substantial amounts. A recent article in a San Francisco newspaper charged that it seemed Yosemite National Park was "being run for the protection of bears and not for the protection of tourists." Likewise, sweeping California were rumors that hundreds of people had been injured—some very seriously—by Yosemite's bears. "While these reports are grossly exaggerated," Tresidder himself admitted, "nevertheless there is sufficient truth in them to do us a great deal of harm."[26]

Of course, by *harm* Tresidder was referring to the company's profits. Indeed nowhere in his letter was there any hint of resolving the bear problem from a biological point of view. Nor did he acknowledge the company's complicity in attracting bears to Yosemite Valley through continuing publicity stunts such as the evening bear show. The problem again was not *human* ignorance or expedience; rather, all penalties should be extracted from Yosemite's bears alone.

If ever there was a conflict of interest between profit and preservation— between the Park Service as protector of the resource or as facilitator of company gains—this was it. "With the present lack of protection outside of the park we can very well go to some little trouble to raise a few bears," Carl P. Russell, the park naturalist, confided to Joseph Grinnell. "I beg you," he therefore repeated, "don't start anything that will encourage killing of Yosemite bears." Russell saw it too; the company, rather than biologists, had management's undivided attention. "We have had quite a number of suggestions as to how the bear situation might be relieved," E. P. Leavitt, acting superintendent, reported to Washington on October 8. Yet it was Tresidder's letter of September 30 that Leavitt enclosed for the director to review. Similarly, in his own letter to Park Service headquarters, he in effect corroborated Tresidder's insinuation that Yosemite was being run for bears instead of for park visitors. "While I am personally opposed to killing off bears if there is any other practical solution," Leavitt remarked, "conditions are fast reaching the stage where we must determine whether the Valley is being administered for the use and enjoyment of the people or for the use and enjoyment of the bears."[27]

As Russell vehemently argued, the responsible answer was that the park was for the enjoyment and preservation of both. But that approach required managing people as well as park animals, and this the Park Service

147

was most reluctant to do. Complaints about bears were bad enough without inviting further denunciations from unhappy visitors perhaps penalized for feeding bears and other park wildlife. "There must be some remedy," began the standard complaint, in this instance from a camper anguished about losing sleep during three nights spent fending off bears. "As far as I am concerned I don't care if you drive them all out of the Park or kill them en masse." Either way it seemed "high time that something was done, not only in Yosemite but in the other National Parks to relieve the campers of this pest." Otherwise the National Park Service should "drop the slogan about 'the people's playground' and call the Parks plainly what they will soon be—'the bear playground'."[28]

The question begged again was, why should there be any distinction? Why not have parks that were refuges for both? Because, as Carl Russell and Joseph Grinnell had both sadly discovered, the Park Service lacked the fortitude and conviction to insist that preservation came first. "My references to my esteemed fellow-workers are quite confidential," Russell appended his letter, further acknowledging that park biology was the least of his colleagues' concerns.[29] And indeed, articulate champions of biological conservation such as Russell and Grinnell were still few and far between. When all was said and done, people far outnumbered animals, and that was the only statistic the Park Service consistently found compelling. Like the Park Service, moreover, the concessionaire served people. Inevitably, as a result, there was a hidden if not obvious partnership linking the management of the two. Their goal was the same—to satisfy visitors. The resource, it followed, would continue to suffer the expense.

* * *

Like any bureaucracy, the Park Service bent to the wishes of its constituents, and among them, visitors and concessionaires were the two most vocal and insistent. The observations of Carl P. Russell were therefore all the more significant; in 1947 he would become superintendent of Yosemite, holding that post until 1952. With a Ph.D. in ecology and a lifetime interest in western history (his books included the first significant study of Yosemite National Park), he was among that small minority of scholars and scientists promoted to higher management rank.[30] Harold C. Bryant was another, rising to the superintendency of Grand Canyon National Park.[31] Otherwise management personnel tended to have more "practical" experience and training, generally years of association with engineering, maintenance, law enforcement, or some combination of those and other operations-related skills. A military background, such as that of Superintendent "Colonel" Charles Goff Thomson, was also a career plus. Scientists were not discouraged; they were just in the minority. But even scientists were expected to have Park Service aims at heart. And the most important was the standard operating dictum that the comfort, convenience, and safety of the visitor came first.

Joseph Grinnell, outside the Park Service, and Carl P. Russell, inside, symbolized emerging efforts to redistribute the balances of management more evenly and equitably. Even if people obviously did come first, must all but the most benign resources rate a distant second? Wildlife in general, and predators in particular, had yet to be understood, let alone achieve some semblance of legal standing. Rather, the tendency persisted to judge animal behavior strictly in terms of human values. In this vein E. P. Leavitt, acting superintendent, reported in December 1927 that Jay Bruce, the state lion-hunter, "made a very successful trip to the South Fork of the Merced River below Wawona on November 29 and 30. He killed an average-size female lion and captured her three kittens, which were about four months old." That made ten lions killed in the Wawona district during 1927, "and a grand total of 43 killed by Mr. Bruce during the current year. He has killed close to 400 lions," Leavitt concluded, "since he has been engaged in this work."[32]

Clearly Jay Bruce was something of a hero to Park Service officials. So too Leavitt's replacement, Superintendent Charles Goff Thomson, reported in April 1929 his "authentic information" that a cougar was "very active around Alder Creek; a liver-pancreas-eating savage that is making his nine or ten day circuit with almost daily kills."[33] Obviously Thomson had already made up his mind that extermination of mountain lions in the Yosemite environment had to be continued.

The fate of Yosemite's bears remained equally problematic. The love-hate relationship that had finally evolved was dependent for the most part on the whims of park visitors. Residents generally considered bears a nuisance; likewise campers tended to side with calls for stricter controls. The average tourist enjoyed bears along the roadside, at least until the moment of inevitable carelessness that resulted in the predictable outcome—scratches or bites. Granted, Superintendent Thomson admitted, people shared the blame. "We cannot go on killing bears that are spoiled by familiarity with tourists," he agreed. Still, he qualified that statement, adding that the Park Service also could not allow "the bears to go unchecked." Once more the contradiction—checking bears without restraining or penalizing tourists—escaped his attention. Rather, he had discovered another rationale for promoting the bear show. Here visitors and animals could meet under strict supervision, separated by the protective gulf of the Merced River. On the one night of July 16, 1929, nearly two thousand visitors in 336 private cars and 4 large buses had filled the viewing stands for the evening demonstration.[34]

In October 1929 Superintendent Thomson reported Yosemite's "latest innovation"—a new "patrol wagon" consisting of a "large piece of corrugated pipe sealed at one end and equipped with a trap door at the other," all "mounted on two auto wheels" and pulled by a truck. Whenever an alarm was sounded that a bear was "disturbing the peace," the wagon was quickly dispatched to the site and detached from the truck. Thomson explained the process that followed: "A piece of meat [is] placed inside. Smelling the meat the bear usually jumps in, the door slams shut, after which the culprit can be transported to the lower end of the Park where he is liberated." Every bear caught was also "daubed with a bit of paint" when released; in that manner the Park Service could determine in an instant which bears were returning to residential areas.[35]

A constant employment of the bear trap over the next several years seemed to help resolve the worst of the bear problem. In 1929, eighty-one people were treated at the valley hospital for bear-inflicted injuries; from January 1 through August 31, 1932, only sixteen people required similar care. By August 1933 the situation had once again deteriorated, with fifty-two injuries reported since January 1. Once more, stepped-up killing of bears seemed the only practical solution. The total number of animals killed was rarely revealed to the public, even in the official monthly reports. In November 1935, however, Superintendent Thomson acknowledged that five "of the worst offenders had to be shot." In June 1936 he reported, "A few bears were quietly disposed of when it was determined that they were endangering persons and property." Finally, in August 1937 came the following admission: "Authority was secured from the Director to increase the number of bears that may permanently be disposed of during the current season from 8 to 14."[36]

In that fashion, wildlife management in Yosemite still swung back and forth between mild tolerance and vigorous control. Whenever trends did seem more positive—that is, whenever evidence of understanding seemed to outweigh the standard prejudices—determined efforts to educate the public, as advocated by Joseph Grinnell and his associates, appeared to make all the difference. Just another example was the Yosemite School of Field Natural History, a summer seminar begun in 1925 to train young men and women as park naturalists and science teachers. A prime objective of its first director, Harold C. Bryant, was to provide more incentive for Park Service personnel to resolve biological issues with greater patience and understanding. And indeed, a review of the twenty or so individuals admitted every year revealed that at least half were—like Bryant—somehow associated with the University of California, with Joseph Grinnell, or, more likely, with both.[37]

The Yosemite Natural History Association, established in 1924, similarly furthered the educational aims of park science and interpretation. Yet again, lasting converts were in the minority. The leading management constant continued to be park development. Although protective measures sympathetic to wildlife might still be controversial, most visitors, politicians, and local business interests could always be counted on to support expanded services and accommodations.[38]

The Great Depression proved a boon to redevelopment. Even as severe economic problems gripped American commerce and industry, Yosemite, as the direct beneficiary of government recovery programs, sailed through the 1930s with barely a ripple in the Park Service's aggressive program of internal restructuring and improvements. All but the heart of the Tioga Road, the park's cross-Sierra highway, benefited from large infusions of new construction capital. By the end of the decade every other major thoroughfare had been widened, straightened, and paved with fresh asphalt. New roads and bridges of modern design and fabrication replaced existing park structures that had outlived their usefulness. Most dramatic were the reconstructed sections of the Big Oak Flat Road, specifically that portion rising up from its new junction with the El Portal highway through a series of tunnels and right-of-ways carved from the precipitous walls of the Merced River Canyon. Similarly, the new Wawona Tunnel, dedicated in 1933, measurably enhanced travel southward on the reconstructed Wawona Road by cutting off the steepest climb out of the valley, past Inspiration Point.[39]

Before, during, and after the Depression, plans everywhere were the same—to accommodate rather than limit the influx of new visitors. Consequently, along with highways all sewage, water, electric, and telephone systems were expanded or modernized. Wherever tourists tended to congregate, new parking lots likely appeared. The Yosemite Park and Curry Company also targeted those sites for a variety of new additions. "We are attaching a blue print showing the refreshment stand we desire to construct and operate at Happy Isles," Don Tresidder, the company president, wrote Superintendent W. B. Lewis on April 26, 1927, for example. Looking forward to the stand's completion in time to serve guests that summer, Tresidder asked for approval "at an early date, in order that we may proceed with the work immediately." Similarly, on November 12, 1927, the company proposed the construction of a new toboggan slide on a site fronting Camp Curry. "In light of the late date at which it has been necessary to make this proposal," Tresidder concluded, "may we please ask that, if it is required, you telegraph Washington at our expense and request a telegraphic reply."[40]

That common brand of anxiety was just another indication that the concessionaire's priorities related strictly to business and not to the environment. Pressure was building, moreover, for any form of development that would appreciably extend the normal travel season. In Yosemite that meant the development of winter sports, and the toboggan slide proposed in 1927 was further proof that the big push was on.

Like the Curry Company, the Park Service embraced winter sports as the perfect solution to year-end declines in visitation figures. Consequently, once more the important distinctions between the regulator and the regulated were consistently blurred. The superintendent's monthly report for January 1930 was just one indication of the campaign's increased influence on Park Service management. So popular were winter sports that the Ahwahnee Hotel, the Yosemite Lodge, and the Camp Curry bungalows all had to remain open. Especially on weekends, when visitation was heaviest, many rangers were also "engaged in winter sports work." Meanwhile, park and Curry Company officials had already met with the California Development Association to discuss the possibility of attracting the 1932 Winter Olympic Games to Yosemite National Park.[41]

The Camp Curry ice rink, touted as the largest in North America, was central to everyone's hopes for winning the Olympics. The Yosemite Winter Club, another Tresidder innovation, further sponsored a broad variety of activities and promotions. In January 1931, for example, Superintendent C. G. Thomson reported the inauguration of the "first annual San Joaquin Valley–Sierra Winter Sports Carnival, sponsored by the State Chamber of Commerce." An estimated 3,700 people entered Yosemite Valley on January 10 and 11 "to witness the carnival and take part in the events." Four years later the winter sports movement reached another milestone at Badger Pass, the site of the Curry Company's downhill ski facility. By December 1935 a ski lift and a lodge were ready for guests. The following January alone, 9,995 people visited the area, proof again that winter sports in Yosemite National Park were a most popular diversion.[42]

Although the park had not been chosen for the 1932 Winter Olympics, the Yosemite Park and Curry Company had achieved its predecessor's historical ambitions—to turn Yosemite National Park into an all-year resort. The missing key for David A. Curry had been better transportation. For Don Tresidder, in contrast, the opening of the All-Year Highway in 1926 made winter sports realistic. He immediately molded that opportunity to the company's greatest advantage, inviting ice pageants, speed-skating championships, college hockey games—whatever the Park Service would allow—to play out their special brand of excitement against Yosemite Valley's imposing mountain backdrop.

* * *

In keeping with precedent, every serious call for less development and more preservation in Yosemite came from outside the government bureaucracy and especially from outside the management circles of the park concessionaire. Another skeptic and critic was Dr. John C. Merriam, president of the Carnegie Institution in Washington, D.C. "It is my feeling," he wrote Stephen Mather in October 1927, "that along with a basic plan for the Valley floor, including all of the administrative and service necessities, it will be essential to go back to a fundamental investigation of the things which are dominant among the greater values of Yosemite." Needed, Merriam elaborated, was "a special commission or group" to determine the future of Yosemite National Park, giving specific attention to the possibility of "developing a plan comparable in some sense to that which is being worked out on broad lines for the National Capital."[43] Put another way, he would return to the principles of Frederick Law Olmsted, reestablishing preservation—and not recreation—as the primary purpose of Yosemite National Park.

Merriam's "special commission" was actually the vision of Duncan Mc-

153

Duffie, president of Mason-McDuffie, a prominent California brokerage firm with headquarters in Berkeley. Merriam not only agreed that such a commission seemed "desirable" but also considered it a virtual "necessity" in every ongoing effort "to develop means for the highest and largest use of Yosemite and at the same time to safeguard its greater values." Although the statement still lacked definition, anyone could see where he thought Yosemite ought to be headed. And that was perhaps the reason for Mather's endorsement. Inviting critics to work with the Park Service was one way of deflecting open criticism of the agency's policies, turning those very critics, as Mather implied, into another group of important "collaborators." Be that as it may, he promptly approved. Such were the origins of the Yosemite National Park Board of Expert Advisers, also known simply as the Advisory Board.[44]

Officially inaugurated on July 1, 1928, the board consisted of three members recognized for outstanding contributions to science, landscape planning, and the national parks. Duncan McDuffie accepted an appointment, as did Dr. John P. Buwalda, a geologist with the California Institute of Technology in Pasadena, and Frederick Law Olmsted, Jr., of Brookline, Massachusetts. The choice of Olmsted was especially symbolic. Like his father, he had risen to become one of the nation's most reputable landscape architects. The senior Olmsted had died in 1903, but in his son the legacy of Yosemite planning had indeed come full circle. Much as Frederick senior had implored nineteenth-century Californians to think far beyond themselves, so Frederick junior insisted that planning always with an eye to the future was still the government's primary responsibility.[45]

Accordingly, over the next several years the Advisory Board met and addressed every issue that might have affected the park's destiny. In the valley those issues included the following: dredging Mirror Lake to preserve its depth and thereby its reflections; constructing cableways from the valley floor to Glacier Point and Mount Watkins; sanitation and sewage disposal; trail location and maintenance; traffic circulation and automobile congestion; and relocating the existing Yosemite Village. Outside the valley the committee investigated construction at Glacier Point, development at Tuolumne Meadows, and the effect of increasing visitation at the Mariposa Grove, among other issues affecting the development and protection of all backcountry zones. As early as August 16, 1928, for example, Frederick Law Olmsted, chairman of the board, reported to Stephen Mather that concerns had arisen regarding the future realignment of the existing Tioga Road west of Tioga Pass. "A careful reconnaissance should at once be made to determine the best ultimate location," Olmsted wrote. Especially at Tuolumne Meadows, the Tioga Road's final realignment would measurably affect the most suitable locations "for camping, for the Lodge and cabins, for the store, garage, and other services, and for the administration headquarters for this part of the Park."[46]

Predictably, however, development pressures kept Yosemite Valley as the focus of attention. Already the Curry Company was falling back on a standard line of argument—there was no parking "problem" in Yosemite Valley that more parking lots would not resolve. Olmsted strongly disagreed and reported on November 7, 1928, "The more we studied it the more keenly we felt that it would be a calamitous loss to obliterate the arm of the meadow in front of Camp Curry by gravelling it and converting it into an automobile parking space." Granted, the Yosemite Park and Curry Company wanted more parking for its guests. Even so, a lot at this location "would be a very serious loss to the attractiveness and value of Camp Curry." Eastward from the meadow in question the view opened "across the Valley toward the Royal Arches and up the Valley into Tenaya Canyon," Olmsted observed. Throughout Camp Curry's history, that was the view patrons had found "so distinguished and so pleasantly memorable." Although many current guests undoubtedly thought first about their cars and not about any particular view, that was all the more reason to resist substituting "for this meadow a necessarily ugly, bare, parking yard, partly or wholly filled with serried ranks of automobiles." Probably nothing else, short of decimating Camp Curry's trees, would do more to destroy its "pleasant association" and to make guests sense that the camp was in fact "overcrowded and overgrown and citified," in short, "not very well worth coming back to." Last, but by no means least, "a great parking yard, as seen from Glacier Point, for example, would seem like desecration."[47]

In his emphasis on protecting the subtler beauties of Yosemite Valley, Olmsted had simply taken up where his father had left off in 1865. He further stated Professor Buwalda's opinion. "The two assets of the Valley which are in a sense most vulnerable, the two which if marred involve the most irreparable injury, are the cliffs and the meadows." At least scars in vegetation had some chance to heal, whereas those "on bare granite [could] never be obliterated." Still, "radical changes in the meadows by filling on them for roads or parking spaces" would also so extirpate the existing "biological conditions that if every shovelful of filling material were subsequently removed a scar would remain for generations."[48]

It followed that driving across the open meadows, also a popular pastime in Yosemite Valley, should be strictly forbidden. Indeed, Olmsted argued, the Park Service should immediately move to make that practice "impossible." Outspoken support for removing the valley's "rather absurd little Zoo," as well as for relocating the Tule elk herd outside the national park, further underscored the Advisory Board's sincerity in defending the priorities of biological conservation.[49]

In an initial response to the committee's recommendations, the Park Service in 1929 inaugurated the so-called moral ditches program. Through the construction of deep trenches bordering the roadsides, motorists were finally prevented from short-cutting across the meadows. In 1930 the Advisory Board challenged the legitimacy of Indian Field Days, last held in 1926 and 1929. "In the midst of the Leidig Meadow," the board's report noted, "almost untouched by other artificial changes, an oval race-track was stripped of turf and slightly graded, to make the surface safer and more convenient for horse-races." That large oval now branded "the whole meadow," especially when viewed from high above along the valley rim. The effect was to suggest management for the sake of "a sporting event" rather than for the protection of "a precious element in one of the great natural landscapes of the world."[50]

The restoration of Leidig Meadow would undoubtedly require "many years, even if much pains be taken to that end." The first priority was to abolish Indian Field Days itself, which, in the committee's estimation, was really "quite absurd." Essentially the event was little more than "a white man's race-meet or rodeo," since Yosemite's Indians historically had never known of such events. In the meantime, any felt need to provide entertainment for government or company employees could certainly be met by "some other device not disregardful of the landscape." Similarly, as an added source of amusement for visitors, Indian Field Days had no more excuse or justification "than the introduction of a county fair or a full blown commercial circus." Indeed the committee undoubtedly "would feel much the same way," Olmsted concluded, about adding "a golf course as a means of 'attracting' or holding in the Valley visitors to whom its essential qualities are insufficiently interesting without such conspicuously artificial elements in the landscape."[51]

Yet again that was precisely the issue—Yosemite Valley was being over-run with such proposals, most of which seemed to originate in the offices of the Yosemite Park and Curry Company. In April 1930 a nine-hole minia-ture golf course was in fact laid out on the grounds of the Ahwahnee Hotel. "So it goes," Olmsted remarked, obviously disgusted, "nibble by nibble!"[52] In 1929 Don Tresidder had also asked for serious consideration of a cable car system running from the valley floor to Glacier Point.[53] In its initial response, the Advisory Board conceded the advantages of such a system for transporting greater numbers of visitors and, bearing equally on Tresid-der's motives, for opening Glacier Point to significant winter access. Quite obviously, however, the esthetic considerations demanded full review. Most troubling, the cableway and cars would be distinctly visible from all parts of the valley facing Glacier Point. Likewise, "the cableway and its fascinating moving cars," the board reported, would undoubtedly become an attraction unto themselves, in brief, "an object of curiosity to almost every visitor in the upper part of the Valley."[54]

The question, then, was simple. Was that distraction somehow out-weighed by the project's intended benefits? If with some reluctance, the Advisory Board firmly concluded no. The movement of the cars and the clear visibility of the cables, "binding the top to the bottom of the cliffs, would involve a critical loss to the majesty of the Valley wall and to its power of stirring the imagination to contemplate the vast geologic units of space and time to whose story the Valley is a key." Indeed "the proposed cableway," Olmsted added the following year, would be located in "pre-cisely that part of the entire Park which is its most distinctive, most famous, and most precious natural feature—the very heart of the Yosemite Valley proper, extending from El Capitan to the Half Dome." Unless that area was fully protected, the cableway was unjustified, regardless of any alleged benefits affecting transportation or convenience. By itself, improved access was no reason to continue "indefinitely the process begun by our pre-decessors of progressively weakening and nibbling away the natural im-pressiveness and natural beauty of this *great central unit of the Valley*." A far wiser choice would be "to admit our limitations and leave some of these problems unsolved," Olmsted concluded, "pending the discovery of solu-tions clearly and certainly free from this fundamental objection."[55]

One by one the fears that his father had expressed as early as 1865 were all coming true. Discernible change was everywhere; even more was in the offing. There seemed no better time to plead again for his father's admonition that preservation come first. "If, by an incredible set of circumstances," he wrote, returning to the line of reasoning used by the senior Olmsted in 1865, "the Yosemite Valley had remained undiscovered by white men until this year 1930, . . . and were entrusted to the National Park Service and its advisers to protect and make available for enjoyment and appreciation by the people of this and future generations, what plans for its treatment would secure the greatest value to mankind in the long run from this marvelous find?" "That," he further answered himself, "is no easy question." But often a planner's only recourse was to pose such a challenge, to insist that people think hypothetically and have the courage to look ahead. That was the big difference between 1930 and 1865; evidence of past mistakes and "the physical damage" they had caused could now be marshaled. The challenge, then, was simply to heed those lessons, to admit, above all, that "nibbling" in Yosemite Valley had been relentless and that sometime—somehow—the Park Service would have to perform its duty and firmly draw the line.[56]

That line, moreover, should be *inside* Yosemite Valley itself rather than somewhere along its periphery, thereby protecting, as Olmsted maintained, the great heart of Yosemite National Park. Otherwise preservation was just an expedience, a temporary lull in the relentless "nibbling" that was still so clearly underway. In fact there was no more room for the common brand of subterfuge, for the argument that development, because it *was* concentrated in the valley, somehow was insurance that the rest of the park would remain wild. That line of argument was the worst expedience of all; it simply justified past mistakes while opening the door to countless new ones. Granted, man-made changes on the valley floor were "trifling" in comparison to those "changes repeatedly wrought there by Nature in the very recent geologic past." But that still was not the point. Taken together, even the most trifling human changes had obviously "contributed to a serious cumulative total impairment of the original and distinctive impressiveness and beauty of the central unit of the Yosemite Valley." The challenge of preservation was to protect the entirety of the park, not just those parts—however large—that were previously undeveloped.[57]

Everywhere, the issue remained joined. Although the scenery attracted visitors, it was the distractions that paid. Both commercially and esthetically, the concept of pure sanctuary was very difficult to sell. If scientists and preservationists did indeed have reason for greater optimism, it lay in the fact that people outside the Park Service, from Joseph Grinnell to Frederick Law Olmsted, were occasionally provided an agency platform for expressing nontraditional points of view. But that was still a major qualification; the Park Service more eagerly served its most influential and supportive clients, especially those for whom Yosemite would remain just another business opportunity. When the scenery no longer entertained, there had to be something more to do. In contrast, the very idea of sanctuary called for resisting such temptations. Grinnell and Olmsted, among others, had tried their best to instill that value in management, to make it paramount rather than just supportive throughout Yosemite as a whole. For preservation to have meaning, they argued, it must always come first. For sanctuary to succeed it must be the *only* objective. To be sure, there could never be any doubt why preservation remained so controversial.

The Science of Sanctuary Redefined

The year that ecology became a serious value in Yosemite National Park would be difficult if not impossible to pinpoint exactly. Ecology certainly did not rise to preeminence at any time during the 1920s, when a combination of predator controls and overtures to increased park development significantly compromised the aspirations of many naturalists and scientists. A more likely candidate for the honor would be some year in the early to mid 1930s. In November 1932, for example, the Yosemite Valley "zoo" was effectively abolished. The following October, in 1933, the Tule elk herd was finally removed to a refuge in distant Owens Valley. Meanwhile, the Park Service was having second thoughts about its predator control programs and was considering halting the extermination of all predatory animals except, in certain instances, the ever durable coyote.[1]

Then, in 1933, came the publication of *Fauna of the National Parks of the United States,* the first officially sponsored, detailed statement about the principles of wildlife management in national park areas. Its three authors, George M. Wright, Joseph S. Dixon, and Ben H. Thompson, all listed intimate ties to Yosemite National Park. Each could lay further claim to a close working relationship with Joseph Grinnell and the Museum of Vertebrate Zoology at the University of California at Berkeley. To be sure, the volume bore the unmistakable imprint of Joseph Grinnell, especially in its underlying conviction that wildlife should be a predominant value of national parks. It further emphasized many of the ideas that Grinnell and

Tracy Storer had formally enunciated nearly two decades earlier in their own pathbreaking article, "Animal Life as an Asset of National Parks."[2]

Fauna of the National Parks had a most intriguing history. George M. Wright, its young senior author, financed the research from his private family fortune. And it was Wright who enlisted Joseph Dixon and Ben H. Thompson in the project. Still, behind everyone stood Joseph Grinnell, constantly providing his young associates with guidance and encouragement. Dixon was a product of the Museum of Vertebrate Zoology, where he had served since 1915 as assistant curator and economic mammalogist. A graduate of Stanford University, Thompson also came to know firsthand Grinnell's rigorous standards and attention to detail. Thus throughout the study's research and subsequent preparation, the professor's influence and ideas were very much apparent. Especially in Wright, Grinnell saw another vital seed for bureaucratic responsibility, for influencing the Park Service to make meaningful changes in resource management from within. The young man's initial opportunity had come in November 1927, when he had reported as ranger naturalist to Yosemite National Park. "Mr. Wright has had two years' experience in museum and field work at the Museum of Vertebrate Zoology, University of California, with Dr. Joseph Grinnell and Mr. Joseph Dixon," the superintendent's monthly report briefly noted, further suggesting the significance of those university ties. Obviously, as a result, Wright would "be a valuable addition" to the park staff.[3]

The publication just five years later of *Fauna of the National Parks* more than confirmed that Wright's talent, like his mentor's, had implications for wildlife research far beyond the boundaries of Yosemite alone. With all of the conviction that imbued Grinnell's own letters and publications, Wright and his colleagues set forth, collectively and park-by-park, the requirements for wildlife maintenance and long-range recovery. "It is true that flora and fauna and even geography itself have been in a state of flux since the continents first rose from the sea," they admitted, "and in this sense there is no one wild-life picture which can be called the original one." That said, "practical considerations" obviously required that some period be established as the ideal set-point for determining how to proceed with restoration in any given area. In the authors' estimation, that period was the one "between the arrival of the first whites and the entrenchment of civilization in that vicinity." To go farther back in time would risk wider and more serious gaps in scientific knowledge. "Consider this from another viewpoint," Wright and his colleagues therefore argued. "The rate of alteration in the faunal structure has been so rapid since, and relatively so slow before the introduction of European culture, that the situation which obtained on the arrival of the settlers may well be considered as representing the original or primitive condition that it is desired to maintain."[4]

The desire itself was nothing new, having surfaced as early as 1916 in Joseph Grinnell and Tracy Storer's article for *Science* magazine. The distinction in 1933 was Park Service sponsorship of the source and its authors. The statement nevertheless was bound to cause problems, especially among purists, who argued that management itself was most definitely artificial. "Recognition that there are wild-life problems is admission that unnatural, man-made conditions exist," Wright and his colleagues wrote, anticipating the likely rebuttal to their report and its views. "Therefore, there can be no logical objection to further interference by man to correct those conditions and restore the natural state." Of course restraint must be exercised to make certain that management did not chance upon "an even more artificial condition in place of the one it would correct."[5]

In an institution of so many ideals, here was yet another, restoring "a balance of nature" to a host of park environments. What, then, was the original composition of those admittedly elusive "balances?" And could they ever be introduced even if reconstructed? Once again Wright, Dixon, and Thompson were forced to make certain concessions to environmental reality. "At present," they admitted, "not one park is large enough to provide year-round sanctuary for adequate populations of all resident species. Not one is so fortunate—and probably none can ever be unless it is an island—as to have boundaries that are a guarantee against the invasion of external influences."[6]

As the basis of Wright's, Dixon's, and Thompson's experiences and research, Yosemite fit that description perfectly. External threats to Yosemite were actually twofold, consisting not only of environmental change but also of a flood tide of visitors. Yosemite, it followed, stood to remain at the forefront of management controversies as the National Park Service wrestled with the provocative list of challenges raised by *Fauna of the National Parks*.

* * *

Inevitably, the early years of environmentalism, defined as the growing awareness of the intricacies of biological systems and the need for their maintenance, were very much consumed with the search for a valid terminology. One popular construct was the so-called balance of nature. The question was whether that concept was either useful or accurate. If the universe revealed any constant, it more likely was change. What biologists seemed to be saying was that nature was self-adjusting. But again, where did those adjustments lead, and precisely what did they portend? The many variables in the natural world were not necessarily always positive or, for that matter, consistently in equilibrium. Whatever theory was offered, it was bound to have exceptions, especially when that theory was either tested or applied directly in the field.

Such uncertainty left proponents of change, even in national parks, free to argue its "naturalness" or inevitability. What *Fauna of the National Parks* therefore tried to establish was that *human* change, at the very least, must be controlled, except in clear instances where intervention was the only certain recourse for restoring natural balances. The conundrum was still obvious: if humans themselves had evolved biologically, was not their presence—and its consequences—perfectly "natural" in its own right? Wright conceded the point in volume two of his report; the distinction was that man had the intelligence to resist destructive change. "He thus becomes capable of self-imposed restrictions to preserve other species against himself." More than anything else, Wright declared, that very human attribute explained the uniqueness of the national park idea. "Within the national parks, man's estimate of the greatest values to be obtained for himself from the sum total of their native resources, dictates that he shall occupy them in such a way as to cause the minimum of modification from the aspect they presented when he first saw them."[7] The question, then, had come full circle: What levels of change were either desirable or appropriate in the national parks, and who, when all the arguments were in, would be making those decisions?

As the focus of debate further shifted from wildlife to vegetation, Yosemite was once again in the center of the controversy. In a future of increased biological awareness, the Mariposa Grove of giant sequoias served as another perfect illustration of probable consequences for management. For decades, protection had consisted mainly of constructing firebreaks around the grove and fences around individual trees, as well as occasionally cleaning up fallen branches and other debris. Otherwise the trees were considered a grand novelty rather than an irreplaceable biological resource. In

163

1881, for example, the Wawona Tree was hollowed out to allow stage-coaches to pass through the base of its trunk. And in the years that followed, chambers of commerce, veterans organizations, and university clubs, among other civic groups, prevailed upon park officials to name the biggest trees and adorn them with suitable plaques. "I agree with you that a tree in the Mariposa Big Tree Grove should be named for Bret Harte," Major William Forsyth replied to one such request in August 1911. If the sponsor would send the major "the name painted in gilt letters four inches high on a strip of zinc six inches wide, one-eighth inch thick, and painted black," he would have it fastened "on the tree you mention near the tree named Tennessee." A June 11, 1912, inventory of the grove's largest sequoias revealed that the obvious assortment of wartime heroes, American presidents, and literary greats had already been similarly honored.[8]

By the late 1920s, illegal as opposed to legal vandalism had become the bigger problem. "I know you will be particularly interested in the device I finally hit upon for the protection of the Grizzly Giant against vandals," Superintendent Charles Goff Thomson proudly reported to Park Service Director Horace M. Albright in November 1930. "I have puzzled nearly two years over a way to protect this tree and yet not impose unsightly fences et cetera into the foreground." The solution came to him while recalling his military service during World War I. "Out of a vivid memory of my days in France, I finally hit upon the scheme of putting in a low parapet wire entanglement and we have just accomplished this." The entanglement was "of the low German type with long triple-barbed wire strung crisscross between steel posts standing at a maximum of a foot from the ground." The barrier surrounded the Grizzly Giant in a maze twenty feet wide "but no nearer than about twenty feet at the closest point to the trunk." Heavy plantings of ferns, azaleas, and snowbrush were intended to conceal the wires "except upon close scrutiny."[9] Apparently Thomson had not stopped to consider the possibility that someone other than vandals might, as a result of that camouflage, accidentally become ensnared in his World War I masterpiece.

Rather he was convinced that he had not only thwarted potential vandals but also, in the process, further solved the perennial problem of soil compaction. "The entire area about the tree had been made a desert by trampling people," he observed. Consequently, that area as well had been replanted with native flowers and shrubbery. "The effect is simply splendid as now the Grizzly Giant rears its great bulk out of an area of lush vegetation. A narrow trail encircles the tree at a reasonable distance," he concluded, "reducing the hazard to its root system to the absolute minimum possible."[10]

The pursuit of technical solutions to biological and social problems was also much in evidence as Superintendent Thomson stepped up the so-called vista clearing in the Mariposa Grove. By October 1933 over three thousand trees, mostly white fir, had been cut at ground level and completely hauled away. "No evidence of the clearing appears," Chief Ranger F. L. Cook confidently reported. "Unless one knew that the clearing had been done he would think that it were a natural condition of the forest." The esthetic results, in either case, were most gratifying and dramatic. From the loop road through the grove it was now possible, literally for the first time, to view giant sequoias, both singly and in groups, from practically every angle. "The trees are more readily visible and one gets a better impression of size, majesty, and numbers while riding along the road," Ranger Cook added by way of elaboration. The impression overall was of greater openness and spaciousness, the appearance, in effect, of a "park-like" forest. The removal of logs, branches, and other "unsightly" debris further contributed to the freshness of that sensation.[11]

Only a few years earlier Cook's assessment probably would have ended there. Traditionally, after all, the Park Service had been most concerned about how resources *appeared* to the general public. But *Fauna of the National Parks* was just the latest reminder that appearances could be deceiving. "Arguments against removal of the trees are not so easy to find," Cook therefore added, acknowledging the possibility of biological considerations. He himself was not a scientist and made no pretense to speak "with authority." He doubted that removing white fir from among the sequoias would affect the giants "during their long span of life"; still, he noted, no one could say for certain what effect the firs might have "on the ecological condition of the forest through the centuries."[12]

The distinction was that trees were "living things." Unlike traditional park landscapes, "such as canyons, waterfalls, mountains, lakes, geysers, caves, etc.," biological resources undoubtedly called for "an entirely different set of factors" in their management. However beneficial vista clearing might seem to be from an esthetic point of view, by allowing visitors in the Mariposa Grove, for example, to "have a much greater appreciation of the number, size, and grandeur of the Sequoias," the fact remained: Such clearing probably changed "the natural condition and appearance of the forest."[13]

Much as Cook did not seem fully aware of fire's past importance in periodically "clearing" the Mariposa Grove, through lightning strikes or Indian burning, George Wright himself urged caution in sequoia vista clearing projects. "I believe that any competent ecologist," he wrote the Park Service director, with copies to the superintendents of Yosemite and Sequoia national parks, "would consider the removal of an associated species such as white fir, and the establishment of clearings, as something to be viewed with alarm." Certainly no intensive project should be carried out "without years of preliminary experimentation in areas of minor importance." Besides, "in a national park we are both obligated and should desire to present Sequoias exactly as found in nature. The only permissible deviation relates to the practical necessity of making the groves accessible to visitors. Extensive vista clearings do not, in my estimation, fall within this category."[14]

How opinions would change. Meanwhile, Wright was a victim of what he *believed* to be natural. For all his statements that wildlife relationships should approximate their condition just prior to pioneer contact, he relied on his perception of the sequoia groves as *he* had always known them. That perception alone, rather than scientific evidence, formed the basis of his statement that sequoias should be protected "exactly as found in nature," again, just as he had first seen them and therefore knew them best. The contradiction was so obvious that Superintendent Thomson challenged it immediately. "Mr. Wright . . . apparently assumes that our careful and effective *management* of fauna may not be so applicable to flora," he too wrote the director. Wright's perception of the sequoia groves was no less false or idealistic. Park Service "suppression of naturally-caused forest fires has resulted in enormous and menacing jungle growths that threaten our best exhibits, including the Big Tree groves," Thomson declared. As early as the 1850s, "Galen Clark cleared not only a goodly portion of Wawona, but his biggest job in the Mariposa Grove was the clearing away of manzanita and ceanothus and other shrubs and brush about the bases of the Big Trees. I could go on and on," he concluded. "Primeval conditions, indeed . . ."[15]

In the course of the debate, an important subtlety had emerged. Wright argued for restoring a period long vanished and yet also revealed his potential for being distracted by the environment he personally knew. Yet it was still Wright, and not Thomson, who called for further study, sensing, in the end, science's overarching significance. Thomson was perfectly willing to move forward with what he had. "I propose to complete a thesis which I already have in rough draft," he wrote, further defending his own assumptions, "conclusively demonstrating the fact that primeval conditions have long passed from most of the Parks; that there is no good in assumptions to the contrary."[16] In other words, he simply preferred his own theories. The greater depth in Wright's argument was that management must follow science. Thomson alone seemed comfortable with the thought that because of existing inroads on national park environments, management need not always wait until more scientific evidence had been gathered.

In this instance, at least, Thomson's assumptions had been correct. The sequoia groves had already been extensively altered by the exclusion of fire. However, he used that fact not as a rationale for reintroducing fire but rather as a justification for his vista clearing efforts. Wright did not initially mention fire but sensed science's larger importance, namely that with more information there might evolve a truly consistent pattern of management, rather than one based in any way on momentary—and perhaps illusory— contemporary preferences.

The persistence of assumption underscored the absence of scientific knowledge. Complete data on past environments and biological relationships was simply unavailable. Among the few exceptions, Joseph Grinnell and Tracy Storer's *Animal Life in the Yosemite* had appeared late in park history, long after major alterations to the environment were already well advanced. What elements had composed the so-called original environment? The descriptions of explorers, journalists, and early tourists aside, the truth of the matter was that no one could say with absolute biological certainty.

* * *

If debate about the Yosemite environment was still best described as a groping for awareness, nowhere were the standard prejudices and inconsistencies more evident than in decisions affecting wildlife. Activists still struggled to give priority to wildlife conservation, attempting, specifically, to raise the level of appreciation above the excitement of seeing wildlife to full acceptance of the restraints required for the perpetual coexistence of people and animals. Especially in the opinion of concerned scientists, most notably Joseph Grinnell and his associates, wildlife was the natural resource that made Yosemite so thrilling and so captivating. Landscapes, however spectacular, were shorn of uniqueness without "the witchery of movement." Wildlife was that resource of action, national parks' one feature that by its constant mobility invited the fullest sense of anticipation and the drama of encountering the unexpected. A full recognition of the role of predators was also central to that philosophy. Here again, parks would be incomplete as representative examples of the original American wilderness if they were devoid of those animals whose "witchery of movement" included the excitement of the chase.[17]

The perception of wildlife as innately dangerous to humans thwarted not only reform but also bureaucratic maturity. The amazing irony of that perception was its distortion of common sense, especially its tendency to sensationalize threats from wildlife while distracting attention from the real sources of danger in the park, namely the far greater chance of death or injury caused by a careless park visitor or—even more probable still—by personal disregard of basic safety precautions. The potential for death and injury spanned the entire range of human frailty, from automobile and climbing accidents to drownings and sunstroke.[18] Park Service rhetoric, nonetheless, tended to promote the standard biases. Only animals killed "cruelly" and "savagely"; humans suffered "fate."

Whether or not park rangers had the courage to mold public opinion, to emphasize the contributions of Yosemite's wildlife rather than sensationalize those rare moments of risk to visitors, again depended almost entirely on who was in charge. An especially revealing incident occurred on July 12, 1931, when a woman hiking with four companions in Tenaya Creek Canyon was alleged to have died from a rattlesnake bite. "I believe this is our first fatality from rattlesnake venom since the Service took over this Park," Superintendent Thomson informed the director. Yet the significance of that statistic escaped him entirely. By his own admission, the chances of being killed in Yosemite by a rattlesnake were extremely remote. Nevertheless the order went out immediately to kill every rattlesnake on sight.[19]

Anticipating the reaction of certain horrified biologists, Thomson moved to deflect criticism by justifying extermination as a prerequisite for public safety. Granted, there were "one or two members" of the National Park Service with "a friendly feeling toward rattlesnakes." Be that as it may, "the safe-keeping of all visitors" was of far greater priority. He maintained that no "casual interpretation of park values," for example, protests against disturbing so-called "balances of nature or other hypothetical or similar theories should ever restrain our employees from a firm resolve to destroy every possible rattlesnake." The recent "sad occurrence" had only strengthened his own resolve "to war against them throughout my superintendency here."[20] So much for the fact that apparently in the past fifteen years no other visitor had died under similar circumstances.

Nor could it be proven that a rattlesnake bite had been the cause of death. Joseph Grinnell quietly investigated the incident, writing Charles W. Michael, his contact in Yosemite, for "the inside" of the story featured in the press. "I was able to learn that there is no positive evidence that the woman was actually struck by a rattlesnake," Michael replied. "She felt a sharp pain in her leg and thought at first that she had stepped into a thorny bush of some kind. Then she got the notion that she had been struck by a rattlesnake. The rest of the party ridiculed the idea as no snake had been seen or heard." The woman's leg swelled badly, however, and she was treated for snakebite at the valley hospital, where she died several hours later. "As you say, that rattlesnake story will remain inconclusive—in the minds of those of us who are critical of evidence," Grinnell declared, also refusing to succumb to the emotionalism of the moment. "But it will go down in history as an actual death from rattlesnake bite," he admitted, finally resigning himself to its consequences for biological conservation. "I don't see how it could be headed off now."[21]

It was, as Grinnell lamented, another missed opportunity for balancing everyday sensationalism with biological common sense. At times any animal, humans included, could be dangerous and unpredictable. The challenge was to educate park visitors to see themselves as part of, not apart from, the natural world. Some risk was inevitable. Even so, were the biological risks found in national parks any greater than the personal risks normally encountered in civilization? The concept of biological sanctuary called for that very level of commitment—for the complete willingness to abandon at the park gate all preconceptions of human society. Inside Yosemite, biological order had to prevail. And that meant an environment not just for park visitors but for every species of wildlife, potentially dangerous or otherwise.

If as yet rarely expressed so forcefully, environmental philosophy was tending in that direction. Gradually, tolerance was building for mountain lions, coyotes, and even the dreaded rattlesnake.[22] It was just another case of building such a conscience outside the Park Service rather than principally from within. Granted, Joseph Grinnell had seeded Park Service officialdom with his best and brightest pupils. But their influence was still decades in the making. Besides, even added to others with a similar biological point of view, his students were, and would remain, a distinct if articulate minority. Otherwise the Park Service leaned heavily toward its traditional roots and perceptions, few of which more typified the prejudice that scientists still faced than did Superintendent Thomson's declaration of war on every Yosemite rattlesnake.

* * *

In keeping with precedent, conservation in Yosemite National Park was still least controversial in direct proportion to the distance that the resource to be protected was from the centers of visitation and development. Attention, for example, had turned to Yosemite's boundaries. Ever since the park had been reduced by a third of its territory in 1905, preservationists had expressed dismay over the extensive cutting of the old-growth timber in the ceded areas, especially in the yellow and sugar pine forests that had originally formed the park's western side. As logging operations accelerated during the 1920s, a concerted effort arose to purchase several thousand acres of timber and return them to the park. John D. Rockefeller, Jr., America's leading park philanthropist, contributed nearly $1.7 million to the campaign; Congress further passed legislation agreeing to match all private donations. Accordingly, in 1930 the so-called Rockefeller Purchase, comprising more than twelve thousand acres of timber straddling the Big Oak Flat Road and providing a critical buffer for the Tuolumne and Merced groves of giant sequoias, was designated for restoration to Yosemite National Park.[23]

The biological significance of those lands was considerable. The same could be said of the 8,765 acres in the Wawona Basin that likewise were added to the southwestern corner of the national park, in 1932. These properties also benefited from private donations and government matching funds. At least for Yosemite's boundaries, it appeared that the environment was slowly but steadily gaining in priority.[24]

Indeed still more land, the Carl Inn Tract, was added west of the Rockefeller Purchase between 1937 and 1939, again thanks to private donations and government matching funds. However, each of the new additions had its traditional as well as biological argument. Planned improvements along the length of the Big Oak Flat Road west to the park boundary dictated that the National Park Service should control more properties in the vicinity of the Rockefeller Purchase and Carl Inn. Similarly, reporting the Wawona additions in August 1932, Superintendent Thomson was quick to balance the esthetic gains against the possibility of appropriating some of that new territory for additional park improvements. "The Wawona Basin is an excellent area in which to develop campgrounds and cabin accommodations," he cheerfully remarked. Thus the park would be able "to meet the ever increasing demand for cheaper accommodations—developments not possible in Yosemite Valley."[25]

From the perspective of park officials, management might be a balancing act, but it still tended toward development. Indeed the gradual shift in favor of protection was once again traceable to George Wright and his colleagues. *Fauna of the National Parks* summarized in a single report the biological imperatives facing Park Service personnel. In that regard any additions to Yosemite were only to be applauded, even if portions of those lands would later be developed. Yosemite, like every park, was nowhere near biological self-sufficiency. Larger wildlife species in particular frequently roamed far beyond the boundaries of even the original national park. Whatever the rationale or however small the acreage, any increase in the size of the park was therefore greeted as another step in the right direction.

Biologists' efforts through the remainder of the 1930s and beyond were almost totally consumed in ensuring that no more habitat was lost to the park. Development, they argued, should be held to present levels to prevent further deterioration in wildlife's chances for recovery. Here too, *Fauna of the National Parks* listed a number of examples. "Many have already expressed a wish to see Yosemite National Park restocked with mountain sheep," Wright and his colleagues observed, highlighting just one of the projects requiring significant additions to existing habitat. "A gradual return of the southern remnant is the ideal solution, and there is a fighting chance that this will take place if it continues to increase and reoccupies its range northward along the crest of the mountains." One "serious obstacle" worked against that possibility—the continuation of "heavy grazing by domestic sheep between Yosemite and Mount Whitney." Eventually, as a result, reintroducing mountain sheep to Yosemite National Park would probably require Park Service intervention.[26]

Then again, the sheep were not likely to survive unless critical habitat adjoining the park was protected. Yosemite's eastern boundary ended abruptly along the crest of the Sierra. "The park unfortunately does not include the east slope, which is the habitat preferred by the sheep. They are particularly dependent on this side during the period of heavy snow, and would be without the benefit of park protection at such times."[27]

For the moment, the men observed, the wisest course of action was patience and vigilance. The southern band of sheep was still too small to risk capturing some of the animals and transporting them to Yosemite, especially since the prospects for their recovery just outside the park were obviously very slim. At least the project was legitimate and eventually "should be planned for, because the native form is still in existence." Meanwhile, the Park Service should "do nothing now except to watch the Mount Whitney sheep until either they work back naturally, or, failing that, become sufficiently abundant for a restocking experiment to have a chance of success."[28]

Whatever its remoteness, the crest of the High Sierra otherwise failed as suitable habitat for sustaining free-roaming bands of native sheep. The problem, to reemphasize, was domestic livestock that grazed on lands immediately bordering the park. Turning their attention to Yosemite Valley, Wright, Dixon, and Thompson noted that wildlife problems there were different but that the outcome was much the same—the dislocation of certain species. Animals were killed by automobiles, only one of the unforeseen consequences of allowing cars in the valley. Just one "striking example" involved "the gray squirrel colony near the foot of El Capitan," apparently "the only remaining colony in Yosemite Valley after the great epidemic of 1920." And yet, "for a number of years practically all of the potential increase was accounted for as automobile fatalities." Once again "the way must be found," Wright concluded, "to reconcile the conflicts arising from joint occupation of the national parks by men and animals without impairment of any major park value."[29]

The reward for Wright's efforts was the establishment in 1933 of the Park Service's Wildlife Division. Yet the battle for biological legitimacy was still all uphill. In February 1936 George Wright, then only thirty-two years of age, was killed in New Mexico in an automobile accident. Perhaps no single event cost wildlife conservation in the national parks more of its zest and momentum.[30] Everywhere, it appeared, the ideal of sanctuary came practically to a standstill. Thus Joseph S. Dixon, as field biologist, predicted in 1940 that visitors to Yosemite in 1990 would "want to know why on earth didn't the Park Service have vision and fortitude enough to keep commercial developments off the Valley floor so that it could be kept as a natural sanctuary or shrine." Given the evolution of visitor services, his answer was indeed prophetic. "At the present rate the investment in commercial buildings will become too great to be moved."[31] Wildlife Division or not, the Park Service hierarchy still followed its traditional agenda.

That agenda during the 1930s had been further swept along on the winds of the Great Depression. The government's priority nationwide had been to put people back to work. In effect, from the moment of its inception in 1933, the Wildlife Division of the National Park Service had competed for attention with the Civilian Conservation Corps, President Franklin D. Roosevelt's famous Depression Army. By the end of 1933, five separate camps had been established in Yosemite. Invariably, the ccc's make-work priorities promoted a development outlook. Until it was disbanded in 1942, the ccc devoted the vast majority of its efforts to constructing roads, bridges, firebreaks, shelters, picnic sites, and trails. Often projects were proposed and advanced with no real attention to their biological implications. In the rush to economic recovery, the environment was again that much easier to forget.[32]

Thus the 1930s concluded on another crest of park development. Instead of seriously addressing the advantages of perhaps limiting visitation, the Park Service searched for more ways to accommodate the inevitable. The key word was *planning*. Dr. E. P. Meinecke, for example, an influential park consultant, suggested that overcrowding in the valley might be eased substantially by restricting camping to individually designed and designated sites, thus ending the free-for-alls commonly used in the past. The Curry Company, arguing that congestion was only periodic, also saw the solution in expanding park facilities rather than imposing limitations on future public access.[33] Amid the signs of emerging environmental restlessness, these viewpoints continued to be the constant. Tradition, not ecology, still held the upper hand.

* * *

Like George M. Wright's untimely passing in 1936, the death of Joseph Grinnell three years later symbolically closed the era of environmental awakening in Yosemite National Park.[34] The next quarter century would

173

also be characterized by intermittent periods of ecological awareness followed by a return to traditional policies openly favorable to development. One noteworthy reform occurred in the fall of 1940, when Yosemite joined other national parks in abolishing its bear-feeding show. During the summer of 1943 Superintendent Frank A. Kittredge briefly revived a substitute, for which he was reprimanded severely by Park Service headquarters. "It is regretted that this situation has occurred," wrote Regional Director O. A. Tomlinson, for example. Kittredge was therefore advised that "the bear feeding ground and all appurtenances to the 'bear show'" were to "be obliterated" immediately.[35]

Yet the damage, in retrospect, had long since been done. An entire generation of park visitors had grown up with the idea that bears in national parks were not really "wild" animals. Indeed, as late as the summer of 1937, warning signs in Yosemite read as follows: "CAUTION: DO NOT FEED THE BEARS FROM THE HAND." By implication the message was twofold—bears might otherwise still be fed. The inevitable rise in injuries among thoughtless or careless visitors finally forced the Park Service to word its warnings more decisively. Thus Joseph S. Dixon, in his capacity as field biologist, recommended that every sign in the park should immediately be changed. Superintendent Lawrence S. Merriam emphatically agreed, reporting to the director that henceforth every sign would state: "DANGER: DO NOT FEED THE BEARS"—*period*.[36]

Nonetheless the problem, to reemphasize, had long since been created. In Dixon's estimation, artificial feeding was largely responsible for a bear population on the floor of Yosemite Valley "at least *four times what it was under original natural conditions*."[37] Policy in the early 1940s shifted accordingly, emphasizing artificial feeding outside of the valley in the hope that more bears would be enticed to leave developed areas. In the meantime, the irony of Dixon's statement was still lost on Park Service officials, Dixon included. Simply, who dared insist that Yosemite Valley's *human* population should also approximate those alleged "original natural conditions"? In the words of *Fauna of the National Parks,* the ideal "natural" period fell somewhere "between the arrival of the first whites and the entrenchment of civilization in that vicinity."[38] But obviously that standard applied to the environment only. For if it applied as well to the level of visitation (by 1941 approaching six hundred thousand people annually),[39] all but a few hundred visitors, equivalent to either the original native or the original pioneer population, would have to be turned away at Yosemite's gates.

The seeming futility of trying to revert to past landscapes while at the same time moving to accommodate increasing numbers of visitors lay at the heart of biological debates during the 1940s and 1950s. "We construct roads and trails and buildings one moment and cry 'spoliation' the next," Dorr G. Yeager, the acting regional naturalist, observed in 1943, penetrating to the heart of management's greatest irony. "Our limits now are intangible and the abeyance or concurrence of a project usually is governed by the persuasiveness of the argument presented by the advocate of the project." In short, persistence paid off and preservation further suffered. As inspiration for his remarks, Yeager noted the completion of Park Forester Emil Ernst's "Preliminary Report on the Study of the Meadows of Yosemite Valley." Ernst seemed to present conclusive evidence "that the forest is rapidly engulfing the meadows." How, then, should the Park Service react? "It occurs to me that these problems cannot be solved," Yeager concluded, "until we have established an over-all development policy from which we shall not deviate." Meanwhile the Ernst report would "only add fuel to the controversy" concerning the direction and appropriateness of future park development.[40]

An immediate example of that controversy was how best to retain the valley's stunning views. With the forest closing in all across the valley floor, many of the finest vistas of cliffs and waterfalls were rapidly becoming overgrown. "These views must be kept open if a visit to the valley is to be worth while," argued Thomas C. Vint, chief landscape architect for the National Park Service. Still, the method he offered was both comforting and familiar. "I doubt if anyone would advocate the practice of burning"; rather, the problem called for simply cutting and removing vegetation by hand. "I very strenuously oppose any consideration of broadcast burning within the forest growth of Yosemite Valley," Chief Forester G. D. Coffman declared, agreeing that Ernst's historical documentation could be interpreted too literally. After all, just because "the Indians used fire in Yosemite Valley as a means of maintaining open conditions," that was no justification "for returning to such a haphazard practice."[41] And so the issue, although debated, obviously remained. At what point in the valley's history should its appearance be suspended, and how, in the final analysis, should that objective be pursued?

Unlike Joseph Dixon, few government officials flirted with the one criterion that might have made a real difference—restricting visitation to a level consistent with existing park facilities. Rather, Superintendent Frank

A. Kittredge concluded in April 1945, "Yosemite Valley will be deluged with visitors as soon as the war is ended and gas rationing relieved." The situation was "inescapable."[42] The prophecy, in short, was still literally self-fulfilling. More provisions for visitation only spurred visitation all the more. If Yosemite was to be managed with ecology uppermost in mind, determining the proper methods was left to yet another generation.

* * *

Among all of the scientific issues raised in postwar Yosemite, no other rose to greater prominence than the protection of its wilderness values. By *wilderness* was meant not only preserving solitude but also protecting wild country's chain of biological relationships. Although the issue was no longer new, it seemed that the stakes had measurably increased. Led by booms in population and in technological innovation, postwar America was undergoing some very dramatic changes. Inevitably some would have an effect on Yosemite. In September 1944, for example, Superintendent Kittredge reported the first experiments with a new insecticide known as DDT. A small amount in both powder and liquid form had been given to the park by the Chemurgie Corporation of Richmond, California. "It appears that after the war the DDT chemical, now used effectively by the military in insect control, may be made available for civilian use," Kittredge remarked enthusiastically. "In that event it is possible that it may be of great assistance in Yosemite National Park in control of the fly nuisance."[43]

Given Yosemite's long history of insect abatement, the proposal made sense. For years it had been common practice to spray a film of oil over stagnant pools of water, thereby suffocating any mosquito larvae growing in the pools. The invention of new methods and chemicals similarly invited experimentation. Thus in July 1935 Superintendent Charles Goff Thomson had reported the successful application of one thousand gallons "of Arsenical spray mix" over "all of the accessible Alders" in the Mariposa Grove in an attempt to eradicate the alder flea beetle, "responsible in the past for considerable defoliation." The mix had also been applied to the elms at Old Village, trees apparently brought into the valley by James Mason Hutchings. Those trees as well had been "badly defoliated." "The trees now," Thomson had proudly stated, further underscoring the chemical's effectiveness, "have a beautiful dark green healthy color."[44]

But *should* wilderness be picture perfect? And were not Hutchings's elms themselves exotic? Finally, were not insect infestations just another form of

IV. *Wildlife Management and Ecology*

28. Its reputation as one of the largest national parks aside, Yosemite failed to provide adequate refuge for many wildlife species, especially those competing with human motives and pursuits. The bighorn sheep, for example, were long since extinct in Yosemite when Assistant Park Naturalist Ed Beatty posed with an ice-preserved carcass, thawed from Lyell Glacier, October 1933. Bighorn sheep were reintroduced to Yosemite in 1986. Courtesy of the Yosemite National Park Research Library.

29. Early efforts to protect giant
sequoias from soil compaction and
vandalism focused on the Grizzly
Giant, estimated to be 2,700 years
old. Superintendent Washington
B. Lewis and the Baron Rothschild
Party encircle the tree, June 4,
1922. The fence apparently was
meant to discourage only unofficial
access. Courtesy of the Yosemite
National Park Research Library.

30. Lewis's successor, Colonel
Charles Goff Thomson, borrowed
from his field experience in World
War I and replaced the fence with a
barbed-wire entanglement, pho-
tographed on August 5, 1934.
Courtesy of the Yosemite National
Park Research Library.

31. Visitors' fascination with "approachable" animals, especially bears, led to inevitable confrontations and further serious inroads on Yosemite's effectiveness as a wildlife preserve. Courtesy of the Yosemite National Park Research Library.

32. Since the mobile bear trap was first used in 1929, bear management in Yosemite has relied heavily on capturing and relocating so-called problem bears. Initially, rangers branded released animals with a daub of white paint to identify those that returned to developed areas. Modern techniques of identification include ear tags and tattoos, applied after capture while the animal is under anesthesia. Courtesy of the Yosemite National Park Research Library.

33. In Park Service reports, deer grown tame from being fed by tourists were often called "beggar" or "pauper" deer; most such animals, like "garbage" bears, were quietly captured and killed. Quite obviously, the Park Service itself was also to blame for feeding and spoiling wild animals. Ranger Bill Reyman with a herd of Yosemite deer, ca. 1930. Courtesy of the Yosemite National Park Research Library.

34. Park Naturalist Bert Harwell offers a tidbit to a friend, April 5, 1930. Courtesy of the Yosemite National Park Research Library.

35. From his desk at the Museum of Vertebrate Zoology, University of California, Berkeley, Professor Joseph Grinnell campaigned vigorously for responsible methods of wildlife management in Yosemite and other major parks. Courtesy of the Museum of Vertebrate Zoology, University of California, Berkeley.

36. Critics, most notably Joseph Grinnell, of wildlife policy in Yosemite objected to caging and displaying native animals best enjoyed in natural surroundings. Above, the infamous Yosemite Valley "zoo," ca. 1930. Courtesy of the Yosemite National Park Research Library.

37. Exotic animals, in biologists' opinion, also had no place in national parks. Yosemite Valley's exotic elk herd, above, was relocated to the Owens Valley in 1933. Note visitors petting, and probably feeding, one of the animals beside the enclosure to the right. Courtesy of the Yosemite National Park Research Library.

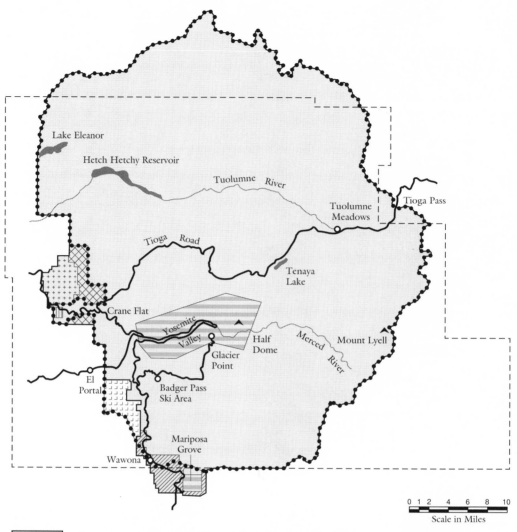

Lake Eleanor

Hetch Hetchy Reservoir

Tuolumne River

Tuolumne Meadows

Tioga Pass

Tioga Road

Tenaya Lake

Crane Flat

Yosemite Valley

Half Dome

Merced River

Mount Lyell

Glacier Point

El Portal

Badger Pass Ski Area

Mariposa Grove

Wawona

0 1 2   4   6   8   10
Scale in Miles

Yosemite National Park

San Francisco

Present area and boundaries of Yosemite National Park

Yosemite Grant of 1864

Boundary as established October 1, 1890

Boundary as altered February 7, 1905

Land Exclusion of 1906

Land and Timber Exchange of 1914

"Rockefeller Purchase" of 1930

"Wawona Addition" of 1932

"Carl Inn Addition" of 1937

predation, one whose short-term esthetic effects would nonetheless be erased by the new plant growth sure to follow? The point again was that those kinds of questions were just beginning to be asked. In the meantime, by June 1949 infestations of needle-miner moths in the lodgepole pine forests surrounding Tenaya Lake and Cathedral Creek reached epidemic proportions. Spraying was begun shortly afterward using a combination of airplane, helicopter, and hand applications. Again most prophetically, the chemical used was DDT.[45]

Predictably, doubts that spraying was either advisable or effective surfaced most often among trained biologists, especially those associated with preservation groups. The Sierra Club was most vocal; so too, faculty members of the University of California at Berkeley still frequently advised Park Service officials. Generally that role, like Joseph Grinnell's in the past, remained strictly unofficial. Stepped-up spraying for needle-miners in the late 1950s nevertheless provoked more widespread and even more outspoken comments. If only indirectly, scientists obviously still served as a most important conscience for government managers, who were not always as deeply committed to natural resources.[46]

By 1959 Yosemite's needle-miner infestation covered tens of thousands of acres surrounding Tuolumne Meadows and Tenaya Lake. The damage was most visible in the browned and dying trees seen from everywhere along the Tioga Road. "It may appear foolish to let a tree die, or to let part of a forest die," wrote David Brower, of the Sierra Club, summing up the consensus among Park Service leaders. "But," he added, immediately interjecting the opinion of knowledgeable scientists and preservationists, it appeared foolish "only in the short view." He next turned philosophical. "God made the lodgepole pine. God also made the needle miner. To oversimplify badly, He may have made both to prevent either from overrunning too much of the earth." Whatever God's reasoning, Yosemite during the past sixty years had been through three such epidemics. "The lodgepoles . . . are still there," Brower observed, "needle miners or no." Indeed one would need "an expert" to determine precisely "where the first epidemic of this century ran its course." Likewise people "might very easily pass the second one without seeing it." Brower continued, "*Because* of both of them, and similar epidemics in the previous century, you may have seen more meadow than you would otherwise see, and more mountain hemlocks." The lesson was "unmistakeable," he concluded. Nothing had been

177

lost to Yosemite National Park; rather, the resources and their relationships were simply in constant change.[47]

Those changes, moreover, were perfectly natural. Indeed Brower's observations might just as easily have been Joseph Grinnell's. "Our fathers before us were taught that predators were bad actors, varmints, evil animals and birds which should be shot," he remarked, taking a page from Grinnell's earlier text. "We are not more enlightened than our fathers when we try to evaluate what the good actors are, and what the bad, in the forest." Rather the Park Service should "hesitate before assuming that a needle miner is no good and that we must therefore try to poison all needle miners in Yosemite—killing off we don't know what else in the process."[48]

Yet the argument got nowhere. During the summer of 1959 alone, 3,400 acres were sprayed, including the Tenaya Lake and Tuolumne Meadows campgrounds. In July 1961 another 4,872 acres were sprayed in the same vicinity, using three helicopters. And in 1963 the procedure was still continuing, with smaller acreages treated at Tuolumne Meadows and Glen Aulin.[49]

It was, as Joseph Grinnell had so often lamented, another prime example of the failure of bureaucracy to catch up with biology. Two momentus signs of catch-up came in 1962. The first was the publication of *Silent Spring* by the biologist Rachel Carson. Originally serialized in the *New Yorker*, the book provided Americans with a comprehensive warning about the dangers of pesticide use. *Silent Spring* was indeed a national bombshell, selling five hundred thousand copies during its first six months in print.[50] Also in 1962, Secretary of the Interior Stewart L. Udall appointed five distinguished scientists to a special Wildlife Management Advisory Board. In the board's chairman, Professor A. Starker Leopold, the legacy of Joseph Grinnell had once more come full circle. Leopold held a Ph.D. in zoology from the University of California at Berkeley. Two years after obtaining that degree in 1944, he had been appointed assistant professor and conservationist at the Museum of Vertebrate Zoology (formerly Grinnell's own), where he had risen to become associate director in 1958. He still held that post in 1962, when Secretary Udall appointed him to the special wildlife commission.[51]

On March 4, 1963, the committee submitted its official report. No one seemed to notice, but the document bore the unmistakable imprint of Joseph Grinnell's ideas. "As a primary goal," the committee suggested, "we would recommend that the biotic associations within each park be maintained, or where necessary recreated, as nearly as possible in the condition that prevailed when the area was first visited by the white man." In short the scientists concluded, "A national park should represent a vignette of primitive America."[52]

Grinnell and Tracy Storer had originally argued the point as follows: "Herein lies the feature of supreme value in national parks: they furnish samples of the earth as it was before the advent of the white man." The ideal was next promulgated in George M. Wright's collaborative study, *Fauna of the National Parks*. "The American people intrusted the National Park Service with the preservation of characteristic portions of our country as it was seen by Boone and La Salle, by Coronado, and by Lewis and Clark." Thirty years after Wright, and nearly fifty years after Grinnell, the ideal was unchanged. For Leopold as well, the survival of national parks rested primarily on a most basic assumption—that Americans would learn enough humility to maintain an ecological masquerade. "A reasonable illusion of primitive America could be recreated," the Leopold Committee argued, "using the utmost in skill, judgment, and ecologic sensitivity."[53]

The ideal of sanctuary was certainly winning its share of converts. If parks were to survive, they had to be managed for their resources as well as for more visitors. There was, for example, the latest "serious question," that of "the mass application of insecticides in the control of forest insects." Similar applications "may (or may not) be justified in commercial timber stands," Leopold and his colleagues observed, "but in a national park the ecologic impact can have unanticipated effects on the biotic community that might defeat the overall management objective." Simply put, spraying was "potentially dangerous." At the least, it seemed "wise to curtail this activity" pending research on a "small scale" to test for possible adverse results.[54]

The message was unequivocal: If the parks were to remain biological sanctuaries, then the resource must always be considered first. Granted, like Wright's and Grinnell's works, from which it drew such obvious inspiration, the Leopold Committee report was not entirely free of untested hopes and pure assumptions. Still, it did form another working basis for elevating park resources to higher and higher levels of management priority. "In essence," the committee acknowledged, "we are calling for a set of ecologic skills unknown in this country today."[55] The point again was that scientists

179

were not afraid to admit those limitations and, simultaneously, to set the highest standards for translating research into management on the framework of what *was* known.

As the classic proving ground for such debates, Yosemite National Park was still in the forefront of controversy. For the third time in fifty years a team of distinguished scientists, inspired by a zoologist linked with the University of California, had examined Yosemite's management structure and again found it wanting. The Leopold Committee had said it tactfully—ecology was inexact. Yet the message between the lines was still troubling and sobering. Ecology might be imperfect, but at least it offered reliable standards. The National Park Service continued to follow its traditional agenda, rating the accommodation of people first and the management of resources only a distant second. From the standpoint of ecology, those priorities were skewed. As in the past, the biggest problem facing scientists was not how to handle imperfect data but rather was how to convince the Park Service to look away from people long enough to see where science was heading.

Self-Interest and Environment

CHAPTER TWELVE

Any resource open to everyone is eventually destroyed. So in 1968 Garrett Hardin, a professor of human ecology at the University of California, Santa Barbara, addressed the futility of pleading for voluntary self-restraint to protect the environment. Such appeals, he noted, impress those individuals with a real sense of social responsibility but fail to sway anyone intent on maximizing personal gain. The result is the tragedy of the commons, the inevitable overexploitation of collectively held resources in the relentless pursuit of economic self-interest.[1]

Extending that thesis to Yosemite, Professor Hardin argued that perhaps access should be denied to anyone unwilling to walk the prerequisite distance for ensuring that the park would not be overused or overdeveloped.[2] Although labeled as elitist, the idea did have broad appeal, especially among preservationists, who considered resource conservation to be the only legitimate purpose of national parks.[3] Development in any form was therefore illegitimate, if only for the reason that structures, roads, and everyday services were commonplace throughout America, whereas Yosemite was one of a kind. There had evolved, in either case, the unwritten standard that whatever Americans could do elsewhere in the country should not become common practice in national parks. Further bearing on Professor Hardin's thesis, setting priorities for conservation required that every interested party, from government officials and visitors to park concessionaires, give up insisting that access standards should be self-determined and

181

thereby begin reassuring that Yosemite's role as a natural sanctuary would be enhanced.

Once more the issue hinged on the fundamental duality in park legislation, legal sanctions that provided, in effect, that Yosemite be managed for both private profit and resource conservation. Self-interest and the public interest (however defined) went hand in hand. But was coexistence realistic? Historically, the behavior of park concessionaires especially had suggested the many possibilities for serious contradictions. Regulated or not, concessionaires as a group had put profit ahead of preservation. As businessmen, they sought expansion, not only of facilities but also of saleable visitor services. Amusements were labeled "needs" and not merely luxuries. More often than not the subterfuge worked, allowing concessionaires to distance themselves from their own intensive campaigns for increased park development. The hostility of preservationists was all the more reason not to label the profit motive for what it was but instead, feigning concern for the environment, to plead again that meeting the demands of expansion was done only with considerable reluctance and, to reemphasize, at the insistence of the public.

If any single commodity ever sold in Yosemite cast doubt on the sincerity of that argument, most certainly that commodity was alcohol. Hardly had the first tourists begun arriving in the valley when tent saloons started popping up alongside popular overlooks and trails.[4] As we have seen, the artist Charles D. Robinson was among the more notable Yosemite publicists who labeled its bars as "necessities." The military later disagreed and for a time restricted the sale of alcoholic beverages to drinks by the glass in hotel rooms or with meals only. The return of civilian control in 1914 presaged another brief period of general sales; soon afterward, however, all sales were banned.[5] National prohibition, imposed in 1919 by the Eighteenth Amendment to the Constitution, effectively sealed the debate for the next decade and a half and, in the process, clearly reinforced the Interior Department's earlier decision to halt all liquor sales in national parks.

With the repeal of national prohibition in 1933, there was an opportunity to review, at the very least, the advisability of resuming the sale of alcoholic beverages in public parks and refuges, in effect requiring visitors to ask of themselves beforehand whether or not bringing liquor in was worth the inconvenience. It would be just one more thing to worry about, just one more thing to carry. Yet the question had hardly been asked when the ban on sales was lifted. Although obviously pleased, concessionaires once more found it expedient to hide their support behind the standard words of subterfuge, insisting again that *public* demand was the chief source of persuasion.

It remained for Don Tresidder, the president of the Yosemite Park and Curry Company, to lift that legerdemain to new heights in a lengthy memorandum dated June 20, 1934. "We wish to state emphatically," he began, "that this Company is not going into the liquor business with the intention of developing a trade that will be as profitable as possible." The remainder of his two-page document continually underscored that promise, indicating that although prohibition in national parks had just been repealed, his company intended to forbid anything suggestive of promoting alcohol consumption. To the contrary, the sale of alcoholic beverages would be kept strictly low-key and tastefully conservative.[6]

As of 1988 there were thirty-five outlets in Yosemite National Park selling beer, wine, or liquor, twenty-three of those outlets on the valley floor alone.[7] The Yosemite Park and Curry Company further promoted sales through modern bars, expansive shelf displays, and various types of advertising, including using company-operated buses and tours to point out the location of lounge facilities. Quite obviously, sometime in the fifty years following Tresidder's memo, his promise had been completely scuttled.

The point again was that Tresidder himself had laid the foundations for the swift and total abandonment of his promise. In retrospect, his memorandum of June 20, 1934, was simply the standard attempt to shift responsibility for a decision that he too so visibly wanted and supported. External pressures, he implied, had *forced* the decision on him. Indeed it was "not without some misgiving" that he had agreed to the "experiment." And so he continued to plead for sympathy and understanding. "It is believed that an intensive and aggressive selling of liquor would jeopardize the goodwill which has been built up among our guests and in the end would have a disastrous effect on our investment in hotels, transportation, etc.," he wrote, further underscoring his commitment to a wholesome park environment. "We have sought to provide facilities under such conditions that families with children would feel free to live in tents or open quarters without fear of being molested or exposed to many undesirable elements and practices found in large cities."[8]

Then why had the Curry Company even agreed to allow this "experiment"? Opening his memo with the punch line to his subterfuge, Tresidder answered that the company was simply responding "to a recognizable public demand on the part of our guests and upon the written authority of the Secretary of the Interior, who has sole and exclusive jurisdiction." Any fault, in other words, lay entirely elsewhere. Again the company was merely satisfying the "public demand" and, by implication, the wishes of a senior government official. The idea—hence the responsibility—belonged to someone else. If, therefore, through the sale of alcoholic beverages Yosemite slipped under greater influence from "undesirable elements and practices found in large cities," no one could blame the Yosemite Park and Curry Company, including its president, for also being party to the prerequisite self-interest perhaps responsible for that result.[9]

Barely another year elapsed before Tresidder revealed his true sentiments regarding alcoholic beverages. On July 13, 1935, Superintendent C. G. Thomson reported privately to the director and the park advisory board that a "new drinking room" had just been completed on the second floor of the Ahwahnee Hotel. The company had "tried to achieve a convivial atmosphere" with a decor suggesting the gold rush period of 1849. And that, in Thomson's view, was inappropriate. "It strikes me as a false note," he declared. "In my opinion, it is a decided let-down in the Ahwahnee atmosphere, and out of place in a national park." Even more to the point, it was his distinct "impression that we were to serve liquor merely as a simple service to the public, but not to accentuate it in any way." That indeed had been Tresidder's manifesto the previous year. "No special emphasis should be placed upon it," he had pronounced in his memo, further warning company employees that "merchandising alcohol" was to be conducted "in the same manner" that the company used to "sell canned goods or other items." For example, he added, "no window displays or alluring showcase displays will be permitted." Rather, everyone was to be on notice: "Any employee seeking to promote the sale of liquor beyond meeting the legitimate and unsolicited quests of our guests will be considered to have violated the clearly defined policy of this Company."[10]

Tresidder, of course, did not fire himself for approving the construction of the El Dorado Room, even though, as Superintendent Thomson noted, the room did seem purposely designed "to compete with the rash of 'cocktail lounges' . . . in many hotels in California." Because building the bar was "an interior change" it had not at the time required Park Service approval.[11] It had, however, most certainly required Tresidder's. Thomson, meanwhile, left no doubt that had the decision been his alone he would not have allowed the El Dorado Room addition.

The incident graphically symbolized the manner in which the manipulation of self-interest tended to compromise Yosemite's distinctiveness as an uncommon resource. Tresidder's memorandum of June 20, 1934, was just another clever ruse, another purposeful attempt to deflect potential criticism even as the Yosemite Park and Curry Company moved forward with plans to promote—and not simply provide—alcoholic beverages. The kinds of limitations to be imposed on any products or services was an issue that few but preservationists had honestly addressed. Yosemite, accordingly, still wavered between preservation and civilization, with the latter still winning out in practically every telling respect.

* * *

For those in the postwar era who considered visitation itself a threat to Yosemite's scenic and biological resources, the park's first moment of truth came on December 31, 1954, when total visitation for the preceding calendar year stood at 1,008,031 people. It was but a few months short of a century since James Mason Hutchings had brought the first party of tourists to Yosemite Valley in 1855. Yet just thirteen years later, in 1967, the figure stood at two million and was rapidly climbing. Only twenty more years were needed to top three million visitors annually; the estimate in 1987 was 3,244,512, bypassing the previous year's estimated total of 2,982,758 by a whopping margin of 261,754 people.[12]

The lingering reaction among preservationists was one of vindication mixed with deep regret. Protection's first outspoken prophet, Frederick Law Olmsted, had predicted, in 1865, precisely the future that Yosemite was now experiencing. Ansel Adams added to Olmsted's interpretation. "When there was a vast reservoir of wilderness," he wrote to David Brower, "when areas such as Yosemite were difficult of access, there was a different kind of visitor; he came primarily for the *experience of the place*" and, even more significant, "was willing to sacrifice certain comforts and undergo considerable difficulties to gain this experience." Suddenly development in Yosemite National Park attracted every kind of individual, not just people resigned to discomfort in the best interest of preservation. So-called services had also become "more general" as the character of visitors had changed. Among those "services" were more and more "entertainments" intended by park operators "to cover a wide and often unjustified range" of public whims and desires. The result, Adams concluded, was "a 'resort' enterprise to which people are attracted for other reasons than the simple experience of the Natural Scene."[13]

In Adams's estimation the fault resided in park management, both public and private. "I know the perfidy of the Company and the weakness of the Park Service as you will never know them," he had already confided in 1952 to his Sierra Club colleague William E. Colby. "You would be shocked if you knew how many times you have been duped by a smooth protestation of virtue on the part of the operators and the weak acquiescence of the Government people." Such were the harsh opinions that often undermined reformers' efforts. "Not many of the individuals in the Park Service have the vision and imagination to grasp what is actually happening," Adams remarked five years later in his letter to Brower, still refusing to back down. "One situation begets another—a rapidly ascending curve of exploitation and 'development' has now brought Yosemite to the brink of disaster—and the insensitivity in evidence here threatens to spread to other Parks."[14]

His list of management failures was seemingly endless. "There is no excuse for typical urban installations in Yosemite," he began. "I am in complete agreement with the idea of removing from Yosemite ALL unnecessary operations, buildings and activities." First among them was camping. "Sympathetic as I am to such an experience, I simply do not see how camping on the floor of the Valley can be long continued without hopelessly affecting its appearance and mood." Yet the elimination of camping should be just the beginning. "People, things, buildings, events, and evidence of occupation and use simply will have to go out of Yosemite if it is to function as a great inspirational natural shrine for all our people. That means me, you, hotels, stores, bars, shops—everything but the barest service necessities."[15]

Adams noted, for comparison, the distinction between Yosemite and the National Gallery of Art, both public institutions supported by Americans. The gallery's "attendance has been . . . good—but the important fact is that the attendance is based solely on Art and the basic attraction of ART, and not on dances, bars, movies, nightly firefalls and vaudeville, swift roads, super-comfortable beds and adequate food, coca-cola stands, 'dude' rides

186

and atrocious curios." The National Gallery "serves [only] *those who wish to attend* for the purpose of getting experience in art. Why cannot the National Parks be planned and operated along the same logical lines?"[16]

What one million visitors foretold for Yosemite was the difficulty of substituting logic for historical self-interest. To be sure, Ansel Adams himself was part of the complex entanglement that affected every rationale for resisting decisive changes in the park's management or infrastructure. Simply, tradition was not that easy to erase. "I may be guilty of a contradiction of my own principles," he finally confessed, "in continuing to support the Christmas Bracebridge Dinner at the Ahwahnee Hotel." Writing years later in his autobiography, he still had no illusions that the event had not originated in pursuit of the profit motive. "The winter season was always slow for the concessionaires; tourists were almost nonexistent. To increase visitation Don Tresidder, the president of YPCCO, began a program of winter sports." In 1927 Tresidder further "suggested a theatrical Christmas dinner at the Ahwahnee as a key focus for family winter vacations." Two years later he asked Adams to direct the entire affair, with the help of an architect, Jeannette Spencer. Adams agreed, "provided we could make it professional in concept and performance." The result was a Yuletide pageant, "an account of an English squire's Christmas entertainment," modeled after Washington Irving's *Christmas at Bracebridge Hall*.[17]

Clearly, no importation into Yosemite Valley could have been more foreign or artificial. The point was that *this* particular display of artificiality was Ansel Adams's own. "I plead guilty to this," he further confessed to David Brower. He nonetheless still excused himself. "Elements of art can be logically associated with the elements of the Natural experience—both concern the spirit and the emotions." Even on the eve of his death in 1984 his opinion was unshaken. He wrote in his autobiography, "I feel a certain pride about the Bracebridge; its aesthetics and style directly relate to the emotional potential of the natural scene."[18] Just paragraphs earlier he had admitted that increasing visitation was Bracebridge's true intent; suddenly all that seemed forgivable because he, and not the Curry Company, had designed the event.

Could this be the same Ansel Adams who had described the Curry Company as perfidious and the Park Service as weak just because neither had embraced his reasoning that Yosemite Valley should be restored by strict limitations on visitation and development? Here was the critic himself making a case for his opponents, arguing that not all development was necessarily intrusive or inappropriate. "As long as the Ahwahnee exists," he wrote, further conceding that point, "it offers the opportunity to express certain events of a definite spiritual character." Put another way, without the Ahwahnee there would be no special meaning to the Bracebridge Dinner, no grand stage on which Adams's proud creation could be played out to the fullest. The Ahwahnee "also, unfortunately, supports evidences of advanced urbanism which create a dichotomy in the Yosemite scene," he immediately added, still obviously wrestling with his original concern.[19] Then which was it to be—complete naturalness in Yosemite Valley or just enough urbanization to allow for Bracebridge?

In microcosm, the emotional tug-of-war of such a dedicated and outspoken preservationist was very telling evidence of the power of inconsistency. Faced with the thought of losing a Yosemite tradition so dear to his heart, Ansel Adams too was forced into rationalizing why he had diminished his lifetime scale of values. That very lapse in fortitude was precisely what Frederick Law Olmsted had had in mind when he wrote in 1865 of the need to adopt strict rules of conduct that would, without compromise, govern every park visitor. Ever since Olmsted, the search for those proper rules of conduct had been Yosemite's historic and endlessly debated challenge. Finally affected by the presence of Olmsted's predicted "millions," that search had indeed become all the more difficult. Ansel Adams was just another example of the futility of asking for commitment without effective coercion. For Adams, it was also too easy to slip into the comfortable excuse that whatever existed in one's own name was somehow legitimate, whereas developments and activities proposed by others were strictly impositions.

Olmsted's admonishment was to treat everything as impositions, unless something had originally been part of the natural scene. Otherwise the danger arose of accepting development itself as natural, further imposing layer upon layer of artificiality over the landscape. Garrett Hardin said it differently, but his conclusion was much the same. The acceptance of change need not be total; it need simply be present. The only way out of the tragedy of the commons was universal coercion. Everyone must accept the same standard, or the standard would fail.[20]

So Ansel Adams, whatever the purity of his motives, had succumbed to the very kind of inconsistency that was so easily turned around into defense for *greater* park development. Historically, the potential for inconsistency had resided in hundreds of visitors, then thousands, then hundreds of thousands. Now, for the first time, those inconsistencies might be expressed in the millions. Soon, it followed, more evidence would appear supporting Olmsted and Hardin, suggesting that the mere possibility of increased compromise would in fact erode whatever remained of the nation's commitment to protect Yosemite, "inalienable for all time."

* * *

On August 7, 1945, Newton B. Drury, the director of the National Park Service, challenged the Yosemite Advisory Board to address the issue of park development head on. "I should like the Board to consider particularly the possibility of moving as much as possible of the Government facilities out of the Valley," he wrote. "I should also like," he added, "the Board to give serious consideration to the proposal of eliminating Yosemite Lodge, broadening the range of service at the Ahwahnee, and eliminating the resort-type entertainment featured at Camp Curry, thereby reducing the tourist impact on the Valley Floor." To compensate for those services and facilities removed from the valley, he endorsed the proposal to "build up the facilities at Wawona, or at Big Meadow," on the southwestern and western borders of the park, respectively. Here could be located "the entertainment and other resort features that might be considered a normal part of the life of a community whose activities are based on desires other than those of seeing and enjoying the natural features of the Park."[21]

Thus Drury set the theme for the next forty years of park planning and debate. The following June he acknowledged receipt of the Advisory Board's report and noted his disappointment that it in fact disclosed "no opportunity for the elimination of activities and the removal of the accompanying facilities from Yosemite Valley." He suggested more review again to determine if "specific activities of both the Government and the Concessioner" should be moved to a location other than Yosemite Valley proper. "It might be expected," he conceded, "that there would be some loss of efficiency, or a small increase in operating costs." Those possible drawbacks, however, "should be balanced against the benefits that would accrue in decreasing the congestion on the Valley floor."[22]

Superintendent Frank A. Kittredge was most sympathetic, writing his own lengthy memorandum to the regional director and stressing the commercialization of Camp Curry. Visitors historically had found Camp Curry to be "delightful, homey, and wholesome," he remarked, appealing to the family values of an earlier age. Then the major concessionaires were consolidated in 1925, after which "the previous gradual increase in tents was pyramided," under the auspices of the newly formed Yosemite Park and Curry Company. As a result, a widening area "not intended for great numbers [of people] was stretched out at the foot of the mountainside." To draw still more patronage, "the beautiful evening campfire program of singing and story telling was enlarged by the addition of paid entertainers." Next came even more amusements, including "a huge dance hall" built "adjacent to the tents and cabin sleeping quarters." And all this was in addition to a modernized "dining room and cafeteria constructed to serve not only the guests of Camp Curry but visitors from other units and from the campgrounds."[23]

Consequently, in place of Camp Curry's original mood, there now prevailed a "carnival atmosphere." Additional "town amusements" had seemed the "logical" answer to accommodating "a village or town of summer residents." Tents and cabins provided housing for as many as fifteen hundred people nightly "in an area not originally planned for such numbers." In short, the concessionaire had "thrust" upon Yosemite Valley and the National Park Service "an area of great concentration," everywhere accented by "exotic entertainments" intended solely as a means "to draw and to hold crowds."[24]

Like Director Drury, Kittredge saw the solution in "decentralization," which, in his view, would once again "substitute a simple camp atmosphere for the present urban conditions and carnival aspects." Similarly, the Park Service should pursue the "elimination of the resort or 'fairground' amusements and the introduction of appropriate amusements." Ultimately, it followed, people seeking "jazz or city type" activities would "soon label the Park as 'dead' and remain away of their own volition."[25]

That itself, of course, was the enforcement of a standard, and as Drury and Kittredge realized, the concessionaire was consistently opposed to preservation by exclusion. Greater visitation was still the basis for greater profits. Accordingly, Drury in particular feared even stronger pressure for developing Yosemite Valley unless management effected "some rather drastic changes in general operations." Nor did preservationists have long to wait for the Curry Company's standard rebuttal to Drury's bold proposal. "Probably what troubles me most," wrote Hilmer Oehlmann, general manager, "is the apparently unqualified assumption that the people who operate concessions in the national parks would subscribe to any form of desecration of these areas for the sake of additional profit." However legitimate that interpretation, Oehlmann knew how best to attack it. Simply, his response was to undermine preservationists themselves by insinuating that their aims were no less selfish or self-serving. "Our critics know in their hearts that they have a deeper appreciation of beauty than the mass of their fellows and discount accordingly any real or fancied enjoyment which shallower mortals may derive from a visit to a park," he declared. That reaction proved nothing but the existence of another "type of snobbery." Like it or not, Oehlmann warned, postwar America was "on the move" and would "not be denied access" to the national parks. "To ascribe the presence of such throngs to the existence of man-made recreational facilities is patently absurd," he concluded. "With ten thousand people in Yosemite the dancehall holds a few hundred, the two cocktail bars together contain fewer than a hundred, while for every swimmer in the pools there are a hundred in the river."[26]

Oehlmann, of course, had conveniently omitted a complete inventory of all company-sponsored and promoted activities, from bicycle rentals and horseback riding to the annual Bracebridge Dinner. The second pillar of his argument was equally selective and once again suggested that preservationists alone were guilty of misreading park history. "Cocktail bars have been mentioned by our critics," he noted, returning to that most familiar example, "frequently with the intimation that the present concessioner started them." Yet everyone "familiar with the early history of the Valley" knew for a fact "that the first hotels had saloons and that the tourists who came here enjoyed the evening pleasures of gin-slings, juleps and other concoctions."[27] But again, he failed to mention prohibition, which had abolished all legal sales of those items. After prohibition it was the Curry Company, not persuasive appeals citing early park history, that had effectively restored the sale of alcoholic beverages to Yosemite National Park.

The sophistry, in either case, always ended predictably—whatever the company sold was provided strictly to appease public demand. "How we could conduct our liquor business on a more restricted basis than at present and still give any reasonable measure of service in that field, I do not know," Oehlmann declared, pleading again that concessionaires did nothing to dictate visitors' tastes. But his succinct statement of principles forcefully

191

suggested otherwise. "I am opposed to the philosophy that all human pursuits beyond eating, sleeping and enjoying nature should be interdicted, if only because they can be followed somewhere outside a national park."[28]

Under Newton B. Drury, a committed preservationist, the National Park Service itself had finally called for a study of that very standard of visitation. Yet Oehlmann remained confident that precedent in Yosemite was to his advantage. "Aside from the concessioners themselves, railroads, bus lines, travel agents, and oil companies will inevitably continue their efforts, and it is not to be expected that the Park Service itself will aspire to confront the Appropriations Committees with statistics of declining travel."[29] Granted, his statement was mildly threatening and obviously self-serving. But this time the weight of Yosemite's past was firmly behind him. Throughout history, self-interest had been more persuasive than preservation, and self-interest was not confined to concessionaires. The future of Yosemite still seemed locked in historical patterns. Even more simply put, Hilmer Oehlmann was right.

* * *

Although pressure was still strongest for development in the valley, the high country did not escape closer scrutiny of its potential for increased visitation. Symbolically, the realignment and modernization of the old Tioga Road foretold the invasion of preservationists' backcountry hideaways. Meanwhile, the Yosemite Park and Curry Company had released some disturbing signals of its own. On September 8, 1955, for example, Hilmer Oehlmann wrote Superintendent John C. Preston in response to a Park Service memorandum regarding bears at Merced Lake. "I realize that the indiscriminate killing of bears could bring criticism against the Park Service," Oehlmann remarked. "However, it has been my observation over the years that the pleasure of a motorist who observes a bear along the highway is not shared by the camper subject to nightly raids." He did not say which the company was more concerned about—that visitors would not be safe or that bears raiding camps would scare off potential customers. Yet no one could doubt his feelings about the animals themselves. "The well nigh unanimous opinion of persons who stay in bear-infested areas is that the critters are an unmitigated nuisance which should be abated."[30]

There was nothing in Oehlmann's memo about people infestations, a reversal of perspective that might have given him greater sympathy for preservationists' concerns. Rather, he held steadfastly to his position that more development in Yosemite was not only good but also inevitable. That the bear "nuisance" might have to be "abated" was simply facing reality. In a similar vein, he protested the consideration of the Wilderness Preservation Bill, introduced in Congress in 1956. He immediately wrote Senator Thomas H. Kuchel of California and requested a copy of the legislation. "You kindly sent me the Bill," Oehlmann wrote, with thanks, on January 7, 1957, "and in your letter of transmittal . . . you stated your conviction that the proposed legislation was meritorious." Oehlmann strongly disagreed. "For my part, I question whether it is either necessary or free from danger." "The danger that I see," he reemphasized, "is that the legislation would create an official group 'loaded' with wilderness enthusiasts, and the counsels of extremists might easily prevail." Again his reasoning was most familiar. "With the country growing at its present rate and with the need for optimum use of our material and recreational resources, I would be wary of radical counsel on the side either of development or preservation." Yet no one could doubt that Oehlmann sided with development, even if that meant preempting some of Yosemite's existing wilderness. "The principle of 'the greater good,'" he concluded, "should govern here as elsewhere."[31]

That principle, quite obviously, was but another rationale for allowing more people into wilderness areas. Accordingly, Oehlmann could not help but be opposed to the wilderness bill. The likelihood that its provisions would be applied first to parks with large backcountry zones, especially Yosemite, could jeopardize further opportunities to expand visitor facilities. The Park Service itself had just launched Mission 66, a ten-year program to upgrade park roads, campgrounds, visitor centers, and accommodations by 1966, the agency's fiftieth anniversary. The program was especially controversial among preservationists, who favored lessening rather than expanding those facilities, at least in backcountry areas where existing levels of construction and access were still rudimentary. Wrote Ansel Adams, "It is not so much what is *wrong* with Mission 66 as what is *missing!*" Instead of reaffirming the principles of national parks, the Mission 66 report "stressed the physical plants and planning directed towards a Recreational pattern." Bluntly, the report lacked commitment "to the basic problem of security of the National Park Ideal." Instead "the term 'Inspirational,'" Adams argued, "is used with a glib obligation to impart some veneer of spiritual purpose. But I get the feeling that those in charge have about as much true grasp and understanding of the Intangible as a Red Indian has of an IBM Calculator!"[32]

In preservationists' estimation, the reconstruction of the Tioga Road, which crossed Yosemite from east to west, only reconfirmed their worst fears about the future of park wilderness. As early as 1933 the Sierra Club had questioned several Park Service options for making the historic mining road a modern, paved thoroughfare. Reconstruction nonetheless soon began on that section of the Tioga Road from Crane Flat to McSwain Meadows in the west and from Cathedral Creek to Tioga Pass on the road's eastern extremity. World War II halted construction; so too, reductions in the Park Service's budget after the war delayed final action on the heart of the highway, that twenty-one-mile portion between McSwain Meadows and Cathedral Creek. That was the portion targeted as a top priority for Mission 66 and, consequently, for preservationists' claims that Mission 66 was overly committed to bigger roads and bigger development.[33]

Pressure for improving the Tioga Road was even stronger in outlying communities, especially those along the park boundary to the east, where reopening the Tioga Road every spring signaled the revival of lifeless tourist economies. "Conservatively, 50 percent or more of the business of Lee Vining is derived from tourist travel over Tioga Pass," noted Marjorie M. Gripper, the president of the Lee Vining Chamber of Commerce. That fact was for the benefit of Superintendent John C. Preston, whom she had written on January 19, 1954, pleading the community's annual case for the earliest possible opening of the Tioga Road. "I believe," she added, "that you can see why the setting of the opening date by you is of such great importance to the economy of Mono County." Would the Park Service therefore begin clearing the road of snow just as early as possible?[34] Other communities east of the park perennially asked the same question and now added their concern that the twenty-one miles of unimproved roadbed be immediately upgraded to modern highway standards.

The Park Service, in other words, was still caught between two opposing forces. It had helped encourage both, but only one—preservation—was unquestionably a legitimate purpose of national parks. The other force, commercialism, had been courted in the interest of building up visitation. Inside the parks, commercialism had taken the form of concessions, which ostensibly were under the full control of Park Service personnel. Outside the parks, however, the Service had little or no influence over the designs of commercial interests. During the 1920s, enlisting those interests up and down the state of California had seemed the best route to boosting visitation to Yosemite and hence boosting agency support. Invariably, as a result, the park superintendent spent a good deal of time meeting with business and civic leaders and reassuring all of them that travel to Yosemite would spill over into their surrounding communities. The unforeseen consequence was the growing dependence of nearby cities and towns on sustaining that travel. Consequently, the superintendent could look forward every winter to a barrage of letters insisting that the Tioga Road be plowed as quickly as possible, not because an early opening did anything to promote preservation but, quite the contrary, because it virtually guaranteed that visitation—hence business—would peak that much sooner.[35]

Even when the road had opened, the flood of letters from the east side never abated; in summer the subject of special urgency merely switched from plowing snow to promptly completing the highway's renovation. Marjorie Gripper, for instance, pressed her attack. "We wish to point out that this highway . . . is a disgrace to the Park Department and an imposition on the travelers." And just to make certain that her point had gotten across, she sent copies of her remarks to leading politicians, from Dwight D. Eisenhower, the president of the United States, to Norris Poulson, the mayor of Los Angeles. "Now, [we have] another problem," agreed Ted Gardner, executive secretary of the Bishop Chamber of Commerce. After thanking Superintendent Preston for opening the Tioga Road in time for the 1954 Memorial Day weekend, he added, "What can we do, what pressure can we exert, to secure the completion of the 21 mile stretch of poor road in the Tuolumne area between Yosemite and Lee Vining?"[36] Here again, only someone totally unfamiliar with the issue might have concluded that somehow his request was motivated by a hidden concern for the protection rather than the commercialization of Tuolumne Meadows.

Understandably, preservationists blamed the Park Service for simply caving in to people like Marjorie Gripper and Ted Gardner, individuals who seemed to equate convenient access with increased business opportunity. "The case of the Tioga Road illustrates our point," argued Richard M. Leonard, the president of the Sierra Club. "The Yosemite National Park speed limit is very appropriately 35 mph, quite adequate for park display and internal park travel roads. Why then adopt the standards of the Crane Flat road section?" That portion, already modernized, "invites speeds of 50 to 70 mph, so that the man who wants to travel at 35 mph and see the scenery is in danger of being hit in the rear by those who are not interested in scenery." And still, in his opinion, the case against roads was even more basic. "We don't build public thoroughfares through museums, libraries, art exhibits or cathedrals. Let us not build them through our parks." Alex Hildebrand, Leonard's successor, agreed. "A highway down the center aisle of a cathedral would enable more people to go through it, but it would not enable more people to come there for peace and spiritual inspiration." Nor would Hildebrand concede "that the correlation between the cathedral and a national park" was, as proponents of development so often stated in rebuttal, "very far-fetched."[37]

It was, however, most revealing that Hildebrand, unlike Marjorie Gripper, did not send a copy of his letter to any major politician. Rather, he directed all carbons to preservation community members only, among them Edgar Wayburn, Ansel Adams, and Alfred A. Knopf.[38] The oversight was, in and of itself, a significant revelation of the difference between the lobbying efforts of the Tioga Road's protagonists. Members of the Sierra Club apparently spent too much time preaching among themselves. And precedent, of course, was still on the side of those favoring Mission 66. The new Tioga Road was swiftly approved and pushed through to completion.

In one last moment of esthetic outrage, the Sierra Club was able to halt construction briefly, in August 1958. Climbing southwest of Tenaya Lake, the right-of-way cut through and across a long granitic escarpment, considered to be one of the most beautiful formations of its kind in the park. Yet following his inspection of the project on August 19, Park Service Director Conrad Wirth ordered that construction be resumed immediately. Sierra Club leaders present during his inspection, among them David Brower, won no major concessions regarding the road's design or alignment. In retrospect the Sierra Club concluded that it had reacted far too late. "The rampant bulldozer scrapes, and having scraped ramps on," Brower declared. "Nor all our piety and wit shall lure it back to cancel half a line, nor all our tears wash out a mark of it." The Tenaya Lake "we knew, the 'Lake of the Shining Rocks' the Indians knew, is dead. Please let us allow no one to forget what the experts killed there, needlessly, in large measure because we who knew they were wrong held our tongues."[39]

The Park Service, in its own defense, shot back at preservationists with its traditional arguments, noting, for example, that the Tioga Road was already there and in obvious need of improvement. The road's original width barely allowed for two cars to pass safely; similarly, its original alignment was too steep, too twisting, and otherwise in need of major adjustments. Even more to the point, the Park Service was obligated to please all of its constituents, not just preservationists and especially not just a few disgruntled members of the Sierra Club. "Brower is a paid employee of the Club and has been on the Service's back almost continually since he became permanently employed," Superintendent John C. Preston remarked, opening a speech before Park Service officials in January 1959. He conveniently ignored that he too was a paid employee of the organization whose position he was defending against compensated preservationists. Preston intended, like Hilmer Oehlmann, to imply that only the Sierra Club and not the Park Service was guilty of conflict of interest. At the very least, he hoped to shift any blame for selfishness and self-interest onto the Park Service's critics. Indeed, once other groups had learned of the Tioga Road controversy, they had rallied to the government's support. "This support," he observed, simultaneously revealing its sources and its biases, "came from the California State Chamber of Commerce, local city and county chambers of commerce, such as Merced, Fresno, and others, County Supervisors, State Senators and Assemblymen, as well as other groups and organizations." His conclusion was obvious: "All this reaction pointed up the fact that groups other than the Sierra Club are extremely interested in what goes on in National Parks."[40]

What Preston failed to clarify was just how that long list of commercial interests better served the needs of Yosemite National Park. Consequently, he represented instead the reluctance of Park Service officials to concede that most of the agency's support outside the preservation community was motivated largely by materialistic ambition. Park Service thinking was back in the 1920s, when it was still being argued that materialism and preservation might be compatible after all. The Tioga Road controversy was just another indication that the marriage of commerce and conservation might have been doomed from the start. Even so, given its long history of fostering that relationship, the Park Service understandably refused to consider suggestions that a breakup might be necessary.

The classic lesson in Garrett Hardin's thesis had yet to be considered. In the tragedy of the commons, a public field in a hypothetical village is eventually overgrazed because each villager makes an individual decision to

197

exceed his allotment and to sneak more cattle onto the field. The promotion of self-interest destroys the resource for everyone. Accordingly, the tragedy is inescapable. Merely the knowledge that a common resource is open to everyone encourages each individual to exploit the resource as much as he can. After all, whatever that individual might save out of a sense of social responsibility will only be consumed by others who have no similar commitment to the welfare of the group.[41]

In its abruptness and completeness, the change of heart exhibited by Ansel Adams seemed to confirm Hardin's thesis. Critical of park development throughout the 1950s, Adams seemed, by the following decade, to have softened considerably. Most notably, by 1971 the flow of visitors through the park no longer distressed him; rather, he now vehemently argued in *favor* of greater numbers, pointing out that Yosemite Valley was "one of the great shrines of the world." However uncharacteristic of Adams in the past, that argument now underlay his support for additional means of access, including cableways and helicopters, "all less damaging than roads." Yosemite Valley, "belonging to all our people," had to "be appropriately accessible" both now and in the future. "Any attempt to reduce Yosemite Valley to a wilderness area would be futile—socially and politically, and would be a real disservice to the people at large," he wrote. "The maximum number of people should see Yosemite and should experience its incredible quality. To shut it off from the world would be somewhat similar to closing St. Paul's Cathedral for the sake of the architecture!"[42]

That assessment, to be sure, was from the same man who twenty years earlier had denounced even camping in Yosemite Valley as an unwarranted intrusion. Now he stood for the very things he had once so strongly opposed—increased development and easier access in the interest of visitation. Nor did he believe that wilderness values would unduly suffer even if visitor facilities were expanded elsewhere in the park. "The present High Sierra Camps do not, in my opinion, violate wilderness qualities as they now exist," he observed, for example. "I personally feel that a High Sierra Camp near the north rim of Yosemite Valley would be a logical link of the chain," he further maintained. "Likewise, establishment of more public camp grounds along the existing Tioga Road and the Glacier Point Road, and at Wawona, would not violate wilderness."[43]

That Adams had changed course was abundantly clear; less obvious was his reasoning, indeed his self-interest. Perhaps the key can be found in his ownership of a photographic studio in Yosemite Valley, a concession that he and his wife had inherited from her father, the artist Harry C. Best. The early 1970s, unlike the 1950s, found Ansel Adams a rising star on photography's center stage. Suddenly his years of personal sacrifice and hard work had all come together. And Best's Studio, renamed the Ansel Adams Gallery in 1972, was the preservationist-turned-businessman's bridge to his growing and adoring public.[44]

In short, like every other concessionaire in Yosemite's long history, Adams may simply have discovered the equation between people and profits. His studio was strategically located immediately adjacent to the valley visitor center. The more people the Park Service attracted, the more people that passed through his studio as well. In microcosm, that relationship was no different from the one enjoyed by the Yosemite Park and Curry Company. At least one thing was evident: Adams now also seemed to advocate wilderness preservation in direct proportion to the distance of that wilderness from the valley floor.

Granted, he may simply have changed his mind. Or, as suggested by Garrett Hardin's thesis, Adams may have fallen victim to the predictable double standard. Typically, he now defended his symbolic cows on Yosemite's commons while attacking those of others. The Ahwahnee Hotel, the Bracebridge Dinner, the Ansel Adams Gallery—these he had come to accept as "elements of art" and "spiritual character." But it was just that these were *his* sacred cows on Yosemite's public lands. His descriptions reveal a distinct bias between those activities he defended and those he opposed. "Obviously phoney enterprises such as the Firefall and the Chief Lemy Dances at the Museum," he declared in 1952, already discounting his own inconsistencies, "should be discontinued. The latter immediately! . . . It is pure, unadulterated FAKE. The National Park Service should be ashamed of itself!!!!!"[45] Adams was right, of course; both the Indian dances and the firefall were purely contrived events. But so too was the annual Bracebridge Dinner, and that contrivance was not based on even a shred of Yosemite history. More to the point, the fakery of Bracebridge was Adams's own. He added to Yosemite's commons what he found appealing, conveniently ignoring that his impositions, whether or not he defended them as art, were no more legitimate environmentally than were the impositions of anyone else.

The fact remained: *Whatever* was added to Yosemite in the name of

199

commercialism was somehow artificial. Most certainly no plant or animal had evolved with commercialism in mind. For Yosemite to be a refuge, the environment always had to come first, exclusive even of attempts to equate art with biology.

Realistically, development justified as art was just another means for rationalizing self-interest. Selling the Yosemite experience, whatever the rationale, still elevated someone's economic privilege above the park's larger public role. The assumption, of course, was that Americans agreed what that larger role should be. And just by singling out Ansel Adams, we can see that they did not. His struggle for consistency was symbolic of the nation's own. Perhaps Yosemite could accommodate both development and the wilderness; Adams's now esthetically pleasing "shrine" could have just enough wilderness to maintain the illusion of sanctuary. Then again, the tragedy of the commons so clearly suggested otherwise. Self-interest and the environment could never coexist; commercialism would always find a way to extract more and more concessions from Yosemite's common lands. Ultimately, any kind of enterprise would actively seek its own expansion. Outside Yosemite, expansion might be tolerable, indeed even legitimate. Once inside, however, expansion might overwhelm everything the park was supposed to represent. Self-interest and refuge moved on different paths, converging only when self-interest was unquestionably altruistic. Inside Yosemite, refuge demanded that the norms of civilization be reversed, allowing the principles of ecology—and not self-interest—to set every standard for proper conduct.

❧ *Management Adrift*

Although the boundaries of significant trends are often indistinct, the quarter century beginning in 1963 unquestionably witnessed several great moments of truth in Yosemite's long and intriguing history. The period began with the release of the Leopold Committee Report, thus ushering in another burst of ecological commitment and awareness. When the quarter century closed, it did so incredibly, swept along on a proposal by the secretary of the interior himself that the Hetch Hetchy dam finally be dismantled, allowing all of the valley to revert to its original condition.

Both mileposts, to be sure, were followed by their share of anticlimax and disbelief. Practically everything in the Leopold study had been urged by biologists before; what reason was there now to believe that those proposals would finally get priority? And as for tearing out the dam that had flooded Hetch Hetchy, that indeed seemed a plan almost too good to be true. Again preservationists could not help but wonder what the hidden catch might be. The Park Service itself seemed to have changed very little. Ideally it was supposed to be an agency with the highest of standards, a bureau committed to pushing its own management and the public in responsible directions. In practice, however, it was still very much the same, especially in its distrust of anything deeply scientific. Inevitably, the result was more vacillation and confusion, more buffeting by those external and internal forces that the Park Service theoretically should have controlled.

Preservationists who expected decisiveness again prepared for disappointment. And if actions spoke louder than words, that pessimism was fully justified. Even more suddenly than it had been resurrected, the plan to drain Hetch Hetchy died. Similarly, the Park Service's bold plan to restore Yosemite Valley became stalled, then was scuttled. Preservation, it seemed, was back to square one. Another era seemed to be closing precisely as it had begun—more visitors to take care of but otherwise so little yet resolved.

* * *

Like any cautious bureaucracy, the Park Service reacted slowly to any suggestions for needed change. Finally, during the late 1960s, portions of the Leopold Committee Report were adopted, most notably directives that fire should be restored to the giant sequoia groves. In contrast, fire on the cliffs of Yosemite Valley was finally to be abandoned. In 1968 came the abolishment of the firefall, ending the century-long tradition of crowd-pleasing spectacles. And growing crowds were precisely the reason the Park Service had been forced into that decision, for the agency itself could no longer ignore the obvious: the firefall simply attracted too many spectators, who brought too many cars and who left behind too much litter, automobile exhaust, and trampled vegetation.[1]

The preparation of yet another management plan was also begun in 1968. Preservationists' arguments remained the same—it was time to rethink the advisability of allowing essentially unlimited access into Yosemite Valley. Just two years later, in the so-called Fourth of July riots, the wisdom of increased restrictions appeared to be confirmed. Throughout the holiday weekend hundreds of youths, fed by resentment over the Vietnam War and other anti-establishment sentiments, had gathered in the park, threatening violence. On July 4 the situation erupted as rioting spilled over from Stoneman Meadow into nearby campgrounds and parking lots. In Stoneman Meadow proper, mounted rangers rode into a crowd of youths and pushed them back by force. Rock throwing, fights with rangers, and attacks on patrol cars continued throughout the evening. Even the national parks, it was apparent, were not invulnerable to urban tensions and social problems.[2]

There were few incidents more ugly and few more prophetic. Never before had attention been so diverted from the historical role of national parks as sanctuaries of nature. Traditionally, the Park Service had balanced that mandate with encouraging visitation. Here was troubling proof that crowds could be mean and not just well-meaning, that not every park visitor was interested in scenery and wildlife. Granted, the Park Service had done nothing to encourage rioters, but it had encouraged crowds. Finally, park officials conceded, substantive changes were necessary. In perhaps the most dramatic departure from the automobile-orientation of Mission 66, in 1970 the eastern third of Yosemite Valley and the Mariposa Grove were closed to motor vehicles. Instead both areas would be served by public transportation, by trams and shuttle buses powered by clean-burning propane. The objective at last was to get people out of their cars and thereby to rely less on the solution, advocated earlier by Mission 66, of simply modernizing roads and expanding congested parking lots.[3]

The stage had once more been set for sharp disagreement regarding the purpose and future of Yosemite National Park. Debate intensified in 1971 when preliminary reports revealed that the National Park Service planning team had seriously reconsidered two controversial proposals for controlling park access. The first, a plan that would eventually eliminate automobiles from all of Yosemite Valley, won preservationists' ringing endorsement. Yet that proposal had been noticeably compromised by a second, namely the revival of the decades-old suggestion that increased visitation could best be offset by building some type of cableway system from the valley floor to Glacier Point.[4]

The latest projected route would carry passengers from Happy Isles up through the Merced-Illilouette Canyon to a terminus on Illilouette Ridge, then up to Glacier Point proper. Among those strongly opposed was Morgan Harris, a professor of zoology at the University of California at Berkeley. "It seems ironic," he wrote Park Service Director George B. Hartzog, Jr., "that we should be attempting on the one hand to remove automobiles from Yosemite Valley, while proposing on the other the introduction of man-made facilities in an even more sensitive location." Also a member of the Sierra Club, Harris assured Hartzog that getting automobiles off the valley floor had the club's full support. It was "most depressing" to realize that the proposed gondola or tramway "apparently had strong sponsorship and advocacy" from the director's own office, "the Superintendent of Yosemite Park, and even the Secretary of the Interior—supposedly the statutory guardians of our Yosemite heritage."[5]

The apparent seriousness of those endorsements undercut the standard qualification that the cableway had been proposed merely as a management alternative, a point the Sierra Club itself conceded in a 1971 policy state-

203

ment. In the absence of unequivocal reassurances to the contrary, preservationists could only conclude that the so-called alternative was in fact the Park Service's preference. That cloud of suspicion continued to darken until 1973, when the Music Corporation of America, a Los Angeles conglomerate, purchased the Yosemite Park and Curry Company and openly announced support for further expansion of park facilities. Charges flew that MCA had pressured the Park Service to include development alternatives favorable to the company in the preliminary draft of the final master plan. Preservationists were incensed and in the storm of controversy that followed called for the preparation of another master plan, one entirely free of alleged company influence.[6]

As charged, the Yosemite Park and Curry Company opposed even the notion of limiting visitor access, especially by automobile. "Why is a primary goal to eliminate or substantially reduce automobiles from Yosemite Valley?" asked Edward C. Hardy, chief operating officer. "The costs of such a plan far exceeds any marginal benefits." Thus he attacked the master plan in a seven-page memorandum dated June 12, 1974, submitted on behalf of MCA to Leslie P. Arnberger, park superintendent. At all of the park's attractions, including Yosemite Valley, Glacier Point, and the Mariposa Grove, congestion was a problem only because the Park Service had failed to build enough parking lots. "What is inadequate is the parking in these areas," Hardy observed, leading up to his solution. "Planning should focus on alternate travel options, such as the Aerial Tramway to Glacier Point and increased parking within the valley."[7]

Preservationists were right. The company was pushing, vigorously, to turn the valley into a staging area for a wide range of commercial activities focused on Glacier Point. The tramway alone would be a major profit center. The company, in either case, would have it both ways—cars in the valley and the attraction of a cable ride. "We submit," added Bernard I. Fisher, vice-president for business development at MCA, "that a 32-mile road from Yosemite Valley to Glacier Point carrying thousands of vehicles polluting the atmosphere causes far greater damage to the land and mood of the Park than would an appropriately placed aerial tram-way."[8] Again there was no mistaking where Fisher's argument was headed. If in fact cars were to be abolished from Yosemite National Park, the company preferred that they be prohibited on the road to Glacier Point so as not to jeopardize the maximum use of an aerial cableway.

Leakage of these views to the press and conservationists precipitated a flurry of letters with complaints that MCA was trying to turn Yosemite Valley into a full-scale resort. The Park Service itself had already dropped further consideration of the cable car to Glacier Point as a management alternative. Yet MCA was still insistent. On July 29, 1974, Jay Stein, president of Recreation Services, wrote Howard Chapman, Park Service regional director, and urged that the proposal be restored to the draft and final master plans. Similarly, Stein proposed a serious review of additional facilities at Badger Pass, new parking lots for Yosemite Valley, new or improved accommodations at all major points of interest, and a reconsideration of winter closures of the popular Tioga Road. In brief, MCA's recommendations were indeed motivated by concern for achieving an even greater volume of year-round visitation. The filming in Yosemite of the television series "Sierra" in 1973 lent further credibility to preservationists' charges that MCA's designs in the park were no different from those of its predecessor.[9]

Like the Hetch Hetchy controversy that opened the century, this latest debate was on the verge of generating thousands of letters, volumes of testimony, and other official documentation. In December 1974 the master plan was rejected and planning was thrown open to a drawn-out process of public comment and citizens' workshops. All told more than sixty thousand people participated, most by responding to a mailed survey in the form of a standardized planning kit. Separate portions of the package asked for choices regarding the future of park transportation, visitor use, resource management, and operations. The list of options for major sites in the park spanned a variable range of values, from providing stricter preservation through more limited access to allowing even greater expansion of existing facilities. In 1978 the results of those surveys were incorporated in a revised master plan; following two more years of comment and additional public meetings, the new general management plan was finally released on October 30, 1980.[10]

Reduced to its essentials, this latest debate about the future of Yosemite differed only by degree from similar controversies in the past. The question was unchanged: What should be the primary purpose of Yosemite National Park? If it should be preservation, should not everything tangential to that purpose be removed? In the common spirit of compromise, that proposal was rejected yet again, at least in Yosemite Valley and other developed areas.

Thus the very existence of development continued to promote its self-preservation. So-called nonessential structures would eventually be removed; otherwise only slight reductions or readjustments would affect accommodations and visitor services.[11]

Expansion would be limited, but that option too remained. Basically, the park had escaped the development only of those structures that had never been built in the first place. To be sure, there would be no cable car to Glacier Point. Then again, Yosemite Valley would not be completely restored to an approximation of its appearance in 1851. Instead of guiding the park's undevelopment, the new plan merely suggested redirection. Tradition, quite obviously, had prevailed once again.

* * *

Beyond development, other issues of park management were no less bound by precedent and inconsistency. Especially when it came to managing wildlife, the Park Service, it could still be argued, lacked proper resolve. On November 5, 1970, for example, the minutes of a meeting held in the Yosemite offices of resource management conceded the fact "that the bear management program in Yosemite is lacking at present"; nonetheless, the recommendation was upheld that "until additional funding is available, the present program should be carried on."[12] How was it possible that thirty-one years after the death of Joseph Grinnell, the Park Service could admit, in effect, that its most important wildlife program in Yosemite National Park *still* lacked sufficient funding and the latest scientific information? How, as a result, could such a program even be considered credible?

The scandal broke in the fall of 1973 when newspapers throughout California published articles that finally revealed just how heavily bear management in Yosemite relied on the killing and disposing of the animals. Confronted with the evidence, government officials admitted that more than two hundred bears had been killed in the park between 1960 and 1972. However, the Park Service added, quickly defending that statistic, most had been "garbage" bears, those whose feeding habits especially posed a danger to park visitors. More difficult to explain were revelations confirming that the carcasses had simply been dumped off a cliff along the Big Oak Flat Road. Pictures taken at the base of the cliff, reported the *San Francisco Chronicle,* "showed bloody carcasses wedged in trees or collapsed on rocks where they landed after being thrown from above." Many had been skinned. "I am terribly concerned about the bear killing in the Valley," wrote P. F. Shenk, a frequent park visitor, summing up the reaction of many Californians appalled by the articles. "The bears have always been among the main attractions of Yosemite for me. Now it seems as though we put a label 'garbage bear' on an animal that is behaving only as nature intended, and *ipso facto* it becomes an enemy to be killed and dumped over a cliff."[13]

Predictably, the Park Service took refuge in letters supporting its actions, especially those letters arguing, in effect, that the Park Service, in killing Yosemite bears, had not gone far enough. "*Get rid of more of them*," a San Francisco resident strongly advised. "But you will have to be more discreet in disposing of them," he conceded. "Could not some institutions use that meat and tallow?" Mark Thomas, Jr., a San Jose attorney, also wrote "to support the action of the rangers." Only the previous summer he and his sons, accompanied by friends, had visited the Yosemite backcountry and had left with the conviction that bears "were unbelievable pests." "They destroyed much of our food. They were so brave that to get them to move out of the way yelling and whistle blowing would do no good, and it was actually necessary to throw things at them." Indeed, along the trails he overheard hikers swear "that next summer they would bring guns with them to protect themselves from the bears." The rangers were to be commended instead of condemned. "I certainly hope," Thomas concluded, "that none of the rangers nor the department suffers any detriment for having done a job that was sorely needed."[14]

As concerned preservationists had charged for the past fifty years, this very same callousness infected the Park Service itself. The still haunting observation was that the agency was supposed to know better, was supposed to educate the public rather than succumb to persecuting wildlife under the guise of visitor safety. That excuse too had been terribly abused and distorted. So Galen Rowell, the noted mountaineer and photographer, called in 1974 for courage to address the real issue. "Efforts to deal with the bear problem have been one sided," he observed, further establishing the basis for his rebuttal. Yosemite in 1973 had 2.3 million visitors. "Only 16 were injured by bears," Rowell noted, "and that represented an increase of more than 500 percent from 1972." Property damage in 1973 from 268 "bear incidents" totaled $24,367, or "about 1 ¢ per visitor, and zero warnings or citations were issued tourists for their infractions concerning bears."[15]

How, then, did the Park Service justify having killed more than two hundred bears since 1960? Once more it all depended on who was left in charge. "One of the few obvious correlations in statistics," Rowell added, carefully reviewing past trends, "is between the number of kills and the turnover of National Park Service management. While 39 bears were killed in 1963, only four were killed in 1969, when another regime managed the park." Even more revealing, those same discrepancies could be pinpointed within Yosemite's management structure. In 1972 and 1973, for example, "the Yosemite Valley District reported 173 property disturbances amounting to $17,353 damage." Meanwhile, the "huge Mather District, encompassing everything along the Tioga Pass highway, including Hetch-Hetchy and Tuolumne Meadows, reported 272 property disturbances worth $29,159." In the Yosemite Valley District, twenty-one bears were killed. Yet in the Mather District, even though the number of reported incidents and the amount of property damage was considerably more, "rangers killed none." "Why?" asked Rowell. "Because the ranger in charge of the Mather District believes bears should not be killed except in extreme circumstances."[16]

It was, in retrospect, another case of responsibility imposed on the Park Service from without rather than universally welcomed from within. Between Joseph Grinnell's science and Galen Rowell's exposé, Yosemite National Park had aged by more than fifty years. For all Grinnell's scholarship, however, now supplemented by Rowell's passion, the inescapable conclusion remained: As a rule the Park Service would do nothing unless coerced into change. "Like our armed forces," Rowell concluded, "the Park Service is a powerful bureaucracy with strong resistance to change from its lower ranks and the outside." Granted, the agency had "many good people" and even "a healthy smattering of genuine brilliance."[17] The only problem, preservationists agreed, was that so few of those individuals topped the management ladder.

It was also, to be sure, a matter of one's perspective. Yet there had never been any question that ever since Yosemite Valley had first been set aside, the most influential barometer of a manager's success was the number of visitors passing through the park. It was the one kind of proof requiring no further explanation for management decisions that were otherwise difficult to quantify. Consequently, the historical gulf between preservation and recreation had begun forming from the outset, widening in practically

208

every instance where protection of a resource might jeopardize traditional sources of support. Most important, people were the standard by which the government measured its success. Management would do nothing to disappoint the park visitor.

As Galen Rowell had confirmed, it was the level of appeasement that so troubled preservationists. In any dispute involving wildlife in particular, the Park Service seemed to practice a glaring double standard. Time and again bears that caused problems were linked to human sources of food. Obviously bears were attracted by the sheer abundance of foodstuffs and garbage, especially items left out in the open or carelessly thrown away. Park bears, in either case, were reacting to conditions brought about by human intervention. Yet whenever penalties were assessed, all seemed to fall on the bears, including the ultimate penalty of execution. "In situations involving humans and bears," Rowell bitterly concluded, "rangers have found it more convenient to pick on the bears. No one has to advise them of their rights or worry about due process of law."[18]

In the suggestion that animals, like people, were deserving of due process lay the fundamental difference between those who saw Yosemite as a national playground and those who considered it a natural refuge. Galen Rowell was just the latest in a fifty-year lineage of reformers insisting that the welfare of natural resources should be considered on a par with government, corporate, or individual self-interest. It was small wonder, given park history, that such sentiments were still revolutionary. The logical extension of that philosophy was to eliminate from Yosemite everything having nothing to do with furthering the protection of the natural environment. Or so the argument went, and, predictably, it had yet to be taken seriously.

Not in a generation had there been someone as articulate and convincing as Joseph Grinnell to point out the fallacies and inconsistencies in animal-reduction programs, especially programs biased toward the assumption that animals rather than people were basically at fault for confrontations. It was still all too easy to slip into an evasive terminology disguising the uncomfortable truth that the blame was often the other way around. As early as 1954, another perceptive visitor saw the real problem as simply lax enforcement of park rules and regulations. "A week or two ago I was traveling through the Kootenai National Park in British Columbia," the visitor indicated, "and noticed this sign: 'Penalty for touching or feeding bears maximum $500.00 and imprisonment'." Apparently the Canadians took wildlife conservation far more seriously. A similar law in Yosemite Valley might also save people, the hospital, and the Park Service "a good deal of trouble." That law already existed, replied Ronald F. Lee, the Park Service's chief of interpretation, who then admitted its futility. "The enforcement of the regulation is difficult, however, in view of our very limited ranger force and the great number of visitors, as well as the mulitiplicity of other protection problems."[19]

Lee dodged the obvious question: When had the situation ever been different? For instance, how had bears been treated when the number of visitors had been lower? The answer, at least historically, was that for the better part of a half century the animals had been treated much the same.[20] The issue was not, as he implied, a simple matter of budgets, visitation, or personnel. Rather, as Galen Rowell reconfirmed nearly twenty years later, it remained a complex problem involving management attitudes as well.

By 1973, at least, public awareness forced the Park Service to react to scandal more swiftly and decisively. Finally, bear management in Yosemite would be handled through a combination of scientific research, public education, and stronger law enforcement. Trained scientists rather than park rangers were to be in charge. "As I am sure you realize," Superintendent Leslie P. Arnberger wrote the chief of resources management, Richard Riegelhuth, on May 22, 1975, "our Bear Management Program is one of the most sensitive operations underway in this Park." In other words, the Park Service could no longer afford its historical indifference and methodologies. "Our Bear Management efforts are being watched," Arnberger admitted, "with a great deal of intense interest by numerous individuals and organizations." That scrutiny, and not the bears, had obviously motivated his concern. To be sure, Riegelhuth should understand why "it is essential that the program be carried out with professionalism and that every action taken is fully justified and can stand the test of complete and full disclosure to the public."[21]

The situation, to reemphasize, was another example of reform motivated by the power of scandal rather than a deep sense of agency responsibility. The Park Service had finally moved decisively, but only under the pressure of adverse publicity. "I guess all our heroes have feet of clay," another critic wrote, summing up that observation. And from the pen of a California sixth grader came another bitter assessment. "Bears have a right to live just like you and me and maybe even more. At least they don't kill each other for no reason or pollute air and water like we do." John M. Morehead, Yosemite's chief ranger, signed the standard park reply. "You'd be surprised at how much damage a bear can do—many thousands of dollars a year and, although we are responsible for protecting wildlife, we are also responsible for protecting life and property of visitors to the Park." The young critic, his teacher, "and perhaps your whole class," Morehead concluded, "have based your entire opinions on only one side of the argument."[22]

   * * *

Caught off guard by the intensity of the public's reaction to wildlife problems in Yosemite during the 1970s, the Park Service rediscovered, again to its bureaucratic dismay, that it lacked the necessary information to begin even basic reforms. Among those who addressed the problem straightforwardly was Richard Riegelhuth, chief of resources management. The issue of bears aside, the National Park Service just did not have sufficient data on most wildlife species. He confessed, "The research and management of wildlife species have suffered irregular attention over the years, depending on Park program focus." Consequently, there were "serious voids" in his office's files. Other data critical to management had probably been lost or misplaced. "Suffice to say," he concluded, "too few records of animal movements, distribution, densities, and behavior are now recorded in our files."[23]

Exactly fifty years earlier Joseph Grinnell and Tracy Storer had published *Animal Life in the Yosemite;* it was also forty years since George M. Wright had released his distinguished faunal series. In addition, more than a decade had already passed since the preparation of the Leopold Committee Report. Well might anyone have wondered why Riegelhuth, in his quest for information, would have to turn to former rangers for missing data about the park. "Should you have recollections, notes, or records assembled during your service in Yosemite," he wrote to at least ten such individuals, "that you believe may contribute fact, we would be pleased to make copies and return the originals to you. Of particular interest to us is information pertaining to the bighorn, deer, bear, mountain lion, and the rarer small mammal forms."[24] It was indeed the kind of request that in years past would have prompted Joseph Grinnell to ask, in reply, Why was that research apparently never even started, let alone carried forward to a meaningful conclusion?

Science, of course, had always been near the bottom of the Park Service's list of priorities. Scientists spoke a different language, one increasingly at odds with everyday management decisions. Park Service tradition was built on visitation, not science. Even to entertain the thought of limitations went against the agency's overriding philosophy. Time and again preservationists concerned about Yosemite Valley in particular heard the same rebuttal—the valley floor in the 1970s was far more beautiful than at any date in the past, especially the turn of the century, when horse-drawn vehicles had been the primary means of transportation. "Then the roads were old, unsurfaced, dirty in the dry season, the means of covering all vegetation with dust, and slippery mud channels in wet weather," observed Horace M. Albright, defending the modernization of Yosemite Valley as recently as 1975. In addition, critics should not forget the "barns, stables, fences, hay and manure piles occupying large areas, unattractive buildings, cattle and horses grazing on meadows; no adequate sanitation," and "camping permitted in all parts of the Valley."[25]

Thanks primarily to Park Service intervention, "all of these features of earlier years were gone—roads paved, new bridges built, sanitation facilities installed in camp grounds, sewer systems built, water lines renewed," and no grazing permitted "on the meadows except by native wildlife." Had Yosemite Valley been destroyed? Hardly, Albright concluded. "All visitor accommodations and other facilities, except the road system, were confined to the Eastern part of the Valley, and the Western part beyond the Yosemite Falls area was accessible only to picnickers, and visitors wishing to walk or ride in a wilderness atmosphere."[26]

Finally, by 1959 the old Yosemite Village, originally a motley collection of buildings fronting the south side of the Merced River, had been obliterated, and any necessary facilities, such as the village store, had been removed to locations of far less esthetic sensitivity. "I deplore the continual emphasis on overcrowding and impairment of the natural features," Albright therefore added to his concluding remarks. The fact remained: "Yosemite Valley today is far more beautiful than when our great naturalist explorer and writer, John Muir, saw it and in finest prose glorified it, or when President Theodore Roosevelt visited it in 1903 and enthusiastically praised it."[27]

Park Service tradition, Albright confirmed, leaned heavily toward public works. Yet his comparison distinguished between only two separate stages in Yosemite Valley's history of development and ignored that the valley prior to any construction had suffered from none of the esthetic impairments he had enumerated. Rather, in Albright's estimation, development was a given and therefore became a basis for comparison instead of an object properly targeted for exclusion. Granted, paved roads were better than dirt roads and modern sewage systems better than cesspools. The point he refused to acknowledge was that development itself, whether modern or crude, perhaps should never have been allowed inside Yosemite National Park.

Once development was accepted as legitimate or otherwise necessary, but a small step remained toward tolerating its expansion. Expansion, moreover, could be in one of two forms, either building new facilities or promoting additional services. Closely watched by preservationists throughout the 1970s, the Yosemite Park and Curry Company quickly dropped any outright defense of the former and pleaded instead for privileges aimed at redirection. The goal was still the same—to turn park visitors' spontaneous actions into organized, paid events. On June 2, 1982, for example, Edward C. Hardy, president of the Yosemite Park and Curry Company, wrote Robert Binnewies, park superintendent, requesting "permission to provide raft rentals for use on the Merced River in Yosemite Valley. We believe there is significant demand for this type of activity, and that the activity is ideally suited to Yosemite," Hardy further wrote, justifying company self-interest with that now predictable brand of rhetoric. "We believe that providing a raft rental operation can improve guest safety in Yosemite National Park by assuring that guests are riding with puncture resistant rafts . . . and that all riders are equipped with Coast Guard approved life jackets." Understandably, the word *profit* appeared nowhere in his letter to mar the sincerity of his remarks.[28]

Regardless, his motive was obvious and so again was the question: Was commercial rafting in the best interest of Yosemite National Park? Superintendent Binnewies said yes and therefore approved an initial operation of fifty rental units. His decision, however, went against the reservations of both Charles W. Wendt, the chief ranger, and Richard Riegelhuth, the chief of resources management. "From a resource protection standpoint," noted Wendt in a lengthy memorandum, "fewer numbers of people on the river will mean a reduced amount of trash along the shores and less disturbance of the wildlife." Safety considerations were no less important. "Even with life vests people get into trouble and the persons in the rental boats, without experience, will still have problems and require rescue." Similarly, he argued, "the more spontaneous user who would rent rafts if they were available, tends to drink more alcohol, use more drugs, and is generally more disorderly from a law enforcement standard. Furthermore, they are dirtier from a litter standpoint, and more destructive from a resource management standpoint." And even if none of those concerns materialized, the "aesthetic standpoint" alone was reason to deny the request to start up the entire operation. Simply, did the National Park Service "want an additional flotilla of 50 boats 'doing' the Merced?"[29]

Ironically, just four years earlier, Edward Hardy himself had used Wendt's exact argument to defend the need for swimming pools in Yosemite Valley, specifically the three existing pools targeted for possible exclusion during planning deliberations. "The alternative is swimming in the river," Hardy protested, "and the environmental impact of that activity could be adverse in terms of bank erosion and water pollution. There is also the safety factor in that people are more likely to drown in the river than in guarded pools."[30] Suddenly, in the instance of rafting, he had reversed himself completely and now argued that increased use of the Merced River would not in fact lead to appreciable environmental damage or greater threats to visitor safety. The esthetic effect of the operation he conveniently ignored, along with any admission that his sudden change of heart may also have been motivated by profit.

The procedure, in historical perspective, had been no different for a hundred or more years. Concessionaires would do everything allowable to maintain and expand their operations. Thus whatever the issue, the argument for the moment was the one that seemed to work best. If the aim was to keep swimming pools, the Merced River was fragile or dangerous. If rafting appeared profitable, suddenly the river was durable and safe. Idealistically, the Park Service would then decide once and for all whether either rafting or swimming pools belonged in Yosemite Valley. And that, in the opinion of preservationists, was precisely the problem: Whereas the concessionaire always behaved predictably, asking time and again for the chance to turn a profit, the Park Service was woefully unpredictable, vacillating between departments or from one superintendency to the next on whether or not Yosemite's protection would be firm and uncompromised.

To be sure, the concessionaire's formula for management remained the simpler of the two—ask, ask again, and never take "no" for an answer.

Inevitably, as a further result, new activities were likely to explode. Indeed, hardly had rafting been approved when Edward Hardy returned to the superintendent for permission to increase the size of the following year's fleet. In consultation with Hardy's staff, Superintendent Binnewies "agreed that 80 rafts would be an appropriate number at this time" and, in addition, reassured Hardy that "we are authorizing you to institute the raft rental operation on a permanent basis."[31]

Binnewies's approval, nevertheless, had still been given against the recommendations of resources management. Finally, in a confidential report dated March 1, 1986, the division identified twenty-four separate issues affecting Yosemite's air, water, vegetation, and wildlife. In Yosemite Valley the issue posing special problems was rafting on the river. Use of the Merced had already multiplied three- or fourfold in the brief period since commercial rafting had first begun. Originally, in 1982, there had been few private boats and only fifty commercial rafts. But that level had rapidly escalated. "On an average good weather day in the summer of 1985 there were about 450 rafts, carrying about 1350 people," the report noted. "About two-thirds of these rafts were rentals." Regardless of ownership, the rafts had identical effects. "The current high use levels have resulted in extreme crowding, aesthetic impairment for those wishing to view the Valley from the riverbank or from the Valley rim, litter problems in the river and along the banks, increased trampling and volunteer trails through meadows and erosion on riverbanks, and increased pressure to remove trees in the river on which rafts become entangled and those on the riverbank that may fall into the river." Thus the worst-case scenario predicted by resources management in 1982 was coming true. Indeed crowding was "so great," the report stated, "that at times 25 rafts are visible from Sentinel Bridge and rafts pass a given point an average of every 48 seconds."[32]

Accordingly, the division proposed limiting company rafts "to 90 per day and not more than 20 per hour," that out of a daily total of no more than 180 private and commercial rafts combined. Even if each floated the river twice, the limitation "would restore a minimum level of privacy and slow the rate of resource impacts until a more thorough assessment of those impacts can be made." Without those limits, the report concluded, issuing a subtle reminder about the alleged purposes of Yosemite National Park, "the visitor experience in central Yosemite Valley will continue to shift away from quiet appreciation of the natural beauty of the flowing river, the

215

meadows and riparian vegetation, and the scenic vistas toward a more amusement park atmosphere in which the recreational activity itself becomes the focus of attention."[33]

Here again was the classic argument for a contemplative enjoyment of the park, and here again—in the Curry Company's proposition, its expansion, and the superintendent's approval of both—was another classic example of how completely the Park Service could succumb to periodic blandishments promoting organized (hence profitable) forms of recreation, even those known to compromise the integrity of the resource. In defense of raft rentals, the Yosemite Park and Curry Company underscored the portion of its agreement obligating the concessionaire to conduct a summer-end cleanup of the riverbed and embankments. But was cleanup preservation or just another stark admission that rafting had indeed gotten completely out of hand? "A decision needs to be made soon," resources management argued, further revealing the depth of concern that had provoked its report, "since resource impacts continue to compound with time."[34]

Granted, the division acknowledged, not everything was hopeless. Elsewhere in the park, most notably in the Mariposa Grove, the reintroduction of fire was strong reason for optimism. Until 1972, natural fires in Yosemite had been "routinely suppressed." The biological results had long before been noted: "a denser canopy; dense, stagnant thickets of understory trees; large accumulations of fuels; and species shift toward shade-tolerant trees with declines in shrubs and herbs." In 1970 prescribed fire finally "premiered as a management tool." Over the next fifteen years, "68 prescribed fires burned 26,550 acres." In addition, since 1972 natural fires caused by lightning had been allowed to burn in designated zones covering 78 percent of the park. "From 1972 to 1985, 292 natural fires burned 24,309 acres," the scientists disclosed. "About 26 natural fires burn each year in Yosemite."[35]

The reintroduction of bighorn sheep in 1986 was another apparent success. Turn-of-the-century hunting, as well as competition with domestic sheep, had cost bighorns their historical range in Yosemite; the many proposals to bring them back had never lost a sense of urgency or popularity. As George M. Wright had confirmed during the early 1930s, however, any reintroduction had to await the recovery of herds to the south, lest the remaining population be endangered by an insufficient number of

V. *Urban Distractions and Influence*

38. Bisected by the Tuolumne River and draped with spectacular waterfalls, the Hetch Hetchy Valley was described as a smaller replica of Yosemite Valley proper. Courtesy of the Yosemite National Park Research Library.

39. Neither its similarity to
Yosemite Valley nor its location
within Yosemite National Park
were to spare Hetch Hetchy from
urban encroachment. In 1913
Congress awarded Hetch Hetchy
to the city of San Francisco, which
flooded the valley with this water-
supply reservoir. Courtesy of the
Yosemite National Park Research
Library.

40. The luxurious Ahwahnee
Hotel, opened in 1927, provided
every urban comfort in a wilder-
ness setting. Courtesy of the
Yosemite National Park Research
Library.

41. The distinctive interior of the
Ahwahnee Hotel has tempted the-
atrics designed purely for promoting tourism. The most famous is
Bracebridge, an annual Christmas
pageant and dinner. Contrived
during the late 1920s, Bracebridge
is obviously modeled after English
cultural themes totally foreign to
Yosemite. Courtesy of the
Yosemite National Park Research
Library.

42. Winter sports became the perfect rationale for opening Yosemite National Park to more special events, even those better suited to urban surroundings. Here film crews make motion pictures of the annual Winter Carnival, January 1932. Courtesy of the Yosemite National Park Research Library.

43. The Badger Pass ski area, originally modernized in 1935, brings crowds seeking entertainment rather than greater awareness of the environment. Courtesy of the National Park Service.

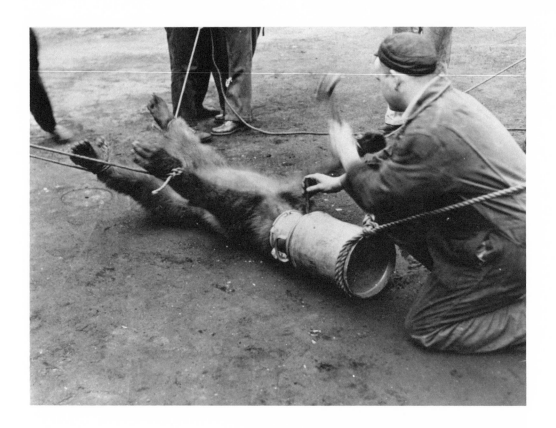

44. For unsuspecting animals, encountering civilization in Yosemite
often ends tragically. Rangers work
to free a bear who stuck his head
in a milk can, 1957. Courtesy of
the National Park Service.

45. Park Service biologists kill a
bear by lethal injection, having
deemed the animal a potential risk
to visitor safety. Courtesy of Resources Management, Yosemite
National Park

46. How visitors *really* die: sign
placed at entrance stations and in
Yosemite Valley, September 1947,
by Superintendent Frank A. Kittredge. Courtesy of the Yosemite
National Park Research Library.

6 NEEDLESS DEATHS
IN 16 DAYS

RECKLESS CLIFF CLIMBING
LIQUOR
CARELESS DRIVING

BE CAREFUL AND LIVE

47. In addition to environmental damage, the development of national parks inevitably leads to big-city social problems, including crime. The modern Yosemite Valley jail, with twenty-two beds, is the type of urban facility every park could do without. Courtesy of Brian Grogan.

48. The greater the presence of serious crime, the greater the need to make arrangements for litigation. The new Yosemite Village Courthouse completed in 1987 processes nearly one thousand cases annually. Courtesy of Brian Grogan.

49. Easy access, preservationists charge, brings both unwanted visitors and needless environmental damage, such as scarring caused in 1958 by the modernization of the cross-park Tioga Road. Courtesy of the Yosemite National Park Research Library.

50. This time exposure of Upper
Yosemite Valley at night, as seen
from Glacier Point in 1963, bears
dramatic witness to the final results
of development. Roads, campgrounds, parking lots, and buildings are all clearly visible. Courtesy
of the National Park Service.

healthy breeding animals. Fortunately, through the years the two native herds surviving in the Sierra continued to do well, finally allowing re-introduction to be attempted beginning in 1979.[36]

These positive trends were not discounted; they just seemed incomplete. And most, like the further designation of wilderness areas in 1984, gener-ally affected more remote portions of the park. The bighorns faced a struggle for survival along the eastern fringes of Yosemite. Natural fires, however beneficial, were also basically restricted to high-country zones. What about Yosemite's heart? What about its "incomparable valley"? Did every living thing have to climb ever upward to find true protection? Did sanctuary belong only to those resources capable of surviving in higher and higher altitudes? There was no escaping biological realities. Yosemite Valley was vital; it was the center of the park. If sanctuary failed there, it would probably fail everywhere.

Then again, Yosemite historically had had two hearts instead of only one. Perhaps that "other Yosemite," the Hetch Hetchy Valley, could finally be drained and eventually be restored. Indeed no fantasy was dearer to the hearts of preservationists. But was it, in fact, just another pointless dream? In 1987 a hopeful answer came from a most surprising quarter. No less than the secretary of the interior, Donald Hodel, proposed that San Fran-cisco find its fresh water elsewhere, allowing the O'Shaughnessy Dam to be dismantled and Hetch Hetchy to recover its wilderness charms. Prelimi-nary studies were cautious, indicating that full restoration would probably require centuries. Regardless, preservationists were not surprised by the government's final verdict. San Francisco, it was obvious, vehemently opposed the plan. Predictably, as a consequence, the idea did not get past its initial bout of aimless if lively publicity.[37]

If Hodel had indeed been serious, the rejection of his proposal was just the latest example of the power that development wielded by the mere fact of its preexistence. In Yosemite Valley too, the question remained: Would Americans be willing to restore the valley floor beyond altering the loca-tions of a few buildings or tearing down outmoded structures? In another moment of revelation, John M. Morehead, park superintendent, an-nounced in 1987 that further efforts to remove major facilities to sites outside Yosemite Valley seemed hopelessly impractical. Even in outlying areas, visitors would literally inundate transportation services and accommodations. That and similar recommendations to depend on staging areas, as enumerated in the 1980 general management plan, had been ill-advised. Accordingly, for all intents and purposes that plan was now defunct.[38]

What might take its place was pure conjecture. Yet if history was again any indication, the replacement would also be lacking in terms of preservation. Every search for management principles consistently protective of the resource had led to frustration and most certainly was inconclusive. Yosemite, even on the eve of its second century as a national park, was still inextricably bound by the compromises governing its first one hundred years.

❧ Epilogue: Reassessment and Future

Every conflict in Yosemite's history, and therefore every suggestion of those conflicts yet to come, can be traced to some compromise of the ideal that a national park first and foremost should exist for the protection of its natural heritage. Even as that ideal evolved, it faced two major obstacles. First, the standards of biological conservation were not original to Yosemite, certainly not in the minds of visitors at large. Spectacular scenery initially drew people to Yosemite, and scenery embellished with accommodations and services seemed perfectly acceptable to early park visitors. Second, park legislation provided, in effect, for a competing rather than complementary set of management values. When visitation was minimal, that duality between access and preservation could more easily be overlooked. Meanwhile, however, the precedent had been established. Development was *inside* Yosemite, where it could not help but exert pressure on the goals of preservation.

From the outset, preservation had failed to win unquestionable legitimacy. Whatever was natural or original to Yosemite did *not* automatically have priority over anything introduced or artificial. Supposedly, naturalness distinguished national parks from every other classification of public lands and resources, not to mention from the forces of civilization itself. The mere presence of development, especially in Yosemite Valley as the heart of the park, arguably broadcast a different message—that no natural resource was special or distinctive enough to warrant that degree of commitment to unswerving protection.

Preservation, it seemed, was an ideal. Undoubtedly it demanded too much, insisting that people come to see the resource only and ask nothing more of Yosemite than what it had been offering for thousands of years. The purposes of Yosemite were inspirational, scientific, and educational in nature. Only by adhering to those standards, not by trying to satisfy every public whim, would Yosemite's natural heritage receive all due consideration.

In that case preservation made unpopular demands, beginning with insistence on humility and total self-restraint. Inside Yosemite, every outside standard of conduct had to be open to question, for if social and personal behaviors were the same both inside and outside the park, there might well be no park, at least not one where natural conditions clearly prevailed. Roles had to be changed, perhaps entirely reversed. Every honest effort for protection rested on accepting standards of biological rather than social equity. Park animals, for example, would not be labeled *good* or *bad;* those terms were strictly human and loaded with social biases. Similarly, the suggestion that park animals were innocent or guilty according to legal custom strained every limit of biological credibility. People would have to have the courage to accept certain risks when entering natural environments, much as they accepted the everyday risks of their fast-paced civilization. Otherwise, growing levels of visitation possibly threatened everything the park was supposed to represent, encouraging instead the opposite impression that Yosemite was indeed just another grand resort.

Much of Yosemite's first century as a national park witnessed that struggle for meaning and consensus, for the recognition of its distinctive qualities apart from anything distracting or intentionally commercial. It was small wonder that research scientists were no less controversial than preservationists and that often the two groups were really one and the same. Science added clout to preservationists' emotions, underpinning those ideals with hard data rather than repetitious good intentions. Research science made it all the more difficult for proponents of development to stay in firm command, to justify, for example, eliminating predators, controlling bears, adding parking lots, or realigning roads. At the very least, scientists embraced preservation for the security it afforded their favorite research subjects. To be sure, Park Service scientists themselves were generally committed to a strict interpretation of the so-called Organic Act, which had established the Park Service on August 25, 1916. Jan van Wagtendonk, for example, a Yosemite research scientist, argued in March 1986: "A reasonable interpretation of the Organic Act indicates that Congress intended the Secretary of the Interior to protect natural conditions in parks, *as an absolute duty,* and to only allow use consistent with that protection. It is questionable whether the Service should determine public desires and attempt to accommodate them" (italics added).[1]

Inside any bureaucracy, even a little such criticism went a very long way. Granted, the Park Service had a sprinkling of research scientists such as Dr. van Wagtendonk, at least in the larger and more visible parks. The Park Service also cooperated with academic scientists in opening the reserves to a variety of seminars, classes, and specialized research projects. Yet the gulf between science and management was still very real. Although scientists might see the parks as great outdoor laboratories, Park Service tradition still had more in common with recreation than with research or preservation.

The Park Service could be pushed slightly one way or the other, but generally it stuck with what it knew, and what it knew best was people. Tradition, in turn, led to further rationales for management policies as they had evolved, most notably the argument that only small portions of Yosemite had been extensively developed. "The National Parks were not created just to hold every acre of their lands in exactly their state when reserved." Thus Horace M. Albright, co-founder of the National Park Service and its renowned second director (1929–33), defended the development of Yosemite Valley as late as 1975. National parks "were created 'for the benefit and enjoyment of the people,'" he added, further paraphrasing the common wording of early enabling acts. "The people must be given fullest consideration up to the point where natural features of a park might be impaired."[2]

In the eyes of preservationists, anything distracting was definitely an impairment, especially, as in Yosemite Valley, when located among the grandest features of a major national park. In 1987, for example, guests checking in at Yosemite Lodge received the following reminder with their room key: "The Mountain Room Bar is the perfect place to rendezvous before and after dinner. Enjoy cocktails and spectacular views of Yosemite Falls from the patio in summer or hot drinks by the fireplace in winter." Nor was that all. "A bigscreen TV," the announcement concluded, "provides added excitement to major sports events."[3]

For more than a century, preservationists had questioned the very process by which something as commonplace as a big-city barroom had won entry into such an uncommon resource. Yosemite Falls, they argued, should be entertainment enough without adding commercial distractions, especially televised sporting events and alcoholic beverages. Perhaps, as advertised, cocktails were "as cool as the mists off Yosemite Falls."[4] But that too was marketing puff and not preservation. The beneficiary was the concessionaire and not the park resource.

Indeed Edward Hardy, president of the Yosemite Park and Curry Company, defined Yosemite National Park as "a destination resort." True, it was also called a national park. "As such," he confessed in March 1986, "it is subject to more regulations, policies, and sensitivities than in most other resorts." But there it was again—the word *resort* instead of *park*. He almost seemed disappointed that the distinction still had to be made. His employees, however, should have no troubling doubts. "Individuals fortunate enough to work in a destination resort enjoy a variety of benefits," he remarked. "Among those in Yosemite are the beautiful surroundings and vast recreational opportunities." For Hardy there seemed to be no difference between the two, no threat to the natural beauty through the vigorous promotion of organized recreation. "Our first responsibility is to our GUESTS," he declared, further implying that most of them wanted company services exactly as offered. "Additionally, there is the responsibility for a private business in a national park to operate in support of the National Park Service goal—to provide for the use and enjoyment of the Park while protecting the Park resource for future generations." But his own priority was dramatically clear. "The guest is our reason for being here and quality guest service is critical." The resource was entertainment. As such, it was there to serve business, not the other way around.[5]

Extrapolating Hardy's definition into the twenty-first century suggested that Yosemite National Park in the future would look much like it had in the past. Development might not swell appreciably, but neither would it visibly retreat. Besides, every effort would still be made to expand park facilities, again relying on the strength of the argument that to turn anyone away from Yosemite would be to deny that person a sacred right.

In preservationists' scenario, levels and means of access would be determined solely by the welfare of the resource. At a minimum, visitors should be willing to leave the trappings and prejudices of civilization behind. Perhaps one answer, then, was more public transportation. Unlike private access, public transportation called for more forethought and planning on the part of the visitor. Choices and decisions would have to be made, for instance, on whether it was more important to bring along the family stereo or another change of clothes. Mandatory public transportation would be a responsible social filter, allowing everyone to have access but nonetheless directing each visitor to ask a most important question: Is the privilege of seeing Yosemite recreation enough?[6]

People seeking organized recreation would be asked to head elsewhere. Similarly, every duality in the management structure would be fully eradicated, allowing no business to compete for attention with the natural environment. The few real necessities of any visitor's experience, namely food, lodging, and perhaps camping equipment, could be provided by nonprofit foundations operating strictly as adjuncts of the National Park Service. The criterion of every product or service would be a compatibility with the goals of preservation. The purposes of Yosemite, as an uncommon resource, would remain strictly educational, scientific, and protective.[7]

Predictably, the Park Service was quick to argue that those goals were already being realized, that indeed the agency had never departed from them in the first place. The Park Service, in effect, hoped critics would forget its history. Granted, some noteworthy changes had recently been made, among them prescribed burning in the Mariposa Grove and sincere (if again belated) attempts to reduce the possibility of confrontations between visitors and wildlife. The painful revelation was how slowly, and under what circumstances, the Park Service had moved to inaugurate a few reforms. As early as 1933, in *Fauna of the National Parks,* George M. Wright and his colleagues had laid down exacting but fair principles for wildlife management in sensitive areas, including Yosemite. Yet not until the 1970s did wildlife management in general, and bear management in particular, even begin to approximate the standards justified, in absorbing detail, by Wright and his coauthors. "The fallacy of spreading an inviting feast for bears and then 'taking them for a ride' to remote sections is evident," the biologists had written. "The bears travel in a vicious circle, but obviously it is man who keeps them running on that path." The solution was obvious: "If man is to live in close proximity to bears he must protect his property by devices which bears can not break." But of course "bear-proof refuse containers and food safes" would be "an expense," although one no less important than "road construction and police protection." This much was very evident: "If food is not available around human habitations, bears will not stay there long."[8]

In the end, however, scandal—more than biological common sense—provoked genuine reform. A pile of bear carcasses at the base of a cliff along the Big Oak Flat Road was exposed by the national media in 1973 and did far more to restructure bear management in Yosemite than did any ecologist's pleas. For much the same reason, the most effective reformers were people outside rather than inside the National Park Service. George M. Wright, Harold C. Bryant, and Carl P. Russell, among other committed scientists, did pursue Park Service careers, and highly successful ones. But again, these men were the exceptions. Their avoidance of misleading stereotypes, such as "garbage" bears, "killer" rattlesnakes, and "blood-thirsty" lions, reflected considerable sensitivity and training. They were also fortunate to have had Joseph Grinnell as a friend, confidant, and teacher and, equally important, to have received periodic endorsements from the Museum of Vertebrate Zoology. Grinnell also extended research space, financial assistance, and conceptual advice. Even the distinctive faunal series, begun in the early 1930s by George Wright and his colleagues, rested in large part on Grinnell's earlier work and ideas.

The requirements of biological sanctuary were consistently clear and straightforward—people were welcome, but the resource must come first. Beyond simply admitting crowds of visitors, the National Park Service should be educating resource stewards. Yes, bears could be dangerous, but generally only if provoked. The danger was also relative. As of 1988 no visitor in Yosemite's recorded history had ever been killed by the common black bear, and the grizzly in Yosemite was long since extinct.[9] Undoubtedly many more people had been killed or injured on highways leading into Yosemite than had been harmed by wildlife—or any other natural phenomenon—inside the park. No less than James Mason Hutchings, the leader of the first party of tourists into Yosemite Valley in 1855, met his death in 1902 along the Big Oak Flat Road, where he was killed when his horses suddenly bolted, throwing him from his wagon to the ground.[10] For the next three-quarters of a century, accidental drownings, automobile and motorcycle wrecks, drunken driving, climbing mishaps, and overexertion killed literally hundreds of other park visitors and residents. Bears, to reemphasize, killed absolutely no one.

Yet any concerned visitor, reviewing the files at Yosemite park headquarters, could easily draw exactly the opposite conclusion. Even with better funding and trained biologists, bear management in Yosemite still relied heavily on killing "problem" bears. As of October 18, 1988, for example, eight animals had been put to death in that year alone, and several weeks remained before the bears would be hibernating.[11] The deaths, however justified, were still visible proof of the failure of sanctuary. Park resources, and not visitors, continued to pay the ultimate price for every lapse in sound judgment and equitable rules of conduct.

The first biologists to seek reform, among them Joseph Grinnell and George M. Wright, themselves had conceded the necessity of killing individual animals that had habitually become aggressive.[12] As scientists of conscience, however, they still asked that biological reasoning everywhere substitute for momentary expedience and emotion. Thus Grinnell and his followers kept stressing education, even to the point of insisting that every park visitor learn the basics of resources and ecology. Stronger ethics and greater awareness would have to be taught. The prerequisite for responsible behavior was a better knowledge of the environment. "To educate people to this point of view, for their own safety and pleasure, may take several years, but there seems to be no other course," Wright and his colleagues observed in 1933. "It is easier to make the human adjustment to a new circumstance than to coerce the animals." Park visitors, accordingly, had to be contacted and informed.[13]

The assumption was basic—people should accommodate the resource. And that was asking a lot of an agency still so committed to accommodating people first. Granted, some of Yosemite's original distractions, among them the firefall and the bear show, had eventually been abolished. Others, like the cable car to Glacier Point, had been seriously considered but never actually built. The point was that an evening in Yosemite Valley was still likely to remind perceptive visitors of a night spent in any city or resort. Rangers patrolled park highways much as policemen cruised city streets, checking for speeders, drunken drivers, and the occasional stranded motorist. Robbery and rape were no longer uncommon. The worst-case scenarios might in fact be exceptions. Or so the Park Service, and especially the concessionaire, consistently argued. Then again, by 1987 Yosemite Valley's jail had been expanded from sixteen to twenty-two beds while, nearby, construction had also been completed on a new courthouse for the magistrate. Something, it was safe to argue, was visibly out of control in Yosemite

Valley, if by the term *national park* all visitors should expect the best and not the worst of every human endeavor.[14]

Further borrowing from Garrett Hardin's thesis, the tragedy of the commons, we might see the problem simply as one of easy and unrestricted access. There was still no effective social filter, no physical or mental barriers, to make visitors ask themselves the question, Is the privilege of seeing Yosemite recreation enough? Rather, opponents of change still successfully argued that change was too expensive or, even if cost-effective, then much too impractical. For example, estimates for completely restoring Yosemite Valley by removing its major buildings and facilities ranged in the hundreds of millions of dollars.[15] And what would be the fate of those historic structures which themselves were now clearly identified with the park and its past? Conceivably, future generations of visitors would also value those buildings for their own sake, regardless of their location or alleged intrusion on the environment. Certainly structures of such style and elegance as the Ahwahnee Hotel would, if torn down, never be replaced, even on lands just outside the national park.

The problem involved more than buildings, preservationists conceded; it remained one of compatible user standards. If in fact people were universally conscientious about the natural resource, where they ate or slept might have no lasting influence. But if more and more visitors, by constantly gravitating toward any distraction or commonplace amusement, regularly displaced others more committed to the environment and its needs, then indeed Yosemite's distinctive base would continue to be compromised.

That might, as was often charged, sound selfish or elitist. It also might, as preservationists rebutted, be the salvation of Yosemite. Every institution is somehow selfish and selective, if only by practicing one kind of activity to the exclusion of every other kind. For Yosemite to remain distinctive, management must practice—not just preach—those forms of behavior ensuring that distinctiveness. Every landscape shared differences; few rose to such uniqueness. That uniqueness, in 1864, had allowed Americans to herald Yosemite as a symbol of national pride. By the 1920s visitors were finally hearing more about plants, animals, and Yosemite as a refuge of biological diversity. The message had been changing, but the place was always the same. It followed that future generations might repeat the experience, finding new knowledge and values undreamed of by Yosemite's previous visitors and guardians.

226

If so, the gift of preservation is still essential to every future opportunity. Each succeeding generation, like Yosemite's first, must pass the park along, "inalienable for all time." Education, it also follows, is therefore preservation's strongest ally. So often have the standards of preservation been challenged and debated that the idealism of the movement has never been fully sustained. Historically, nonetheless, the moment educators adopted Yosemite National Park, preservation everywhere won greater legitimacy. Once the public was encouraged to learn about natural resources and not merely to observe them, the future of Yosemite was that much brighter and unquestionably more secure.

The theme, if straightforward, remains simple and eloquent. Yosemite is too important to be just another place. Civilization has many undeniable advantages, yet even the most inventive civilization has never built a Yosemite. Yosemite by every imaginable standard is one of a kind. In that perception, and no other, lie the only tried and true principles for guiding the future of the park's natural heritage.

❧ Notes

CHAPTER ONE

1. John Muir, *My First Summer in the Sierra* (Boston: Houghton Mifflin Co., 1916), pp.116–20.

2. Joseph LeConte, "Ramblings through the High Sierra," *Sierra Club Bulletin* 3 (January 1900): 33–35. This is a reprint of his 1875 work, *A Journal of Ramblings,* privately published.

3. Ansel Adams with Mary Street Alinder, *Ansel Adams: An Autobiography* (Boston: Little, Brown and Co. with New York Graphic Society Books, 1985), pp.50, 53.

4. François E. Matthes, *The Incomparable Valley: A Geologic Interpretation of Yosemite,* ed. Fritiof Fryxell (Berkeley and Los Angeles: University of California Press, 1950). This should be supplemented with Jeffrey P. Schaffer, "Pleistocene Lake Yosemite and the Wisconsin Glaciation of Yosemite Valley," *California Geology* 30 (November 1977): 243–48; and N. King Huber, "The Geologic Story of Yosemite National Park" (Bound typescript, Yosemite National Park Research Library, n.d.).

5. Matthes, *The Incomparable Valley.*

6. Elizabeth Godfrey, *Yosemite Indians,* rev. James Synder and Craig Bates (Yosemite: Yosemite Natural History Association in cooperation with the National Park Service, 1977), p.3; Linda Wedel Greene, *Historic Resource Study: Yosemite,* 3 vols. (Washington, D.C.: U.S. Department of the Interior, National Park Service, 1987), 1:1–13. I have also benefited from personal communications with Craig Bates, ethnologist, Yosemite National Park.

7. U.S. Department of the Interior, National Park Service, Yosemite National Park, "Preliminary Report on the Study of the Meadows of Yosemite Valley," by Emil F. Ernst (Typescript, File 880–01, Yosemite National Park Research Library, May 15, 1943), pp.9–16; Godfrey, *Yosemite Indians,* pp.11–13.

8. Godfrey, *Yosemite Indians,* pp.3–4; Greene, *Yosemite,* 1:7,15–17.

9. Godfrey, *Yosemite Indians,* pp.5–7; Greene, *Yosemite,* 1:17–23. These and many other accounts are taken from Lafayette Houghton Bunnell, *Discovery of the Yosemite, and the Indian War of 1851,*

Which Led to That Event (1880; reprint, Freeport, N.Y.: Books for Libraries Press, 1971). It should be supplemented with C. Gregory Crampton, ed., *The Mariposa Indian War, 1850–1851, Diaries of Robert Eccleston: The California Gold Rush, Yosemite, and the High Sierra* (Salt Lake City: University of Utah Press, 1957).

10. Zenas Leonard, *Narrative of the Adventures of Zenas Leonard,* ed. Milo Milton Quaife (Chicago: Lakeside Press, 1934), p.129.

11. Godfrey, *Yosemite Indians,* p.6; Greene, *Yosemite,* 1:22.

12. As quoted in Godfrey, *Yosemite Indians,* p.8.

13. Ibid. See also Bunnell, *Discovery of the Yosemite,* chap.5.

14. Godfrey, *Yosemite Indians,* pp.8–9; Bunnell, *Discovery of the Yosemite,* chap.11.

15. Godrey, *Yosemite Indians,* p.10.

16. Greene, *Yosemite,* 1:25–26; Godfrey, *Yosemite Indians,* p.10; Margaret Sanborn, *Yosemite: Its Discovery, Its Wonders, and Its People* (New York: Random House, 1981), pp.57–60; Carl P. Russell, *One Hundred Years in Yosemite: The Story of a Great Park and Its Friends* (Yosemite: Yosemite Natural History Association, 1957), pp.46–48. The differing accounts of Tenaya's death are well treated through a comparison of these sources.

17. Godfrey, *Yosemite Indians,* pp.3–4, 35.

18. Bunnell, *Discovery of the Yosemite,* p.54.

CHAPTER TWO

1. Roger R. Olmsted, ed., *Scenes of Wonder and Curiosity from Hutchings' California Magazine, 1856–1861* (Berkeley, Calif.: Howell-North Books, 1962), pp.v–vii; Francis P. Farquhar, *History of the Sierra Nevada* (Berkeley and Los Angeles: University of California Press, 1965), pp.117–18. Similar brief descriptions of Hutchings and his significance abound. An especially revealing portrait of the man and his early life is Shirley Sargent, ed., *Seeking the Elephant, 1849: James Mason Hutchings' Journal of his Overland Trek to California . . . and Letters from the Mother Lode* (Glendale, Calif.: Arthur H. Clark Company, 1980).

2. Farquhar, *Sierra Nevada,* p.118.

3. As quoted from Olmsted, *Scenes of Wonder and Curiosity,* p.xi.

4. See, for example, ibid., pp.271–88.

5. Horace Greeley, *An Overland Journey from New York to San Francisco in the Summer of 1859* (New York: C. M. Saxton, Barker and Co., 1860), pp.306–9; Thomas Starr King, "A Vacation Among the Sierras," *Boston Evening Transcript,* January 26, 1861, p.1.

6. Alfred Runte, "Beyond the Spectacular: The Niagara Falls Preservation Campaign," *New-York Historical Society Quarterly* 57 (January 1973): 30–50.

7. Albert D. Richardson, *Beyond the Mississippi* (Hartford, Conn.: American Publishing Company, 1867), p.426; Samuel Bowles, *Across the Continent: A Summer's Journey to the Rocky Mountains, the Mormons and the Pacific States, with Speaker Colfax* (Springfield, Mass.: Samuel Bowles and Co., 1865), pp.226–27.

8. Greeley, *An Overland Journey,* pp.311–12; Clarence King, *Mountaineering in the Sierra Nevada* (Boston: J. R. Osgood and Co., 1872), pp.43–44.

9. Farquhar, *Sierra Nevada,* p.122; Olmsted, *Scenes of Wonder and Curiosity,* pp.271–87.

10. H. T. Tuckerman, "Albert Bierstadt," *Galaxy* 1 (August 15, 1866): 679. See also Fitz-Hugh Ludlow, "Seven Weeks in the Great Yo-Semite," *Atlantic*

Monthly 13 (June 1864): 739–54; and Gordon Hendricks, *Albert Bierstadt: Painter of the American West* (New York: Henry N. Abrams, 1974).

11. Carl P. Russell, *One Hundred Years in Yosemite: The Story of a Great Park and Its Friends* (Yosemite: Yosemite Natural History Association, 1957), p.93. There are many other accounts of early development history. See, for example, Linda Wedel Greene, *Historic Resource Study: Yosemite*, 3 vols. (Washington, D.C.: U.S. Department of the Interior, National Park Service, 1987), 1:44–45; and Shirley Sargent, *Yosemite and Its Innkeepers* (Yosemite: Flying Spur Press, 1975).

12. Greene, *Yosemite*, 1:69–71; Margaret Sanborn, *Yosemite: Its Discovery, Its Wonders, and Its People* (New York: Random House, 1981), pp.93–94.

13. The complexities and inconsistencies of frontier land law in the United States may be followed in Roy M. Robbins, *Our Landed Heritage: The Public Domain, 1776–1936* (Lincoln: University of Nebraska Press, 1962). For the Yosemite case in particular I have relied extensively on government documents, cited below.

14. Raymond to Conness, February 20, 1864, Yosemite—Legislation, File 979.447, Y-7, Yosemite National Park Research Library. This is a copy of the original in the National Archives, Records of the General Land Office, Miscellaneous Letters Received, G33572.

15. Ibid.

16. Ibid. Olmsted's probable role in the protection of Yosemite is best summarized in Laura Wood Roper, *FLO: A Biography of Frederick Law Olmsted* (Baltimore: Johns Hopkins University Press, 1973), p.268.

17. Other accounts of the events and deliberations leading up to the preservation of Yosemite Valley are Hans Huth, "Yosemite: The Story of an Idea," *Sierra Club Bulletin* 33 (March 1948): 63–76; and Holway R. Jones, *John Muir and the Sierra Club: The Battle for Yosemite* (San Francisco: Sierra Club, 1965), pp.28–29.

18. *Congressional Globe,* 38th Cong., 1st sess., May 17, 1864, pp.2300–2301. An important summary of the events behind Conness's reference to the giant sequoias is Joseph H. Engbeck, Jr., *The Enduring Giants* (Berkeley: University Extension, University of California, in cooperation with the California Department of Parks and Recreation, Save-the-Redwoods League, and the Calaveras Grove Association, 1973). Also relevant is Farquhar, *Sierra Nevada,* pp.83–87.

19. *Congressional Globe,* 38th Cong., 1st sess., May 17, 1864, pp.2300–2301.

20. U.S., *Statutes at Large,* 13 (1864): 325.

21. Ibid.; State of California, *Report of the Commissioners to Manage the Yosemite Valley and the Mariposa Big Tree Grove,* by J. D. Whitney (Sacramento: D. W. Gelwicks, State Printer, 1867), p.3.

22. *Report of the Commissioners* (1867), pp.3–4. The act of April 2, 1866, is reprinted in its entirety in State of California, *Biennial Report of the Commissioners to Manage the Yosemite Valley and the Mariposa Big Tree Grove for the Years 1874 and 1875* (Sacramento: G. H. Springer, State Printer, 1875), pp.7–8.

23. *Report of the Commissioners* (1867), p.4. Galen Clark's colorful life and career may be followed in Shirley Sargent, *Galen Clark: Yosemite Guardian* (San Francisco: Sierra Club, 1964).

24. *Report of the Commissioners* (1867), pp.6–8.

25. Ibid., p.7.

26. Ibid., p.8.

27. Ibid.

28. State of California, *Message of Gov.*

H. H. Haight, Transmitting the Report of the Yosemite Commissioners [1868/69] and Memorial of J. C. Lamon (Sacramento: D. W. Gelwicks, State Printer, 1870), p.3.

29. *Congressional Globe,* 40th Cong., 2d sess., June 3, 1868, p.2816.

30. Ibid., p.2817.

31. U.S. Congress, Senate, Committee on Private Land Claims, *S. Rept. 185 to accompany H.R. 1118,* 40th Cong., 2d sess., July 23, 1868, pp.1–2.

32. Ibid.

33. Ibid.

34. Ibid.

35. I have further discussed this distinction in *National Parks: The American Experience,* 2d ed. (Lincoln: University of Nebraska Press, 1987), p.47.

36. Predictably, those complaining the loudest were Hutchings and Lamon.

CHAPTER THREE

1. Frederick Law Olmsted, "The Yosemite Valley and the Mariposa Big Trees: A Preliminary Report," ed. Laura Wood Roper, *Landscape Architecture* 43 (October 1952): 17, 22–23.

2. Laura Wood Roper, *FLO: A Biography of Frederick Law Olmsted* (Baltimore: Johns Hopkins University Press, 1973), p.287.

3. Olmsted was indeed very familiar with Niagara Falls, having visited the cataract as early as 1828 and 1834. See ibid., pp.6, 14, 378.

4. Olmsted, "Report," pp.16–17, 22.

5. Ibid., pp.16, 22.

6. Roper, *FLO,* pp.288, 301. Olmsted returned, in 1886, to visit the Mariposa Big Tree Grove but did not, for reasons impossible to explain, go into Yosemite Valley. Ibid., pp.407–8. A further analysis of Olmsted's commitment to the protection of natural vegetation is Alfred Runte, "Beyond the Spectacular:

The Niagara Falls Preservation Campaign," *New-York Historical Society Quarterly* 57 (January 1973): 30–50.

7. Olmsted, "Report," p.24.

8. Roper, *FLO,* p.301, 302.

9. State of California, *Report of the Commissioners to Manage the Yosemite Valley and the Mariposa Big Tree Grove,* by J. D. Whitney (Sacramento: D. W. Gelwicks, State Printer, 1867), p.5.

10. Olmsted, "Report," pp.17, 20–21.

11. Ibid., p.22; *Report of the Commissioners* (1867), p.5.

12. State of California, Geological Survey, J. D. Whitney, State Geologist, *The Yosemite Book; A Description of the Yosemite Valley and the Adjacent Region of the Sierra Nevada, and of the Big Trees of California* (New York: Julius Bien, 1868), p.9.

13. Ibid., pp.11, 20–22.

14. State of California, *Message of Gov. H. H. Haight, Transmitting the Report of the Yosemite Commissioners [1868/69] and Memorial of J. C. Lamon* (Sacramento: D. W. Gelwicks, State Printer, 1870), pp.3–4.

15. U.S. Congress, Senate, Committee on Public Lands, *Memorial of J. M. Hutchings Praying A grant of lands in the Yosemite Valley, California,* 41st Cong., 3d sess., February 21, 1871, S. Mis. Doc. 72, p.1. See also U.S. Congress, House, Committee on the Public Lands, *J. M. Hutchings, J. C. Lamon,* 41st Cong., 2d sess., January 18, 1870, H. Rept. 2 to accompany H.R. 184, pp.1–10.

16. Hutchings v. Low, 82 U.S. (1872), pp.78, 94.

17. State of California, *Biennial Report of the Commissioners to Manage the Yosemite Valley and the Mariposa Big Tree Grove for the Years 1874 and 1875* (Sacramento: G. H. Springer, State Printer, 1875), pp.10, 17. This report is also an excellent summary of the Hutchings-Lamon case.

18. Olmsted, "Report," p.22.
19. See, for example, Raymond F. Dasmann, *The Destruction of California* (New York: Macmillan, 1965).
20. A superb overview of these changes is Robert P. Gibbens and Harold F. Heady, *The Influence of Modern Man on the Vegetation of Yosemite Valley* (Berkeley: University of California, Division of Agricultural Sciences, 1964). The standard primary source is U.S. Department of the Interior, National Park Service, Yosemite National Park, "Preliminary Report on the Study of the Meadows of Yosemite Valley," by Emil F. Ernst (Typescript File 880–01, Yosemite National Park Research Library, May 15, 1943). Ernst provides an excellent introduction to Yosemite's early aboriginal and settlement history.
21. L. H. Bunnell to John P. Irish, September 9, 1890, as quoted in State of California, *Biennial Report of the Commissioners to Manage Yosemite Valley and the Mariposa Big Tree Grove for the Years 1889–90* (Sacramento: State Printing Office, 1890), pp.10, 12; Galen Clark to Board of Commissioners, August 30, 1894, File 880–01, Yosemite National Park Research Library. Portions of these quotations are also contained in Ernst, "Preliminary Report," pp.5, 11–12.
22. This point is exhaustively documented in Ernst, "Preliminary Report," pp.9–16.
23. Gibbens and Heady, *Vegetation of Yosemite Valley,* pp.10–20, passim.
24. Olmsted, "Report," pp.22, 24.
25. Ernst, "Preliminary Report," pp.18–19.
26. State of California, *Report of the Commissioners to Manage the Yosemite Valley and the Mariposa Big Tree Grove, 1883–84* (Sacramento: State Printing Office, 1884), p.22.
27. Olmsted, "Report," p.24.
28. Many of these photographs are in-cluded with Ernst, "Preliminary Report." See also Gibbens and Heady, *Vegetation of Yosemite Valley,* pp.2–17.
29. Gibbens and Heady, *Vegetation of Yosemite Valley,* pp.21–24; Ernst, "Preliminary Report," pp.20–60, passim.
30. *Report of the Commissioners* (1867), p.10.
31. State of California, *Biennial Report of the Commissioners to Manage the Yosemite Valley and Mariposa Grove of Big Trees,* by William Ashburner (Sacramento: T. A. Springer, State Printer, 1871), pp.3–5.
32. *Report of the Commissioners* (1883–84), p.22.
33. Ernst, "Preliminary Report," pp.38–39.
34. See again Olmsted, "Report," p.24.
35. William Hammond Hall, *To Preserve from Defacement and Promote the Use of the Yosemite Valley* (Sacramento: California State Printing Office, 1882), p.5.
36. Ibid., pp.21–22.
37. Ibid., pp.8–9.
38. Gibbens and Heady, *Vegetation of Yosemite Valley,* pp.21–25.
39. Hall, *Yosemite Valley,* pp.24–25.

CHAPTER FOUR

1. *United States Statutes at Large,* 26 (1890): 651. The latest scholarship on the origins of Yosemite National Park is Richard J. Orsi, "'Wilderness Saint' and 'Robber Baron': The Anomalous Partnership of John Muir and the Southern Pacific Company for Preservation of Yosemite National Park," *Pacific Historian* 29 (Summer/Fall 1985): 136–56. Orsi masterfully proves assumptions about the Southern Pacific's role in the establishment of the park, as previously discussed in Holway R. Jones, *John Muir and the Sierra Club: The Battle for Yosemite* (San Francisco: Sierra Club, 1965), pp.46–47; Alfred Runte, *Na-*

tional Parks: The American Experience, 2d ed. (Lincoln: University of Nebraska Press, 1987), p.61; and idem, *Trains of Discovery: Western Railroads and the National Parks* (Flagstaff, Ariz.: Northland Press, 1984), pp.39–40.

2. State of California, *Report of the Commissioners to Manage the Yosemite Valley and the Mariposa Big Tree Grove, 1883–84* (Sacramento: State Printing Office, 1884), p.8.

3. William Hammond Hall, *To Preserve from Defacement and Promote the Use of the Yosemite Valley* (Sacramento: California State Printing Office, 1882), pp.5–6.

4. Ibid., pp.6–8.

5. Jones discusses these early legislative failures in *John Muir and the Sierra Club,* pp.41–42.

6. Accounts of Muir abound. Recent scholarship includes Stephen Fox, *John Muir and His Legacy: The American Conservation Movement* (Boston and Toronto: Little, Brown and Co., 1981); Michael P. Cohen, *The Pathless Way: John Muir and American Wilderness* (Madison: University of Wisconsin Press, 1984); and Lisa Mighetto, ed., *Muir Among the Animals: The Wildlife Writings of John Muir* (San Francisco: Sierra Club Books, 1986). The long-accepted biography is Linnie Marsh Wolfe, *Son of the Wilderness: The Life of John Muir* (New York: Alfred A. Knopf, 1945).

7. This most popular insight into Muir's genius is best told in Fox, *John Muir and His Legacy,* pp.20–22.

8. Ibid., p.22.

9. John Muir, *My First Summer in the Sierra* (Boston: Houghton Mifflin Co., 1916), p.116.

10. A creative addition to analyses of the significance of his term is Lisa Mighetto, "John Muir and the Rights of Animals," in Mighetto, *Muir Among the Animals,* pp.xi–xxviii. See especially p.xvii.

11. A complete inventory of these claims, including location, size, price per acre, ownership, and original date of sale, may be found in U.S. Department of the Interior, *Report of the Acting Superintendent of the Yosemite National Park for the Fiscal Year Ended June 30, 1903* (Washington: Government Printing Office, 1903).

12. See, for example, Robert Underwood Johnson, "The Case for Yosemite Valley," *Century Magazine* 39 (January 1890): 478.

13. Jones, *John Muir and the Sierra Club,* p.33.

14. Ashburner v. California, 103 U.S. (1880), pp.575–79. The decision is also reprinted in *Report of the Commissioners* (1883–84), pp.31–32.

15. Jones, *John Muir and the Sierra Club,* pp.37–38. The charges are fully listed in State of California, Legislature, Assembly Committee on Yosemite Valley and Mariposa Big Trees, *In the Matter of the Investigation of the Yosemite Valley Commissioners,* 28th sess., February 1889 (Sacramento: State Printing Office, 1889), p.3. Brief Senate hearings were also conducted.

16. California, Legislature, Assembly, *Investigation of the Yosemite Valley Commissioners,* pp.345–79.

17. Ibid., pp.208–15.

18. Ibid., pp.41–42, 45.

19. Ibid., pp.41, 44.

20. Many of these structures are discussed in ibid. For a complete inventory, see Linda Wedel Greene, *Historic Resource Study: Yosemite,* 3 vols. (Washington, D.C.: U.S. Department of the Interior, National Park Service, 1987), especially vol.1.

21. State of California, *Biennial Report of*

*the Commissioners to Manage Yosemite
Valley and the Mariposa Big Tree Grove
for the Years 1889–90* (Sacramento: State
Printing Office, 1890), p.15. The entire
report was a defense of the commission
and its management practices.

22. See Fox, *John Muir and His Legacy,*
p.10.

23. Robert Underwood Johnson, *Remem-
bered Yesterdays* (Boston: Little, Brown,
1923), pp.279–80; Jones, *John Muir
and the Sierra Club,* p.43.

24. *Biennial Report of the Commissioners*
(1889–90), pp.15–27.

25. John Muir, "The Treasures of the Yosemite," *Century Magazine* 40 (August
1890): 487–88; idem, "Features of the
Proposed Yosemite National Park,"
ibid. (September 1890): 666–67; Orsi,
"'Wilderness Saint' and 'Robber
Baron,'" p.147.

26. Orsi, "'Wilderness Saint' and 'Robber
Baron,'" p.147.

27. Ibid.; Jones, *John Muir and the Sierra
Club,* p.43.

28. Jones, *John Muir and the Sierra Club,*
pp.44–45; Orsi, "'Wilderness Saint'
and 'Robber Baron,'" pp.147–48.

29. Orsi, "'Wilderness Saint' and 'Robber
Baron,'" p.148; "Proceedings of the Sierra Club," *Sierra Club Bulletin* 1 (January 1896): 275; *United States Statutes at
Large,* 26 (1890): 650–52.

CHAPTER FIVE

1. U.S. Department of the Interior, *Report
of the Acting Superintendent of the Yosemite National Park* (August 31, 1891),
52d Cong., 1st sess., 1892, H. Ex.
Doc.1, vol.3. Hereafter cited as Acting
Superintendent, *Yosemite Annual Report*
(date). The standard history of the cavalry's role in national parks is H. Duane
Hampton, *How the United States Cavalry Saved the National Parks* (Bloom-

ington: University of Indiana Press,
1971).

2. State of California, *Biennial Report of
the Commissioners to Manage Yosemite
Valley and the Mariposa Big Tree Grove
for the Years 1889–90* (Sacramento: State
Printing Office, 1890), pp.8, 14.

3. State of California, Legislature, Assembly Committee on Yosemite Valley and
Mariposa Big Trees, *In the Matter of the
Investigation of the Yosemite Valley Commissioners,* 28th sess., February 1889
(Sacramento: State Printing Office,
1889), p.42.

4. Ibid., pp.42–43.

5. Ibid., p.43.

6. Acting Superintendent, *Yosemite Annual
Report* (1891), p.664.

7. Ibid. (June 30, 1893), 53d Cong., 2d
sess., 1893, H. Ex. Doc.1, pt.5, vol.3,
pp.647–48.

8. State of California, *Biennial Report of
the Commissioners to Manage Yosemite
Valley and the Mariposa Big Tree Grove
for the Years 1891–92* (Sacramento: State
Printing Office, 1892), pp.6–7.

9. John Muir, et al., "A Plan to Save the
Forests: Forest Preservation by Military
Control," *Century Magazine* 49 (Febru-
ary 1895): 630–31.

10. Wood in Acting Superintendent, *Yosemite Annual Report* (1891), p.666; ibid.
(September 1, 1892), 52d Cong., 2d
sess., 1892, H. Ex. Doc.1, vol.3, p.666;
and ibid (1893), p.651. Gale in ibid.
(June 30, 1894), 53d Cong., 3d sess.,
1894, H. Ex. Doc.1, pt.5, vol.3, p.676.

11. Wood in ibid. (1893), p.649; Gale in
ibid. (1894), p.675.

12. Ibid., pp.675–76.

13. Rodgers in ibid. (August 22, 1895),
54th Cong., 1st sess., 1895, H. Ex.
Doc.5, vol.3, pp.843–46. Young in
ibid. (August 15, 1896), 54th Cong.,
2d sess., 1896, H. Ex. Doc.5, vol.3,
pp.736–37.

14. Ibid. (August 26, 1897), 55th Cong., 2d sess., 1897, H. Ex. Doc.5, p.808.

15. Ibid. (June 30, 1898), 55th Cong., 3d sess., 1898, H. Doc.5, pp.1056–57.

16. U.S. Department of the Interior, National Park Service, Yosemite National Park, "History of Fish Management in Yosemite," uncatalogued and undated separate, Yosemite National Park Research Library.

17. Acting Superintendent, *Yosemite Annual Report* (1893), p.652.

18. For the popularity of fishing, see, for example, Leo K. Wilson, "Yosemite Fishing," *Yosemite Nature Notes* 5 (July 31, 1926): 52–53.

19. Acting Superintendent, *Yosemite Annual Report* (1893), p.652.

20. Ibid. (1896), pp.737–39.

21. Ibid. (October 10, 1905), 59th Cong., 1st sess., 1905, H. Doc.5, p.698.

CHAPTER SIX

1. Holway R. Jones, *John Muir and the Sierra Club: The Battle for Yosemite* (San Francisco: Sierra Club, 1965), pp.48–49.

2. U.S. Department of the Interior, *Report of the Acting Superintendent of the Yosemite National Park* (August 31, 1891), 52d Cong., 1st sess., 1892, H. Ex. Doc.1, vol.3, pp.664–65. Hereafter cited as Acting Superintendent, *Yosemite Annual Report* (date). U.S. Congress, House, Committee on the Public Lands, *Yosemite National Park,* H. Rept. 1485 to accompany H.R. 7872, 53d Cong., 3d sess., December 10, 1894, p.1.

3. Acting Superintendent, *Yosemite Annual Report* (1891), p.666.

4. U.S. Department of the Interior, *Annual Report of the Secretary of the Interior for the Year 1890* (Washington, D.C.: Government Printing Office, 1890), pp.123–26.

5. As quoted in Jones, *John Muir and the Sierra Club,* p.44.

6. Acting Superintendent, *Yosemite Annual Report* (September 1, 1892), 52d Cong., 2d sess., 1892, H. Ex. Doc.1, vol.3, p.666; ibid. (June 30, 1893), 53d Cong., 2d sess., 1893, H. Ex. Doc.1, pt.5, vol.3, p.651.

7. Ibid. (June 30, 1894), 53d Congress, 3d sess., 1894, H. Ex. Doc.1, pt.5, vol.3, p.675.

8. Ibid. (August 15, 1896), 54th Cong., 2d sess., 1896, H. Ex. Doc.5, vol.3, p.736.

9. Ibid., pp.742–43.

10. Ibid. (October 28, 1899), 56th Cong., 1st sess., 1899, H. Ex. Doc.5, pt.1, pp.502–3.

11. Ibid. (October 8, 1903), 58th Cong., 2d sess., 1903, H. Ex. Doc.5, pt.1, pp.520–21.

12. Ibid. (June 30, 1904), 58th Cong., 3d sess., 1904, H. Doc.5, pt.1, p.390.

13. U.S. Congress, Senate, *Report of the Yosemite Park Commission,* 58th Cong., 3d sess., December 13, 1904, S. Doc.34, pp.1–2.

14. Ibid., pp.3–4.

15. Hiram Martin Chittenden, *The Yellowstone National Park* (Cincinnati: Robert Clarke Company, 1895); *Report of the Yosemite Park Commission,* pp.4–5.

16. Yosemite Park Commission, *Report of the Yosemite Park Commission,* pp.5–6.

17. Ibid., p.1.

18. Ibid., pp.6, 9.

19. Ibid., pp.8–9.

20. Ibid., p.7.

21. Ibid.

22. Ibid., p.8.

23. Ibid.

24. Ibid., p.1; *United States Statutes at Large,* 33 (1905): 702–3. Discussion of the legislation in Congress was brief and uneventful. See *Congressional Record,* 58th Cong., 3d sess. (December 19, 1904), pp.406–7; ibid. (January

14, 1905), p.889; and ibid. (January 26, 1905), p.1384.

25. *United States Statutes at Large,* 31 (1901): 790–91.

26. *Report of the Yosemite Park Commission,* p.51.

27. Ibid.

28. Ibid.

29. Ibid., p.5.

30. Chittenden to Johnson, November 16, 1908, Box 1, Robert Underwood Johnson Papers, Bancroft Library, University of California, Berkeley. Significant correspondence between members of the Yosemite Park Commission, as well as letters written to the commissioners, may also be found in the Robert Bradford Marshall Papers, also in the Bancroft Library. See especially the Hiram Martin Chittenden and William E. Colby files, both in Box 3.

31. Acting Superintendent, *Yosemite Annual Report* (September 30, 1906), 59th Cong., 2d sess., 1906, H. Doc.5, p.653.

32. *Congressional Record,* 59th Cong., 1st sess. (June 9, 1906), p.8146; ibid. (June 19, 1906), p.8740; Acting Superintendent, *Yosemite Annual Report* (September 30, 1908), in U.S. Department of the Interior, *Reports . . . for the Fiscal Year Ended June 30, 1908,* vol.1 (Washington, D.C.: Government Printing Office, 1908), pp.423–24.

33. The standard account of Forest Service policies in relation to preservation is Samuel P. Hays, *Conservation and the Gospel of Efficiency: The Progressive Conservation Movement, 1890–1920* (Cambridge: Harvard University Press, 1959). On establishment of the Forest Service, see pp.39–44.

34. U.S. Department of the Interior, *Report of the Secretary of the Interior for the Fiscal Year Ending June 30, 1903* (Washington, D.C.: Government Printing Office, 1903), p.156. Historical litera-

ture on the Hetch Hetchy debate is both detailed and voluminous. Two important summaries are Roderick Nash, *Wilderness and the American Mind,* 3d ed. (New Haven: Yale University Press, 1982), chap. 10; and Elmo R. Richardson, "The Struggle for the Valley: California's Hetch Hetchy Controversy, 1905–1913," *California Historical Society Quarterly* 38 (September 1959): 249–58. See also Jones, *John Muir and the Sierra Club,* pp.82–169.

35. *Congressional Record,* 63d Cong., 1st sess. (September 3, 1913), p.4151; ibid., 2d sess. (December 6, 1913), pp.385–86; Nash, *Wilderness and the American Mind,* pp.179–80.

36. *Report of the Yosemite Park Commission,* p.9. On the scheme to maintain Yosemite's waterfalls by placing dams above the valley rim, see also Allen Kelley, "Restoration of Yosemite Waterfalls," *Harper's Weekly* 36 (July 16, 1892): 678.

CHAPTER SEVEN

1. The standard account of the recession campaign is Holway R. Jones, *John Muir and the Sierra Club: The Battle for Yosemite* (San Francisco: Sierra Club, 1965), pp.54–81. Richard J. Orsi adds significantly to Jones's interpretation in "'Wilderness Saint' and 'Robber Baron': The Anomalous Partnership of John Muir and the Southern Pacific Company for Preservation of Yosemite National Park," *Pacific Historian* 29 (Summer/Fall 1985): 148–52.

2. "Sierra Club Statement Concerning the Proposed Recession of Yosemite Valley and Mariposa Big Tree Grove . . . to the United States," by John Muir, et al., in *Congressional Record,* 59th Cong., 1st sess. (June 9, 1906), pp.8146–47.

3. Ibid., p.8147.

4. Appendix B, in *Congressional Record,*

59th Cong., 1st sess. (June 9, 1906), pp.8147–48. Perhaps the strongest opponent was John Curtin, the California state senator who had long disputed the right of federal authorities to deny him grazing privileges inside Yosemite National Park. Curtin was also retained as an attorney by the valley concessionaires. See Orsi, "'Wilderness Saint' and 'Robber Baron,'" p.149; and Jones, *John Muir and the Sierra Club,* pp.48–49, 54–81, passim.

5. Orsi, "'Wilderness Saint' and 'Robber Baron,'" p.151.

6. Ibid., pp.151–52; *Congressional Record,* 59th Cong., 1st sess. (June 19, 1906), p.8740.

7. "Sierra Club Statement," *Congressional Record* (June 9, 1906), p.8147.

8. U.S. Department of the Interior, *Report of the Acting Superintendent of Yosemite National Park* (September 30, 1906), 59th Cong., 2d sess., H. Doc.5, pp.653–54.

9. Ibid.

10. See Paul Schullery, *The Bears of Yellowstone* (Yellowstone National Park: Yellowstone Library and Museum Association, 1980).

11. Sovulewski to William Colby, January 28, 1936, File 921.2 S, Biography—Gabriel Sovulewski, Yosemite National Park Research Library.

12. Souvulewski to Forsyth, November 11, 1910, File 12–13–27, Superintendent's Monthly Reports, Central Files, 1907–39, Records of the National Park Service, Record Group 79, National Archives, Washington, D.C. (hereafter cited as R.G. 79).

13. Erwin to Forsyth, September 10, 1910, same File 12–13–27, R.G. 79.

14. Ibid.

15. Forsyth to Secretary of the Interior, November 4, 1910, File 12–13–27, R.G. 79.

16. Forsyth to Secretary of the Interior, November 11, 1912, File 12–13–38, pt.1, Wild Animals, Central Files, R.G. 79.

17. Robinson to Noble, February 4, 1891, Letters Received, 1872–1907, Yosemite Park, R.G. 79.

18. Ibid.

19. State of California, *Biennial Report of the Commissioners to Manage Yosemite Valley and the Mariposa Big Tree Grove for the Years 1891–92* (Sacramento: State Printing Office, 1892), p.10. The commission, of course, did not mean *controlled* fires. The standard history of efforts to confine the Merced River to a permanent channel is James F. Milestone, "The Influence of Modern Man on the Stream System of Yosemite Valley" (master's thesis, San Francisco State University, 1978).

20. Linda Wedel Greene, *Historic Resource Study: Yosemite,* 3 vols. (Washington, D.C.: U.S. Department of the Interior, National Park Service, 1987), 1:351; Carl P. Russell, *One Hundred Years in Yosemite: The Story of a Great Park and Its Friends* (Yosemite: Yosemite Natural History Association, 1957), pp.111–12.

21. Laurence V. Degnan to Douglas H. Hubbard, January 24, 1959, File Y-22, Firefall Collection, Yosemite National Park Research Library.

22. E. P. Leavitt to Agnes L. Scott, September 20, 1928, File Y-22, Yosemite National Park Research Library.

23. Benson to Secretary of the Interior, July 11, 1907, File 12–13–6, pt.1, Yosemite National Park, Privileges, David A. Curry, Central Files, R.G. 79.

24. Leighton to Director, U.S. Geological Survey, August 22, 1907, File 12–13–6, pt.1, R.G. 79.

25. An original study of contamination was Donald B. Tresidder, "The National

Parks: A Public Health Problem: (thesis, School of Medicine, Stanford University, 1927).

26. Curry to James R. Garfield, August 24, 1907, File 12–13–6, pt.1, R.G. 79.

27. As quoted in William W. Forsyth to J. C. Needham, April 23, 1910, File 12–13–6, pt.3, R.G. 79.

28. Regarding Curry's political astuteness, see File 12–13–6, R.G. 79, inclusive. Many of these same letters and documents may also be found in the Yosemite National Park Research Library under Concessions (Accommodations and Transportation), 1896–1910, File Drawer 8.

29. Curry to W. W. Forsyth, September 21, 1911, File 12–13–6, pt.3, R.G. 79.

30. Ibid.

31. Curry to Raker, February 4, 1913, File 12–13–6, pt.3, R.G. 79; printed circular, David A. Curry to Dear Sir:, April 10, 1914, File 12–13–6, pt.5, R.G. 79.

32. Circular, Curry, April 10, 1914, R.G. 79. See also "Memorandum Upon the Points Touched On in Circular of David A. Curry" (undated), File 12–13–6, pt.5, R.G. 79. The memorandum appears to have been written by Adolph C. Miller, assistant secretary of the interior.

33. See Horace M. Albright as told to Robert Cahn, *The Birth of the National Park Service: The Founding Years, 1913–1933* (Salt Lake City and Chicago: Howe Brothers, 1985), pp.8–9.

34. Circular, Curry, April 10, 1914, R.G. 79.

35. Robert Bradford Marshall, a member of the 1904 Yosemite Park Commission, was a most outspoken advocate for a civilian ranger force. "The soldier . . . has no interest whatever in the park. He simply takes it as a sort of outing and while I hate to say it, I am firmly of the belief that a bottle of whiskey can buy the privilege of killing a buck or carry-ing a gun anywhere within the park. This does not mean the officer—but the troopers." Marshall to Frank Bond, October 25, 1905, pt.1, File 1905, Box 1, Robert Bradford Marshall Papers, Bancroft Library, University of California, Berkeley.

CHAPTER EIGHT

1. A detailed overview of the concept is U.S. Department of the Interior, National Park Service, *Research and Education in the National Parks,* by Harold C. Bryant and Wallace W. Atwood, Jr. (Washington, D.C.: Government Printing Office, 1932).

2. The pros and cons of admitting automobiles into Yosemite Valley are forcefully discussed in U.S. Department of the Interior, *Proceedings of the National Park Conference held at the Yosemite National Park, October 14–16, 1912* (Washington, D.C.: Government Printing Office, 1913), pp.58–92, 109–44. A recent interpretation is Richard Lillard, "The Siege and Conquest of a National Park," *American West* 5 (January 1968): 28–31, 67–71.

3. See again, for example, *Proceedings of the National Park Conference* (1912), pp.46–47, 57–58.

4. Alfred Runte, *National Parks: The American Experience,* 2d ed. (Lincoln: University of Nebraska Press, 1987), chap. 5.

5. Curry to Lane, February 6, 1915, File 12–13–6, pt.6, Yosemite National Park, Privileges, David A. Curry, Central Files, 1907–39, Records of the National Park Service, Record Group 79, National Archives, Washington, D.C. (hereafter cited as R.G. 79).

6. Stephen T. Mather to Franklin K. Lane, November 20, 1915, File 12–13, pt.8, R.G. 79.

7. Curry to Lane, September 29, 1916, File 12–13, pt.8, R.G. 79.

8. Ibid.

9. Curry to Lane, September 29, 1916 (2d letter this date), and October 2, 1916, File 12–13, pt.8, R.G. 79.

10. U.S. Department of the Interior, *Proceedings of the National Parks Conference Held . . . in Washington, D.C., January 2–6, 1917* (Washington, D.C.: Government Printing Office, 1917), p.251.

11. E. Raymond Hall, "Joseph Grinnell (1877 to 1939)," *Journal of Mammalogy* 20 (November 14, 1939): 409; William E. Ritter, "Joseph Grinnell," *Science* 90 (July 28, 1939): 75–76.

12. William T. Hornaday to Grinnell, August 15, 1912, Hornaday File, Records of the Museum of Vertebrate Zoology, University of California, Berkeley (hereafter cited as MVZ). Grinnell replied, "The mountainous areas where the condor is making its last stand seem to me likely to remain adapted to the bird's existence for many years, fifty years if not longer." Grinnell to Hornaday, August 24, 1912, Hornaday file, MVZ.

13. Grinnell to Lane, October 7, 1914, and attached Prospectus, "Natural History Survey of Yosemite National Park," File 12–13, pt.1, Yosemite National Park, Privileges, Joseph Grinnell, R.G. 79.

14. Ibid.

15. Ibid.

16. Grinnell to Lane, November 14, 1914, Lane File, MVZ.

17. Grinnell to Sovulewski, November 11, 1914, Sovulewski File, MVZ; Lane to Grinnell, November 25, 1914, and Grinnell to Lane, December 14, 1914, Lane File, MVZ.

18. Grinnell to Mather, May 17, 1915, and Mather to Grinnell, May 31, 1915, Mather File, MVZ. Grinnell thanked Mather for his "unsought contribution" and promised to apply the money "eco-nomically and explicitly toward the purpose for which you intended it." Grinnell to Mather, May 10, 1915, Mather File, MVZ.

19. Grinnell to Mather, January 13, 1916, Mather File, MVZ.

20. Ibid.

21. Joseph Grinnell and Tracy Storer, "Animal Life as an Asset of National Parks," *Science* 44 (September 15, 1916): 375, 377.

22. Ibid., p.377.

23. Ibid., pp.378–79.

24. Ibid., p.378.

25. Ibid.

26. Ibid., p.379.

27. Ibid.

28. See, for example, Horace M. Albright as told to Robert Cahn, *The Birth of the National Park Service: The Founding Years, 1913–1933* (Salt Lake City and Chicago: Howe Brothers, 1985), pp.121–22. Joseph Grinnell is not even mentioned. A similar oversight is made in Robert Shankland, *Steve Mather of the National Parks,* 3d ed. (New York: Alfred A. Knopf, 1970), pp.258–59. Mather again gets the credit. According to E. Raymond Hall, Grinnell's innate modesty precluded him from seeking such recognition. "He liked to inspire the beginning of a movement, then sit back and watch it grow, fully content with, and even desirous of, anonymity for himself." Hall, "Joseph Grinnell," p.413.

29. A brief history of university field courses is given in Bryant and Atwood, Jr., *Research and Education in the National Parks,* p.45. See also *Proceedings of the National Parks Conference* (1917), pp.93–96.

30. Mather to Grinnell, October 3, 1916, Mather File, MVZ; Goethe to Grinnell, January 27, 1909, and Goethe to Grinnell, October 12, 1916, Goethe File, MVZ.

31. Goethe to Grinnell, October 12, 1916, Goethe File, MVZ.

32. Bryant to Grinnell, June 18, 1917, and Grinnell to Bryant, June 19, 1917, Bryant File, MVZ.

33. Grinnell to Mather, September 1, 1917, Mather File, MVZ.

34. Grinnell to Albright, September 6, 1918, Albright File, MVZ.

35. Grinnell to Mills, March 27, 1919, Mills File, MVZ.

36. Grinnell to Mather, June 6, 1919, Mather File, MVZ.

37. Ibid.

38. Mather to Grinnell, June 14, 1919, Mather File, MVZ.

39. Bryant to Grinnell, July 19, 1919, and Grinnell to Bryant, July 29, 1919, Bryant File, MVZ.

40. Bryant to Grinnell, June 9, 1920, Bryant File, MVZ.

41. Actually, the suggestion that the Yosemite natural history be published by the Park Service originally came from Mather. "I wish a publication of this kind," he wrote Grinnell, "or at least one edition of it could be published through the National Park Service." Mather to Grinnell, February 24, 1919, Mather File, MVZ. But Mather soon changed his mind, pleading insufficient funds for printing. Mather to Grinnell, February 10, 1921, Mather File, MVZ. The University of California Press's offer is revealed in Grinnell to Storer, February 21, 1924, Storer File, MVZ.

42. Grinnell to Mather, April 26, 1924, Mather File, MVZ.

43. See again Hall, "Joseph Grinnell," pp.413, 417.

CHAPTER NINE

1. Grinnell to W. B. Lewis, July 8, 1920, Lewis File, Records of the Museum of Vertebrate Zoology, University of California, Berkeley (hereafter cited as MVZ).

2. See U.S. Department of the Interior, National Park Service, Yosemite National Park, "Superintendent's Monthly Report(s)" (hereafter cited as Monthly Report).

3. Contemporary observations include "The Only Way to Yosemite Valley—Nature's Wonderland," *Merced Evening Sun,* June 1, 1907; "The Travel is Increasing," ibid., June 10, 1907. The completion of the Yosemite Valley Railroad led to a deluge of similar articles throughout California. See also, for example, "To Yosemite By Railroad," *Pasadena News,* June 6, 1907; and "New Scenic Railroad Into Yosemite Carries Thousands to Wonderland," *Oakland Tribune,* July 21, 1907. Magazine articles included Edward H. Hamilton, "The New Yosemite Railroad," *Cosmopolitan* 43 (September 1907): 569–75; and Lanier Bartlett, "By Rail to the Yosemite," *Pacific Monthly* 17 (June 1907): 730–38.

4. "Yosemite Visitors, October 1, 1916 to September 30, 1917," Yosemite National Park, Travel, pt.1, Box 727, Central Files, 1907–39, Records of the National Park Service, Record Group 79, National Archives, Washington, D.C. (hereafter cited as R.G. 79).

5. Monthly Report, September 1926 through September 1927. Rail travel over the period declined on an annual average of 29 percent.

6. Monthly Report, September 1927.

7. Grinnell to Stephen T. Mather, October 26, 1915, and Mather to Grinnell, October 26, 1915, Mather File, MVZ. The incident may also be followed in the Gabriel Sovulewski, Enos Mills, and George V. Bell files.

8. Yard to Grinnell, May 18, 1915, Yard File, MVZ.

9. Ibid.; Grinnell to Yard, July 17, 1915, Yard File, MVZ.

10. Yard to Grinnell, July 21, 1915, Yard File, MVZ.

11. Joseph Grinnell and Tracy Storer, "Animal Life as an Asset of National Parks," *Science* 44 (September 15, 1916): 379.

12. Grinnell to Townsley, January 4, 1915, Townsley File, MVZ.

13. Townsley to Grinnell, January 28, 1915, and Grinnell to Townsley, February 3, 1915, Townsley File, MVZ.

14. Townsley to Grinnell, February 19, 1915; Townsley to Grinnell, March 3, 1915; Grinnell to Townsley, March 4, 1915; all Townsley File, MVZ.

15. Townsley to Grinnell, October 22, 1916, Townsley File, MVZ.

16. Grinnell to Lewis, July 8, 1920; Lewis to Grinnell, July 21, 1920; Grinnell to Lewis, July 28, 1920; all Lewis File, MVZ.

17. Grinnell to Lewis, July 28, 1920, Lewis File, MVZ.

18. Grinnell to Lewis, August 12, 1920, Lewis File, MVZ.

19. Lewis to Grinnell, September 11, 1920, Lewis File, MVZ.

20. Grinnell to Lewis, September 14, 1920, Lewis File, MVZ.

21. Ibid.

22. U.S. Department of the Interior, *Annual Report of the Director of the National Park Service,* October 14, 1920 (Washington, D.C.: Government Printing Office, 1920), p.66.

23. Grinnell to Robert Sterling Yard, May 2, 1919, Yard File, MVZ.

24. "Open Letter," Grinnell to E. P. Leavitt, Acting Superintendent, Yosemite National Park, October 4, 1927, File 710, pt.1, Yosemite Fauna, General, Central Classified Files, 1907–49, R.G. 79. Grinnell published his letter as "Recommendations Concerning the Treatment of Large Mammals in Yo-semite National Park," *Journal of Mammalogy* 9 (February 1928): 76. On Grinnell's preference for California subjects, see E. Raymond Hall, "Joseph Grinnell (1877 to 1939)," *Journal of Mammalogy* 20 (November 14, 1939): 411–12.

25. Grinnell to Charles W. Michael, December 4, 1922, and Grinnell to Michael, March 10, 1923, Michael File, MVZ. The epidemic is discussed in Ernest A. Payne, "The Return of the California Gray Squirrel," *Yosemite Nature Notes* 19 (January 1940): 1–3.

26. Grinnell to Lewis, May 12, 1925, Lewis File, MVZ.

27. Grinnell to Lewis, November 25, 1925, Lewis File, MVZ.

28. Grinnell to Russell, November 25, 1925, Russell File, MVZ, and Grinnell to Mather, November 25, 1925, Mather File, MVZ.

29. Leavitt to The Director, National Park Service, November 14, 1927, File 710, pt.1, R.G. 79.

30. McAllister to Mather, December 30, 1918, File 12–13, pt.2, Yosemite National Park, Wild Animals, General, Central Files 1907–39, R.G. 79.

31. Lewis to Director, April 28, 1919, File 12–13, pt.2, R.G. 79.

32. Lewis to Director, May 22, 1919, and Palmer to H. M. Albright, June 6, 1919, File 12–13, pt.2, R.G. 79.

33. Palmer to Albright, June 6, 1919, File 12–13, pt.2, R.G. 79.

34. Ibid.

35. U.S. Department of the Interior, National Park Service, "Preliminary Report . . . on the Elk Situation in Yosemite National Park," July 5, 1928, by Ansel F. Hall, copy in Hall File, MVZ.

36. Grinnell to Thomson, November 8, 1933, Thomson File, and Grinnell to Cammerer, November 9, 1933, Cammerer File, MVZ. Twenty-seven animals

in all were moved. A contemporary account is A. E. Borell, "Yosemite Elk Herd Moved to Owens Valley," *Yosemite Nature Notes* 12 (December 1933): 107–9.

37. Grinnell to White, December 12, 1927, White File, MVZ.

38. Copy in File 979–447, Y–34, Wildlife and Research Reserves, Yosemite National Park Research Library, and in Grinnell Files, MVZ.

39. Monthly Report, November 1932.

CHAPTER TEN

1. The issue of bears comes up repeatedly in U.S. Department of the Interior, National Park Service, Yosemite National Park, "Superintendent's Monthly Report(s)" (hereafter cited as Monthly Report). The annual reports of the superintendents, both military and civilian, are also instructive. This chapter also relies heavily on materials contained in File 12–13, Yosemite National Park, Wild Animals, General, Central Files, 1907–39, and File 715–02, Yosemite National Park, Bears, Central Classified Files, 1907–49, Records of the National Park Service, Record Group 79, National Archives, Washington, D.C. (hereafter cited as R.G. 79).

2. Frank G. Baker to Mather, May 24, 1924, File 12–13, pt.2, R.G. 79.

3. Mather to Lewis, May 31, 1924, File 12–13, pt.2, R.G. 79.

4. W. H. Perdriau to Stephen Mather, May 31, 1924, File 12–13, pt.2, R.G. 79.

5. Lewis to Mather, June 10, 1924, File 12–13, pt.2, R.G. 79.

6. Ibid.

7. Ibid.

8. Ibid.

9. Ibid.

10. Ibid.

11. Russell to Grinnell, October 7, 1927, Russell File, Records of the Museum of Vertebrate Zoology, University of California, Berkeley (hereafter cited as MVZ). Biographical information on Russell may be found in File 921.2, Biography, Yosemite National Park Research Library, and at the Washington State University Library in Pullman, repository of the Russell Papers, 1920–67.

12. Russell to Grinnell, October 7, 1927, Russell File, MVZ.

13. Ibid.

14. Grinnell to Russell, October 11, 1927, Russell File, MVZ. The "Open Letter" referred to is cited in chapter 9, note 24.

15. Russell to Grinnell, October 7, 1927, Russell File, MVZ.

16. Thomson to Grinnell, July 3, 1929, Thomson File, MVZ.

17. Ibid. Additional examples of Thomson's terminology may be found in the Monthly Report.

18. Michael to Grinnell, July 23, 1927, and Michael to Grinnell, August 17, 1928, Michael File, MVZ.

19. Lewis to The Director, National Park Service, December 19, 1923, Yosemite Miscellaneous, Central Files, R.G. 79.

20. Ibid.

21. The bitterness of the rivalry is extensively documented in File 12–13, Yosemite National Park, Privileges, Central Files, R.G. 79. See in particular the David A. Curry and D. J. Desmond Files.

22. Linda Wedel Greene, *Historic Resource Study: Yosemite,* 3 vols. (Washington, D.C.: U.S. Department of the Interior, National Park Service, 1987), 2:658. The events and concerns leading to the merger are exhaustively discussed in U.S. Department of the Interior, National Park Service, "Report on Fran-

chise Situation—Yosemite National Park," March 27, 1923, by Horace M. Albright and W. B. Lewis, and "Supplemental Report on Franchise Situation—Yosemite National Park," December 1, 1923, by W. B. Lewis, both in File 979.447, Y–16, Yosemite—Concessions, Yosemite National Park Research Library.

23. Monthly Report, July 1927.

24. Tresidder to E. P. Leavitt, September 30, 1927, File 715–02, pt.1, R.G. 79.

25. Ibid.

26. Ibid.

27. Russell to Grinnell, October 7, 1927, Russell File, MVZ; Leavitt to The Director, National Park Service, October 8, 1927, File 715–02, pt.1, R.G. 79.

28. G. H. Billings to W. B. Lewis, September 17, 1927, File 715–02, pt.1, R.G. 79.

29. Russell to Grinnell, October 7, 1927, Russell File, MVZ.

30. See Carl P. Russell, *One Hundred Years in Yosemite: The Story of a Great Park and Its Friends* (Yosemite: Yosemite Natural History Association, 1957). The book was first published in 1931 by the University of California Press.

31. A summary of Bryant's career is Ann and Myron Sutton, "The Man from Yosemite," *National Parks Magazine* 28 (July–September 1954): 102–5, 131–32.

32. Monthly Report, November 1927.

33. Monthly Report, April 1929.

34. Monthly Reports, June and July, 1929.

35. Monthly Report, October 1929.

36. Monthly Reports, August 1932, August 1933, November 1935, June 1936, August 1937. In 1938 the quota was increased to twenty animals; in 1939 twenty-five bears were killed; in 1940 fourteen out of an authorized twenty-five; and in 1941 twenty-four out of another authorization of twenty-five animals. My statistics are compiled

from letters contained in File 715–02, pt.1, R.G. 79.

37. Bryant to Grinnell, June 30, 1925; Bryant to Grinnell, July 14, 1925; Bryant to Grinnell, June 30, 1926; all Bryant File, MVZ. Grinnell frequently served as a reference for field-school students. See, for example, C. A. Harwell to Grinnell, March 27, 1933, Harwell File, MVZ.

38. Joseph Grinnell also took an active role in the Yosemite Natural History Association, serving on its original board of trustees. See H. C. Bryant and Carl P. Russell files, MVZ.

39. Construction activity is best followed in the Monthly Report. See also Greene, *Yosemite,* vol.2.

40. Tresidder to Lewis, April 26, 1927; and Tresidder to E. P. Leavitt, November 12, 1927, File 900–01, Drawer 12, Yosemite Park and Curry Company, Buildings, Yosemite National Park Research Library.

41. Monthly Report, January 1930; for efforts to obtain the Olympics, see Monthly Report, February 1929.

42. Monthly Reports, January 1931, December 1935, January 1936.

43. Merriam to Mather, October 25, 1927, File 201–11, Box 10, Yosemite Advisory Board, Yosemite National Park Research Library.

44. Ibid.; also Mather to Horace M. Albright, December 31, 1927, File 201–11, Yosemite National Park Research Library.

45. I have prepared a brief biographical sketch of Frederick Law Olmsted, Jr., in Richard C. Davis, ed., *Encyclopedia of American Forest and Conservation History,* 2 vols. (New York: Macmillan Co., 1983), 2:507–10.

46. Olmsted to Mather, August 16, 1928, File 201–11, Yosemite National Park Research Library.

47. Yosemite National Park, Committee of

Expert Advisors, "Comments on the Camp Curry Entrance and Parking Problems and Related Matters," by Frederick Law Olmsted, November 7, 1928, File 201–11, Yosemite National Park Research Library.

48. Ibid.

49. "1928 Fall Meeting of Yosemite Advisory Commission in Yosemite Valley" and "Memorandum of Certain Tentative Conclusions in Regard to Yosemite Valley Suggested by Meeting of October 31 to November 4, 1928," drafted by F. L. Olmsted, both in File 201–11, Yosemite National Park Research Library.

50. Monthly Report, June 1929; "Draft Report: Meeting of the Committee of Expert Advisers . . . April 24 and 25, 1930," File 201–11, Yosemite National Park Research Library.

51. "Draft Report . . . April 24 and 25, 1930," File 201–11, Yosemite National Park Research Library.

52. As quoted in ibid.; Monthly Report, April 1930.

53. Monthly Report, February 1929. The idea, however, was at least a half century old. See, for example, State of California, Legislature, Assembly Committee on Yosemite Valley and Mariposa Big Trees, *In the Matter of the Investigation of the Yosemite Valley Commissioners,* 28th sess., February 1889 (Sacramento: State Printing Office, 1889), p.317, for an early reference to the tramway concept.

54. John P. Buwalda to C. G. Thomson, with enclosure, "Glacier Point Cableway," September 13, 1929, File 201–11, Yosemite National Park Research Library.

55. Ibid.; "Draft Report . . . April 24 and 25, 1930," File 201–11, Yosemite National Park Research Library. Olmsted's authorship of these passages is confirmed by Duncan McDuffie to Col.

Thomson, September 7, 1929, File 201–11, Yosemite National Park Research Library.

56. "Draft Report . . . April 24 and 25, 1930," File 201–11, Yosemite National Park Research Library.

57. Ibid.

CHAPTER ELEVEN

1. Thomas R. Dunlap, *Saving America's Wildlife* (Princeton: Princeton University Press, 1988), pp.79–80; Horace M. Albright, "The National Park Service's Policy on Predatory Mammals," *Journal of Mammalogy* 12 (May 1931): 185–86.

2. Joseph Grinnell and Tracy Storer, "Animal Life as an Asset of National Parks," *Science* 44 (September 15, 1916): 375–79.

3. Ben H. Thompson, "George M. Wright, 1904–1936," *George Wright Forum* (Summer 1981), pp. 1–4; U.S. Department of the Interior, National Park Service, Yosemite National Park, "Superintendent's Monthly Report," November 1927 (other reports hereafter cited as Monthly Report).

4. U.S. Department of the Interior, National Park Service, *Fauna of the National Parks of the United States: A Preliminary Survey,* by George M. Wright, Joseph S. Dixon, and Ben H. Thompson (Washington, D.C.: Government Printing Office, 1933), p.10.

5. Ibid., p.21.

6. Ibid., p.37.

7. U.S. Department of the Interior, National Park Service, *Fauna of the National Parks of the United States: Wildlife Management,* by George M. Wright and Ben H. Thompson (Washington, D.C.: Government Printing Office, 1935), pp.14–15.

8. Forsyth to Esther C. Boardman, August 4, 1911, and David Sherfey to W. W.

Forsyth, with enclosure, June 11, 1912, File 701–01.42, Box Y-35, Mariposa Grove of Big Trees, General Correspondence, Yosemite National Park Research Library.

9. Thomson to The Director, November 11, 1930, File 701–01.42, Yosemite National Park Research Library.

10. Ibid. Albright replied: "Your letter of November 11, about your protection of the Grizzly Giant, pleases me immensely. It is achievements like this that are distinguishing the National Park Service." Albright to Thomson, November 18, 1930, File 701–01.42, Yosemite National Park Research Library.

11. F. L. Cook, Memorandum for the Superintendent, Sequoia National Park, October 30, 1933, File 701–01.42, Yosemite National Park Research Library. Cook was actually chief ranger at Sequoia and was reporting with regard to vista clearing in Yosemite.

12. Ibid.

13. Ibid.

14. Wright to The Director, December 11, 1933, File 701–01.42, Yosemite National Park Research Library.

15. Thomson to The Director, February 20, 1934, File 701–01.42, Yosemite National Park Research Library.

16. Ibid.

17. Grinnell and Storer, "Animal Life as an Asset of National Parks," p.377.

18. The Monthly Reports provide graphic descriptions of all deaths and injuries.

19. C. G. Thomson, Memorandum to the Director, July 13, 1931, copy in C. A. Harwell File, Records of the Museum of Vertebrate Zoology, University of California, Berkeley (hereafter cited as MVZ).

20. Ibid.

21. Grinnell to Michael, August 4, 1931; Michael to Grinnell, September 3, 1931; Grinnell to Michael, September 7, 1931; all Michael File, MVZ. Grinnell's request for information to C. A. Harwell, park naturalist, was equally emphatic. "Please give me the *truth* with respect to the enclosed report of someone 'killed' by a rattlesnake in Yosemite." Harwell replied with Thomson's memorandum to the director, further adding, "We shall make every effort to exterminate the rattlesnake in accordance with the policy set down by Superintendent Thomson regarding this venomous snake." Grinnell to Harwell, July 17, 1931, and Harwell to Grinnell, July 24, 1931, Harwell File, MVZ.

22. In Yosemite, however, Superintendent Thomson remained true to his promise to exterminate rattlesnakes wherever found. See, for example, Monthly Report, August 1935. George Wright advocated a more reasonable policy in *Fauna of the National Parks* (1935), p.17. "The rattlesnake is, of course, a traditional enemy but, nevertheless, a greatly overestimated one. The proper practice is to destroy rattlesnakes when encountered at human concentration points but to permit them to go unmolested elsewhere."

23. James V. Lloyd, "Albright's Efforts Save Yosemite Timber," *Yosemite Nature Notes* 9 (July 1930): 65–66. Statistics regarding the involved acreages vary, in large part because early estimates were later revised. I have used the original estimates.

24. Monthly Report, August 1932.

25. Ibid.

26. Wright, Dixon, and Thompson, *Fauna of the National Parks,* p.24.

27. Ibid.

28. Ibid., pp.24–26. Hopes that Yosemite could be restocked with native bighorn sheep were already decades old, and indeed such proposals permeate park files and secondary literature. An especially thoughtful assessment of the situation is

George V. Bell to Joseph Grinnell, September 8, 1915, Bell File, MVZ. Bell at the time was the superintendent of Yosemite National Park.

29. Wright and Thompson, *Fauna of the National Parks,* pp.6, 12. Road kills of wild animals are also frequently listed in the Monthly Reports.

30. Thompson, "George M. Wright," p.4.

31. Joseph S. Dixon, Memorandum for the Regional Director, August 27, 1940, Yosemite Wildlife, 1938–1942, Yosemite National Park Research Library.

32. CCC activities are extensively documented in the Monthly Reports. See also Linda Wedel Greene, *Historic Resource Study: Yosemite,* 3 vols. (Washington, D.C.: U.S. Department of the Interior, National Park Service, 1987), 2:732–50.

33. The Meinecke Plan is discussed in A. Robert Thompson, "Preliminary Report to the Chief Forester on Vegetative Studies at Yosemite National Park," May 18–26, 1938, File Yosemite National Park Wildlife, 1938–1942, Yosemite National Park Research Library. References to the plan also appear frequently in File 201–11, Yosemite Advisory Board, Yosemite National Park Research Library. For Curry Company proposals, see this file and 900–01, Yosemite Park and Curry Company, Buildings, Yosemite National Park Research Library.

34. His colleague E. Raymond Hall noted, "Grinnell's effectiveness as a conservationist, though well-known to a few persons, was much greater than was generally supposed." Hall, "Joseph Grinnell (1877 to 1939)," *Journal of Mammalogy* 20 (November 14, 1939): 413.

35. Lawrence C. Merriam, Memorandum for the Director, November 16, 1940, File 715–02, pt.1, and O. A. Tomlinson, Memorandum for the Superintendent, Yosemite National Park, November 1, 1943, File 715–02, pt.2, Yosemite National Park, Bears, Central Classified Files, 1907–49 Records of the National Park Service, Record Group 79, National Archives, Washington, D.C. (hereafter cited as R.G. 79).

36. Merriam to The Director, October 8, 1937, File 715–02, R.G. 79.

37. Joseph S. Dixon, "Special Report on Bear Problem, Floor Yosemite Valley, California," October 7, 1937, File 715–02, R.G. 79. Dixon, accordingly, saw no conflict of interest in killing bears that caused injuries or property damage.

38. Wright, Dixon, and Thompson, *Fauna of the National Parks,* p.10.

39. Monthly Report, September 1941. Estimated visitation for the travel year ending September 30, 1941, was 594,062.

40. Dorr G. Yeager, Memorandum for the Regional Director, Region Four, May 31, 1943, File 718, Yosemite National Park, Ecology, R.G. 79. The Ernst report, previously cited, may be found in File 880–01, Yosemite National Park Research Library.

41. Thomas C. Vint, Memorandum for the Director, September 1, 1943, and G. D. Coffman, Memorandum for the Director, February 5, 1944, File 718, R.G. 79.

42. Frank A. Kittredge, Memorandum for the Regional Director, Region Four, with enclosure, April 28, 1945, File 718, R.G. 79.

43. Monthly Report, September 1944.

44. Monthly Report, July 1935. Mosquito abatement procedures using crude oil are described in Monthly Report, May 1930.

45. Monthly Reports, June 1949, August 1949.

46. See, for example, David R. Brower,

"The Case Against the Latest Proposal to Control Needle Miners in Yosemite Lodgepoles," June 22, 1959, Wayburn Files, Records of the Sierra Club, Bancroft Library, University of California, Berkeley.

47. Ibid.

48. Ibid.

49. Monthly Reports, August 1959, July 1961, May 1963, July 1963.

50. Rachel Carson, *Silent Spring* (New York: Fawcett Crest, 1964).

51. Leopold Files, MVZ.

52. U.S. Department of the Interior, Advisory Board on Wildlife Management, *Wildlife Management in the National Parks,* by A. S. Leopold, et al., Report to the Secretary, March 4, 1963, p.4.

53. Grinnell and Storer, "Animal Life as an Asset of National Parks," p.377; Wright, Dixon, and Thompson, *Fauna of the National Parks,* p.1; Leopold, et al., *Wildlife Management,* p.5.

54. Leopold et al., *Wildlife Management,* pp.12–14.

55. Ibid., pp.14–15.

CHAPTER TWELVE

1. Garrett Hardin, "The Tragedy of the Commons," in Hardin and John Baden, eds., *Managing the Commons* (San Francisco: W. H. Freeman and Company, 1977), pp.16–30.

2. Garrett Hardin, "The Economics of Wilderness," *Natural History* 78 (June–July 1969): 20–27.

3. An outspoken rebuttal to Hardin is Eric Julber, "Let's Open Up Our Wilderness Areas," *Reader's Digest* 100 (May 1972): 126.

4. Notes Linda Wedel Greene, for example, "The first permanent hotel structure in the valley, begun in 1856, . . . functioned more as a saloon until crushed by snow during the winter of 1857–58." Greene, *Historic Resource*

Study: Yosemite, 3 vols. (Washington, D.C.: U.S. Department of the Interior, National Park Service, 1987), 1:44.

5. Mark Daniels to The Secretary of the Interior, September 1, 1915, File 12–13, pt.1, Yosemite National Park, Privileges, D. J. Desmond, Central Files, 1907–39, Records of the National Park Service, Record Group 79, National Archives, Washington, D.C. (hereafter cited as R.G. 79).

6. Don Tresidder, Memorandum, "Sale of Alcoholic Beverages," June 20, 1934, File 979–447, Yosemite—Concessions, Yosemite National Park Research Library. The memorandum also appears in its entirety as an addendum to U.S. Department of the Interior, National Park Service, Yosemite National Park, "Superintendent's Monthly Report," June 1934 (other reports hereafter cited as Monthly Report).

7. Yosemite National Park Research Library to Author, June 1988.

8. Tresidder, Memorandum, June 20, 1934, File 979–447, Yosemite National Park Research Library.

9. Ibid.

10. C. G. Thomson, Memorandum for the Files, July 13, 1935, File 900–01, Drawer 12, Yosemite Park and Curry Company, Buildings, Yosemite National Park Research Library; Tresidder, June 20, 1934, File 979–447, Yosemite National Park Research Library.

11. Thomson, Memorandum, July 13, 1935, File 900–01, Yosemite National Park Research Library.

12. Monthly Report, December 1954; U.S. Department of the Interior, National Park Service, Yosemite National Park, "3 Million People Visited Yosemite National Park Last Year," News Release, January 7, 1988, Yosemite National Park Research Library.

13. Adams to Brower, January 6, 1957, H. C. Bradley Files, Records of the Si-

erra Club, Bancroft Library, University of California, Berkeley (hereafter cited as Sierra Club Papers).

14. Adams to Colby, September 15, 1952, Sierra Club Office Files, and Adams to Brower, January 6, 1957, Bradley Files, Sierra Club Papers.

15. Adams to Brower, January 6, 1957, Bradley Files, Sierra Club Papers.

16. Ibid.

17. Ibid.; Ansel Adams with Mary Street Alinder, *Ansel Adams: An Autobiography* (Boston: Little, Brown and Co. and New York Graphic Society Books, 1985), pp.182–83.

18. Adams to Brower, January 6, 1957, Bradley Files, Sierra Club Papers; Adams, *Autobiography,* pp.184–85.

19. Adams to Brower, January 6, 1957, Bradley Files, Sierra Club Papers.

20. Hardin, *Managing the Commons,* pp.26–28.

21. Drury to Duncan McDuffie, August 7, 1945, File 201–11, Box 10, Yosemite Advisory Board, Yosemite National Park Research Library.

22. Drury to Duncan McDuffie, June 12, 1946, File 201–11, Yosemite National Park Research Library.

23. Kittredge, Memorandum re: Development in Yosemite Valley, June 25, 1947, File 600, Box 78-A, Yosemite Development, Yosemite National Park Research Library.

24. Ibid.

25. Ibid.

26. Drury to McDuffie, June 12, 1946, File 201–11, Yosemite National Park Research Library; Oehlmann to Charles G. Woodbury, October 20, 1947, Sierra Club Office Files, Sierra Club Papers.

27. Oehlmann to Charles G. Woodbury, January 19, 1948, Sierra Club Office Files, Sierra Club Papers.

28. Ibid.

29. Ibid.

30. Oehlmann to Preston, September 8, 1955, File N16, Yosemite Wildlife Management, 1954–56, Yosemite National Park Research Library.

31. Oehlmann to Kuchel, January 7, 1957, File 3823, Yosemite Park and Curry Company, General Correspondence, 1957–59, Yosemite National Park Research Library. In keeping with general practice, Oehlmann sent copies of the letter to both Park Service Director Conrad L. Wirth and Yosemite Superintendent John C. Preston.

32. Adams, Notes on Mission 66, March 17, 1956, Sierra Club Office Files, Sierra Club Papers.

33. William E. Colby to Horace M. Albright, July 31, 1933, Sierra Club Office Files, Sierra Club Papers; Editorial, "Yosemite's Tioga Highway," *National Parks Magazine* 32 (July–September 1958): 123–24; Ansel Adams, "Yosemite—1958: Compromise in Action," *National Parks Magazine* 32 (October–December 1958): 166–75, 190; Greene, *Yosemite,* 2:762–63.

34. Gripper to Preston, January 19, 1954, File D30, pt.1, Yosemite, Tioga Road, Yosemite National Park Research Library.

35. The Monthly Reports again provide the most detailed information regarding the superintendent's relationship with outside communities.

36. Gripper to The Honorable Ben Johnson, June 22, 1954, and Gardner to Preston, May 25, 1954, File D30, pt.1, Yosemite National Park Research Library.

37. Leonard to Conrad Wirth, April 5, 1955, and Hildebrand to Thomas J. Allen, June 10, 1955, File D30, Yosemite National Park Research Library.

38. Hildebrand to Allen, June 10, 1955, File D30, Yosemite National Park Research Library.

39. "Parks Director Orders Tioga Work Re-

sumed," *Fresno Bee,* August 20, 1958; Brower to Alexander Hildebrand, July 23, 1958, and "The Sierra Club's National Park Road Policy—and Tenaya Lake," in Confidential Memorandum, July 25, 1958, both in Wayburn Files, Sierra Club Papers.

40. Statement of Superintendent John C. Preston before the Region Four Conference held in Death Valley National Monument, January 11–16, 1959, File D30, pt.6, Yosemite National Park Research Library. See also Statement of Director Conrad L. Wirth Before Sierra Club Officials, San Francisco, California, November 24, 1958, File D30, pt.5, Yosemite National Park Research Library.

41. Hardin, *Managing the Commons,* pp.20–21. See especially Hardin's comparison of national parks to the commons, on page 21.

42. Adams to Richard Leonard, June 19, 1971, Carton 163, Sierra Club Papers.

43. Ibid.

44. Adams, *Autobiography,* p.106.

45. Adams to William E. Colby, September 19, 1952, Sierra Club Office Files, Sierra Club Papers.

CHAPTER THIRTEEN

1. U.S. Department of the Interior, National Park Service, *Compilation of the Administrative Policies . . . of the National Park System* (Washington, D.C.: Government Printing Office, 1968), p.20; File Y-22, Firefall Collection, Yosemite National Park Research Library.

2. Jack Hope, "Hassles in the Park," *Natural History* 80 (May 1971): 22–23; Dave Patterson to Author, Oral Interviews, April 21–25, 1988, Jackson Hole, Wyoming. Patterson was a ranger in Yosemite Valley during the riots.

3. "Yosemite: Better Way to Run a Park?"

U.S. News and World Report 72 (January 24, 1972): 56; George B. Hartzog, Jr., "Changing the National Parks to Cope with People—and Cars," ibid., p.52.

4. Yosemite National Park, "History and Summary of Planning Documents," December 13, 1974, File D18, General Management Plan, Yosemite National Park Research Library.

5. Harris to Hartzog, April 13, 1971, Carton 163, Records of the Sierra Club, Bancroft Library, University of California, Berkeley (hereafter cited as Sierra Club Papers).

6. "Sierra Club Policy for Yosemite Master Plan Statement," September 1971, Carton 163, Sierra Club Papers; Yosemite, "History and Summary of Planning Documents," December 13, 1974, File D18, Yosemite National Park Research Library. Preliminary proposals further included a high bridge that would cross the gorge of the Merced River and link the Wawona and Big Oak Flat roads without requiring north-south traffic to flow through Yosemite Valley proper. The Sierra Club also rejected the bypass as "out of place in the park."

7. Hardy to Arnberger, with attachment, "Yosemite Master Plan—Specific Comments," June 12, 1974, File D18, Yosemite National Park Research Library.

8. Fisher to John Cook, July 11, 1974, File D18, Yosemite National Park Research Library.

9. Stein to Chapman, with enclosure, "Yosemite National Park: Suggested Revisions to the Draft Master Plan," July 29, 1974, File D18, Yosemite National Park Research Library; Jack Anderson, "Yosemite: Another Disneyland?" *Washington Post,* September 15, 1974, reprint; Philip Fradkin, "Sierra Club Sees Damage in Yosemite Filming," *Los Angeles Times,* August 28, 1974, pt.1, pp.1, 22; "Yosemite Na-

tional Convention Center Proposed by New Concessionaire," *Sierra Club Bulletin* 59 (September 1974): 29. File D18, Yosemite National Park Research Library, also contains revealing letters of complaint to Park Service officials.

10. U.S. Department of the Interior, National Park Service, *Yosemite Master Plan Workbook* (Washington, D.C.: Government Printing Office, 1975); U.S. Department of the Interior, National Park Service, *Yosemite Master Plan: Update* (June 1976); U.S. Department of the Interior, National Park Service, *Yosemite: Summary of the Draft General Management Plan,* August 1978 (Washington, D.C.: Government Printing Office, 1978); U.S. Department of the Interior, National Park Service, News Release, "Final Yosemite General Management Plan Released," October 30, 1980, all located in the Yosemite National Park Research Library.

11. U.S. Department of the Interior, National Park Service, *Yosemite General Management Plan and Final Environmental Impact Statement* (Washington, D.C.: Government Printing Office, 1980).

12. Minutes, Resources Management Meeting, November 5, 1970, File N16, Wildlife Management, Yosemite National Park Research Library.

13. Charles Petit, "Yosemite Bear Killings Protested," *San Francisco Chronicle,* November 21, 1973; Shenk to L. Thompson, November 23, 1973, File N16, Yosemite National Park Research Library. Other newspaper articles include "Killing of Yosemite Bears is Protested," *Fresno Bee,* November 21, 1973; "Park Aides Explain 'Bear' Facts," *Fresno Bee,* November 22, 1973; and "Over 200 Bears Killed in Yosemite in Last 12 Years," *Merced Sun-Star,* November 21, 1973. These and other press releases may be found in File K34, Box 6, Yosemite National Park Research Library.

14. Lawrence M. Stickney to Chief Ranger, November 21, 1973, and Mark Thomas, Jr., to Ranger Department, November 30, 1973, File N16, Yosemite National Park Research Library.

15. Galen Rowell, "The Yosemite Solution to Ursus Americanus," *Sierra Club Bulletin* 59 (February 1974): 27.

16. Ibid.

17. Ibid., p.30.

18. Ibid., p.31.

19. F. R. Peake to National Parks Division, September 14, 1954, and Ronald F. Lee to Peake, October 15, 1954, File N1427, Mammals, 1953–56, Yosemite National Park Research Library.

20. Another controversial discussion of the issue is Alston Chase, "The Last Bears of Yellowstone," *Atlantic Monthly* 251 (February 1983): 63–73. Also see Chase's *Playing God in Yellowstone: The Destruction of America's First National Park* (Boston: Atlantic Monthly Press, 1986).

21. Arnberger to Riegelhuth, May 22, 1975, File N16, Yosemite National Park Research Library.

22. Acton Cochran to John M. Good, November 21, 1973; Jeff Giller to Jack Morehead, n.d.; John M. Morehead to Jeff Giller, January 16, 1974; all File N16, Yosemite National Park Research Library.

23. Riegelhuth to John Bingaman, March 4, 1974, File N16, Yosemite National Park Research Library.

24. Ibid.

25. Statement of Horace Marden Albright, June 13, 1975, "Yosemite Valley Master Planning and the Importance of Its Concessioner," File D18, Yosemite National Park Research Library.

26. Ibid.

27. Ibid.

28. Hardy to Binnewies, June 2, 1982, File C3823, Concessions, 1979–85, Yosemite National Park, Concessions Management, Yosemite Park Office Records.

29. Binnewies to Hardy, June 18, 1982, and Charles W. Wendt, Memorandum for the Superintendent, June 14, 1982, File C3823, Yosemite Park Office Records.

30. Statement of Edward C. Hardy, December 4, 1978, during Hearing on Yosemite Plan, San Francisco, California, File D18, General Management Plan, Yosemite Park Office Records.

31. Binnewies to Hardy, September 30, 1982, File C3823, Yosemite Park Office Records.

32. Confidential Report to the Superintendent, Division of Resources Management, Yosemite National Park, "Natural Resources Management Issue Statements," March 1, 1986, p.9, Yosemite Park Office Records.

33. Ibid.

34. Ibid. See also Edward C. Hardy to Robert O. Binnewies, August 16, 1982, File C3823, Yosemite Park Office Records.

35. "Resources Management Issue Statements," p.18. I have further discussed the evolution of fire ecology in modern park management in *National Parks: The American Experience,* 2d ed. (Lincoln: University of Nebraska Press, 1987), chap.10.

36. "Resources Management Issue Statements," pp.22–23; Jan W. van Wagtendonk, "Adding to the Bighorn Herd," *Yosemite* 50 (Spring 1988): 5.

37. Philip Shabecoff, "Historic Battle Over a Yosemite Lake is Back," *New York Times,* August 6, 1987, p.1; Kevin Starr, "Hodel's Absurd Dam-Razing Idea," *Seattle Times,* August 12, 1987, p.15; Don Hodel, "Hetch Hetchy Valley: Restoring Part of America's Scenic Beauty," *Seattle Times,* December 24, 1987, p.7; Henry Berrey, "Draining Hetch Hetchy: A Water and Power Struggle," *Yosemite* 49 (Fall 1987): 1–4; Stephen J. Botti, "A Place We Never Knew," *Yosemite* 50 (Winter 1988): 12–15.

38. "Is the Master Plan Feasible?" *Yosemite* 50 (Spring 1988): 1–4; Gene Rose, "1980 Yosemite General Plan No Longer Viable," *Fresno Bee,* November 11, 1987.

EPILOGUE

1. Van Wagtendonk to Chief, Division of Natural Resources and Research, Western Region, National Park Service, March 6, 1986, File N2215, Yosemite National Park Research Library.

2. Statement of Horace Marden Albright, "Yosemite Valley Master Planning and the Importance of Its Concessioner," June 13, 1975, File D18, General Management Plan, Yosemite National Park Research Library.

3. Printed key jacket, "Welcome to Yosemite," May 1987, Author's Collection.

4. Table Placard, Mountain Room Bar, Summer 1983, Author's Collection.

5. Edward Hardy, "A Message from the President: Yosemite Park and Curry Company Service Responsibilities," *Yosemite Sentinel* Book 12, vol.3 (March 1986): 3.

6. The issue of public transportation is creatively, if somewhat improbably, addressed in Christopher Swan and Chet Roaman, *YV 88: An Eco-Fiction of Tomorrow* (San Francisco: Sierra Club Books, 1977). See also my article "Yosemite Valley Railroad: Highway of History, Pathway of Promise," *National Parks and Conservation Magazine: The Environmental Journal* 48 (December 1974): 4–9.

7. Greater reliance on foundations was an idea vigorously pursued by Ansel Adams. See Adams with Mary Street Alinder, *Ansel Adams: An Autobiography* (Boston: Little, Brown and Co. with New York Graphic Society Books, 1985), p.346. See also Adams's correspondence in the H. C. Bradley Files, Records of the Sierra Club, Bancroft Library, University of California, Berkeley, especially Adams to David R. Brower, January 6, 1957.

8. U.S. Department of the Interior, National Park Service, *Fauna of the National Parks of the United States: A Preliminary Survey,* by George M. Wright, Joseph S. Dixon, and Ben H. Thompson (Washington, D.C.: Government Printing Office, 1933), pp.69–70. Wright's reference to food safes is in volume two of the report, *Wildlife Management* (1935), p.23.

9. Telephone reconfirmation by Jeffrey A. Keay, Division of Resources Management, Yosemite National Park, to author, October 18, 1988.

10. Roger R. Olmsted, ed., *Scenes of Wonder and Curiosity from Hutchings' California Magazine, 1856–1861* (Berkeley, Calif.: Howell-North Books, 1962), p.vii.

11. Jeffrey A. Keay to author, October 18, 1988.

12. See, for example, Wright, Dixon, and Thompson, *Fauna of the National Parks,* pp.68–70.

13. Ibid., pp.69–70.

14. Author's personal investigations, March 1987 through October 1988.

15. "Is the Master Plan Feasible?" *Yosemite* 50 (Spring 1988): 1–4.

A Note on the Sources

No single bibliography could ever begin to list the many hundreds of books and articles that cite significant events, people, and places in Yosemite's long and involved history. The following is merely suggestive of the major published works and archival sources that must be consulted by every serious writer. My notes, in turn, should also be consulted for detailed evaluations of primary and secondary materials not mentioned in this essay.

The majority of this book has been written from archival collections. These include the records of the Yosemite National Park Research Library, California; Record Group 79, the files of the National Park Service, housed at the National Archives in Washington, D.C.; relevant collections of the Bancroft Library, University of California at Berkeley, especially the Sierra Club Papers; and the Records of the Museum of Vertebrate Zoology, also of the University of California at Berkeley. Other collections of importance include the Frederick Law Olmsted and John C. Merriam Papers, Library of Congress, Washington, D.C.; the Carl P. Russell Papers, Washington State University, Pullman; and the archives of the Federal Records Center, San Bruno, California.

The richness of these collections is borne out by my notes. However, there are some significant gaps, especially when the subject turns from general management to park science. For this reason, the Records of the Museum of Vertebrate Zoology at Berkeley loom even larger for further research. Joseph Grinnell, the director of the museum between 1908 and

1939, insisted that his students and associates keep meticulous notes, along with copies of everything they wrote as representatives of the university. Grinnell's correspondence by itself is incredibly instructive, containing many insights and much information about the national parks found in no other collection. Clearly, for scientitsts and historians who wish to understand the origins of national park research, the Records of the Museum of Vertebrate Zoology are a mandatory source.

By themselves, the records of the National Park Service show frustrating gaps. In keeping with the history of the agency itself, research was usually concentrated on sources of controversy. For that very reason, however, the material on bears is excellent, both at the National Archives and the Yosemite National Park Research Library. The record is more sporadic for the so-called lesser animals, such as smaller birds, mammals, amphibians, and reptiles. So too, there is not a great deal on vegetational changes in Yosemite, that is, not unless those changes became noticeable. Like wildlife, vegetation generated the most controversy—and therefore increased investigation—when long-standing perceptions were either challenged or rudely shattered.

Important insights into natural resource issues may also be gleaned from the official monthly and annual reports of the park superintendents and, for the earlier period, the biennial reports of the Yosemite Park Commission. Regrettably, the practice of preparing detailed monthly reports, which began under the military supervision of Yosemite National Park (1891–1913), gradually lost favor by the mid-1960s. Afterward such comprehensive analyses of park affairs and problems were all but discontinued. Accordingly, the more recent the report, the less likely it is to contain the same degree of sophistication and specificity. Generally absent, for example, are the former day-to-day observations about weather, animal movements and sightings, important visitors, and the comings and goings of the superintendent and staff. Granted, there is some compensation in the greater volume of other documentation. The point is that researchers looking at the modern period must now pull together many of the events formerly reported as a matter of course.

One way to follow recent events is through California newspapers. The *Fresno Bee,* for example, reports almost weekly on activities in nearby Yosemite National Park. So too, the *San Francisco Examiner* and the *San Francisco Chronicle* are important sources of park history, both past and present. The same may be said of the *Los Angeles Times* and, on occasion, the *New York Times*, the *Washington Post,* and the *Christian Science Monitor.* Of course, the larger any controversy, the more likely it was to have been covered outside California. Newspapers, in that regard, lend further dramatic proof to Yosemite's nationwide significance.

In general, the secondary literature about Yosemite has not lived up to the park's reputation. Almost without exception, historians and writers have concentrated on the nineteenth century, telling and retelling those already familiar tales about Native Americans, the mountain men, John Muir, and Hetch Hetchy. The standard work in this regard is Carl P. Russell, *One Hundred Years in Yosemite: The Story of a Great Park and Its Friends* (Yosemite: Yosemite Natural History Association, 1957). Separate chapters also discuss early tourism, transportation, concessions, interpretation, and administration. There is very little, to reemphasize, about natural resource issues. That omission is somewhat puzzling, since Russell, who loved western history, also held a Ph.D. in ecology. Margaret Sanborn, *Yosemite: Its Discovery, Its Wonders, and Its People* (New York: Random House, 1981), is better organized and more interpretive but still repeats a good deal of the standard information.

Unquestionably, the best human history to date is the massive report by Linda Wedel Greene, *Historic Resource Study: Yosemite: The Park and Its Resources: A History of the Discovery, Management, and Physical Development of Yosemite National Park, California,* 3 vols. (Washington, D.C.: U.S. Department of the Interior, National Park Service, 1987). Unlike her predecessors, Greene does not give short shrift to the natural environment. This remains, however, a government-commissioned study. Some historians, accordingly, will undoubtedly take issue with Greene's interpretations, such as her defense of Park Service realignment of the old Tioga Road. Still, what these volumes may lack in critical insight is largely offset by their comprehensiveness and detail. The research is thorough, and therefore of lasting value to future historians.

Francis P. Farquhar, *History of the Sierra Nevada* (Berkeley and Los Angeles: University of California Press, 1965), is also widely cited for Yosemite's early years. The role of pioneer artists and photographers in Yosemite is another popular topic. David Robertson, *West of Eden: A History of the Art and Literature of Yosemite* (Berkeley, Calif.: Yosemite Natural History Association and Wilderness Press, 1984), is among the more recent compilations and interpretations. Peter E. Palmquist, *Carleton E. Watkins: Photographer of the American West* (Albuquerque: Amon Carter Museum and the University of New Mexico Press, 1983), is also instructive, whereas Gordon Hendricks, *Albert Bierstadt: Painter of the American West* (New York: Henry N. Abrams, 1974), concentrates on the first artist to bring Yosemite worldwide acclaim. Ted Orland, *Man and Yosemite: A Photographer's View of the Early Years* (Santa Cruz, Calif.: Image Continuum Press, 1985), is another book that stays comfortably locked in the earlier period. In other words, the subject is still wide open for additional interpretation, perhaps modeled after Barbara Novak, *Nature and Culture: American Landscape and Painting, 1825–1875* (New York: Oxford University Press, 1980). Giving further attention to the natural environment, Novak masterfully demonstrates what a truly comprehensive history of the art and photography of Yosemite would have to include.

Meanwhile, any history of Yosemite inevitably invites comparison with the history of other national parks. The obvious counterpart is Yellowstone, which shares with Yosemite both longevity and fame. Richard A. Bartlett, *Yellowstone: A Wilderness Besieged* (Tucson: University of Arizona Press, 1985), is the latest professional scholarship. Alston Chase, *Playing God in Yellowstone: The Destruction of America's First National Park* (Boston: Atlantic Monthly Press, 1986), may also invite comparisons with my work and that of Bartlett. Exact comparisons, however, would ignore great differences in style and purpose. A major book with application to both Yosemite and Yellowstone is Stephen J. Pyne, *Fire in America: A Cultural History of Wildland and Rural Fire* (Princeton: Princeton University Press, 1982). Similarly, Susan R. Schrepfer, *The Fight to Save the Redwoods: A History of Environmental Reform, 1917–1978* (Madison: University of Wisconsin Press, 1983), contributes to our understanding of natural resource problems and controversies.

Interpretive insights also improve with a discussion of Yosemite's establishment as a state and national park. Hans Huth, *Nature and the American: Three Centuries of Changing Attitudes* (Berkeley and Los Angeles: University of California Press, 1957), and also his "Yosemite: The Story of an Idea," *Sierra Club Bulletin* 33 (March 1948): 47–78, broke important ground regarding Americans' perceptions that eventually inspired scenic preservation. Likewise, Roderick Nash, *Wilderness and the American Mind*, 3d ed. (New Haven: Yale University Press, 1982), is standard in this regard. My own *National Parks: The American Experience,* 2d ed. (Lincoln: University of Nebraska Press, 1987), is also a social, cultural, and intellectual history of the parks and, inevitably, contains much on Yosemite. John Ise, *Our National Park Policy: A Critical History* (Baltimore: Johns Hopkins University Press, 1961), should also be consulted for management issues in Yosemite and its counterparts.

Traditionally, the Hetch Hetchy debate is the one controversy that always comes to mind. A comprehensive account is Holway R. Jones, *John Muir and the Sierra Club: The Battle for Yosemite* (San Francisco: Sierra Club, 1965). Jones should be supplemented with Elmo R. Richardson, *The Politics of Conservation: Crusades and Controversies, 1897–1913* (Berkeley and Los Angeles: University of California Press, 1962), along with individual chapters in many of the above-mentioned works, particularly those of John Ise, Roderick Nash, and Linda Wedel Greene. Stephen Fox, *John Muir and His Legacy: The American Conservation Movement* (Boston and Toronto: Little, Brown and Co., 1981), also devotes several pages to the controversy and, in the process, reinterprets the importance of John Muir as America's most renowned preservationist.

Other writings by and about Muir are further mentioned in my notes. For Yosemite's early period I have chosen to concentrate on Frederick Law Olmsted, who preceded Muir into Yosemite Valley, both as a philosopher and as a preservationist. Two important biographies are Laura Wood Roper, *FLO: A Biography of Frederick Law Olmsted* (Baltimore: Johns Hopkins University Press, 1973), and Elizabeth Stevenson, *Park Maker: A Life of Frederick Law Olmsted* (New York: Macmillan, 1977). Charles Beveridge, et al., eds., *The Papers of Frederick Law Olmsted,* 3 vols. (Baltimore: Johns Hopkins University Press, 1977–1983), provide another superb introduction to Olmsted and his contributions.

Important biographies of Park Service personnel also yield material on Yosemite. These include Robert Shankland, *Steve Mather of the National Parks,* 3d ed. (New York: Alfred A. Knopf, 1970); Donald C. Swain, *Wilderness Defender: Horace M. Albright and Conservation* (Chicago: University of Chicago Press, 1970); and Horace M. Albright as told to Robert Cahn, *The Birth of the National Park Service: The Founding Years, 1913–1933* (Salt Lake City and Chicago: Howe Brothers, 1985). Biographies, understandably, deal essentially with administration. Similarly, the more autobiographical such volumes tend to be, the more self-serving and less critical they also tend to become. Conrad L. Wirth, for example, in *Parks, Politics, and the People* (Norman: University of Oklahoma Press, 1980), defends his role as director of the Park Service (1951–64), especially his support of internal improvements, including widening and straightening Yosemite's Tioga Road. In much the same genre is George B. Hartzog, Jr., *Battling for the National Parks* (Mount Kisco, N.Y.: Moyer Bell Limited, 1988). Memoirs, in the final analysis, are a very personal perspective on events.

Perhaps least known among Yosemite's defenders is Joseph Grinnell. His life is nonetheless pivotal for understanding the evolution of park management in the twentieth century. Grinnell's most important publication on the park, with Tracy I. Storer, is *Animal Life in the Yosemite: An Account of the Mammals, Birds, Reptiles, and Amphibians in a Cross Section of the Sierra Nevada* (Berkeley: University of California Press, 1924). Also instructive is *Joseph Grinnell's Philosophy of Nature: Selected Writings of a Western Naturalist* (Berkeley and Los Angeles: University of California Press, 1943), a collection of original essays assembled by his friends and associates as a memorial to his career.

Regrettably, few naturalists since Grinnell and Storer have matched the sweep and comprehensiveness of *Animal Life in the Yosemite*. Most of the natural history written in recent times appears in smaller volumes and pamphlets discussing trees, wildflowers, birdlife, or geology. California at large has been somewhat more fortunate. A recent natural history of the state is Elna Barker, *An Island Called California: An Ecological Introduction to Its Natural Communities,* 2d ed. (Berkeley and Los Angeles: University of California Press, 1984). Barker, though covering the entire state, still gives Yosemite its due. Her bibliography of relevant works is also an important checklist for literacy in the biological sciences and includes texts by E. J. Kormondy, E. P. and Howard Odum, and Victor E. Shelford. To her selection I would add Raymond F. Dasmann, *Environmental Conservation,* 4th ed. (New York: John Wiley and Sons, 1976), as well as a broad range of specialized journals, such as *Ambio, Bioscience, Ecology, Journal of Mammalogy,* and *Journal of Wildlife Management.*

Outside the natural sciences, historians of the environment continue to work their favorite themes. Walter L. Creese, *The Crowning of the American Landscape: Eight Great Spaces and Their Buildings* (Princeton: Princeton University Press, 1985), devotes an entire chapter to development in Yosemite Valley. But again, much as his title implies, Creese is not overly critical of the park's early structures. More controversial, and therefore harder hitting, is Michael P. Cohen, *The History of the Sierra Club, 1892–1970* (San Francisco: Sierra Club Books, 1988). Cohen provides a long-awaited sequel to the work by Holway R. Jones, who dropped the discussion of the Sierra Club after the struggle for Hetch Hetchy. Accordingly, although development in Yosemite National Park is just one of Cohen's important topics, there is much that is new here, not only about Yosemite but also about the Sierra Club, definitely the park's strongest advocate in the twentieth century.

In Yosemite and other parks, future trends may be suggested by work still in progress. Scientific research, it appears, is definitely on the rise. Suggestive examples would include David Murry Graber, "Ecology and Management of Black Bears in Yosemite National Park" (Ph.D. dissertation, University of California at Berkeley, 1981); and Theodore C. Foin, ed., "Visitor Impacts on National Parks: The Yosemite Ecological Impact Study" (bound report, Institute of Ecology, University of California at Davis, 1977). Another model study is Richard J. Hartesveldt, "Effects of Human Impact upon *Sequoia gigantea* and Its Environment in the Mariposa Grove, Yosemite National Park, California" (Ph.D. dissertation, University of Michigan, 1962). Normal L. Christensen, et al., "Review of Fire Management Program for Sequoia-Mixed Conifer Forests of Yosemite, Sequoia and Kings Canyon National Parks" (special report to the Western Region, National Park Service, 1987), is another example suggestive of future cooperation between park managers and resource scientists. Allegedly, prescribed burning in the sequoia groves has needlessly scarred many trees, a criticism that led, in 1987, to the Christensen study. Finally, Michael L. Smith, *Pacific Visions: California Scientists and the Environment, 1850–1915* (New Haven: Yale University Press, 1987), reexamines the origins of scientific debate and includes further discussions of Yosemite, although the book is mostly about geology.

Debate about visitation in national parks also continues to sharpen. Don Hummel, for example, in *Stealing the National Parks: The Destruction of Concessions and Public Access* (Bellevue, Wash.: Free Press, 1987), argues that preservationists are closing out the general public and, in the process, excluding necessary services. Hummel, not surprisingly, is a former concessionaire. A less strident view, although no less committed to the opposite argument, is Joseph L. Sax, *Mountains Without Handrails: Reflections on the*

National Parks (Ann Arbor: University of Michigan Press, 1980). Sax maintains that national parks are in fact for preservation. Every visitor, accordingly, must be conscious of the need to protect the environment.

Yosemite, in every case, remains central to these and many other debates, suggesting its continuing importance as a field of investigation into the management of the national park system at large.

❧ Index

Adams, Ansel, 8; and Ahwahnee Hotel, 188, 199; on Bracebridge Dinner, 187, 199; contradictions in philosophy of, 187–88, 198–200; and objections to park development, 185–87; 193–94; and Yosemite Valley, 6–7

Advisory Board, 154–58, 189

Ahwahneechee Indians: customs of, 9; dispossession of, 10–13; origins of, 9; and Yosemite Valley, 9, 30, 37–38, 58–60

Ahwahnee Hotel, 189; and Bracebridge Dinner, 187; and El Dorado Room, 184–85; esthetics of, 187–88; historic significance of, 226; opening of, 145

Albright, Horace M., 114–16, 118, 134; and development of Yosemite Valley, 212–13, 221

Alcoholic beverages: history of, 91, 248 n.4; promotion of, 183–85, 221; sale of, defended, 91–92, 182–85, 191

Alder flea beetle, 176

All-Year Highway, 121, 153

Amusements. *See* Recreation

Animal Life in the Yosemite (book), 117, 167, 211. *See also* Grinnell, Joseph; Storer, Tracy I.

Animals. *See names of individual animal species*

Ansel Adams Gallery, 199

Army, 57–99 *passim;* and alcohol, 182; compared with Yosemite Park Commission, 57–66 *passim;* and concessionaires, 92–98; and fire, 62–64; and fish stocking, 65–66; management of Yosemite Valley by, 83–99; praise for policies of, 61–62; and sheep, 60–61; and troopers, 239 n.35; and wildlife protection, 70–72, 78–80, 86–87

Arnberger, Leslie P., 204, 210

Arsenical spray, 176

Ashburner, William, 29, 31, 39–40, 50

Automobiles: admission of, 101; damage by, 156; effect on visitation of, 121; limitations on, 203; and threats to wildlife, 172; in Yosemite Valley, 203–4

Ayres, Thomas A., 13, 39

Badger Pass, 153, 205

Balance of nature, attempts to define, 162–67, 174

Barnard Hotel, 91

Bars. *See* Alcoholic beverages; *names of individual bars*

Bear management: criticism of, 141–43, 147; early examples of, 89, 136, 141–42, 150; failures of, 142–43, 206; pejorative language of, 142; reform of, 210, 222–23. *See also* Bears